Focus on Psychodrama

The Therapeutic Aspects of Psychodrama

of related interest

Dramatherapy with Families, Groups and Individuals
Waiting in the Wings
Sue Jennings
1990 ISBN 1 85302 048 6 hb, 1992 ISBN 1 85302 144 X pb

Drama and Healing
The Roots of Drama Therapy
Roger Grainger
1990 ISBN 1 85302 048 6

Art Therapy and Drama Therapy
Masks of the Soul
Sue Jennings & Ase Minde
1992 ISBN 1 85302 027 3

Storymaking in Education and Therapy
Alida Gersie & Nancy King
1990 ISBN 1 85302 519 4 hb, ISBN 1 85302 520 8 pb

Storymaking in Bereavement
Dragons Fight in the Meadow
Alida Gersie
1991 ISBN 1 85302 065 6 hb, 1992 ISBN 1 85302 176 8 pb

Playtherapy with Abused Children
Ann Cattanach
1992 ISBN 1 85302 120 2

Symbols of the Soul
Therapy and Guidance Through Fairy Tales
Birgitte Brun, Ernst W Pedersen & Marianne Runberg
1992 ISBN 1 85302 107 5

The Metaphoric Body
A Guide to Expressive Therapy Through Images and Archetypes
Lea Barthal & Nira Ne'eman
1992 ISBN 1 85302 152 X

Focus on Psychodrama
The Therapeutic Aspects of Psychodrama

Peter Felix Kellermann
Foreword by Jonathan D Moreno

Jessica Kingsley Publishers
London and Philadelphia

First published in the United Kingdom in 1992 by
Jessica Kingsley Publishers Ltd
116 Pentonville Road
London N1 9JB

Copyright © 1992 Peter Felix Kellermann

British Library Cataloguing in Publication Data
Kellermann, Peter Felix
    Focus on Psychodrama: Therapeutic Aspects
    of Psychodrama
    I. Title
    616.89

    ISBN 1 85302 127 X

Printed and bound in Great Britain by
Billing and Sons Ltd, Worcester

Contents

To my mother Livia Kellermann
Whose love, support, and mothering have been with me always.
Without her, this book, and I, could not have been.
And to Zerka Moreno
With gratitude
For introducing me to psychodrama

Foreword

Peter Felix Kellermann has given me the extraordinary opportunity to introduce his exciting work on the intellectual contributions of my father, J.L. Moreno, M.D. This systematic and provocative approach to psychodrama theory and therapy remind me of an observation by the great American philosopher, William James. James argued that one's attraction to a certain worldview, among the many candidates to which one may be exposed, has a great deal to do with temperament. In his example, philosophical empiricists (such as John Locke and David Hume) tend to be lovers of facts, while their rationalist colleagues (including for example Hegel) are drawn to system and order. Here, of course, James was speaking as a psychologist, not as a philosopher, for such *ad hominem* explanations are irrelevant to the question of which worldview is the true one—if indeed that is even a proper question.

Yet James' psychological observation is worth reflecting upon in the context of the great dynamic psychiatries of the twentieth century. Consider, for example, the different sorts of people who seem to be attracted, whether as students or patients, to Jung rather than to Freud. Still more striking are the differences between those largely drawn to psychoanalysis, of whatever flavor, and those drawn to more active modalities such as psychodrama.

I speak with some authority on this question since early on I became aware that I was a bit of an oddball in my house. Surrounded as I was by all manner of often brilliant followers of my father's work, I noticed that they tended to be more outgoing and, so to speak, spontaneous than I was. Usually they were people who seemed far more interested in doing than in writing about what they did. My own education in the practice of psychodrama, although in some respects it started early, never came as naturally to me as my interest in its philosophy and theory.

Thus I was excited, while rummaging through my father's library as a college student, to discover that there were once a number of other people like me who were interested in developing the theoretical aspects of psychodrama. These people were around mostly before I was born, from about the mid-1930s to the mid-1950s, and they included a number of prominent social scientists and theologians. Numerous monographs published by Beacon House in those days attest to this: *Psychodrama, Volume 2* provides the best-known example.

It is probably not useful to speculate about why there has been, in my opinion, a relative lull in the development of psychodrama theory for about thirty years. I say 'relative' because I do not at all want to be understood as underestimating the work of those (relative few) who have continued to enlarge our understanding of psychodramatic processes, including especially my mother, Zerka T. Moreno. But the sad fact is that they have been the exception, and there has been a degree of conceptual stagnation in psychodrama.

I recur to my primitive psychologizing about intellectual movements by way of celebrating the possibility that Peter Felix Kellermann is proving me wrong, as I was proven wrong by the work of an earlier generation; that a new generation of psychodramatists has matured and is prepared to disprove the 'obvious' impressions about people who are attracted to psychodrama as lacking the patience for the often solitary labors of scholarship. Indeed, as I have traveled about in the last ten years I have been impressed, particularly in Europe, by a number of younger psychologists and physicians who are committed to the theoretical enrichment of psychodrama.

This brings me to what is perhaps the most important single lesson of this volume, a lesson that is implicit in the project Kellermann has set for himself: that there is in fact a rich and unique theoretical apparatus within psychodrama. Frequently, this theoretical richness has been overlooked, and psychodramatic techniques have been brought under other conceptual rubrics, particularly those of the various brands of psychoanalysis. The trouble with such maneuvers is that they create an artificial separation between theory and technique. Put another way, to think that psychodrama is only a bag of loosely associated therapeutic tricks is to think mistakenly that J.L. Moreno 'invented' psychodrama. But even a cursory inspection of the record will show that psychodrama was developed over time, just as my father's ideas developed over time. While this does not obligate anyone to accept psychodrama theory, intellectual honesty at least requires that the theory not be ignored.

Thus Kellermann has undertaken the formidable task of systematizing and clarifying certain fundamental theoretical and practical aspects of psychodrama. In the course of this project he has also set aside some old myths and broken new conceptual ground. He is able to do this because he has an unusual set of attributes, including an impressive grasp of the literature on psychotherapy at large, extensive experience in the clinical setting, a generous philosophical imagination, and the instincts of an innovator.

It is impossible to underestimate the importance of this sort of work. If psychodrama is not ultimately to be dismembered by other theoretical orientations and recalled merely as a curiosity by intellectual history, it is crucial that it prove its continuing worth as an ongoing source of stimulating new ideas and possibilities. No philosophy or theory has long survived as a living part of the culture unless it has proven rich enough to be rearticulated in ever deeper ways. Otherwise it is merely a bloodless vestige, gone the way of Ptolemaic cosmology or the medicine of humours, or hundreds of lesser-known attempts to understand and control.

Readers of the psychodrama literature have for a decade been aware of Kellermann's telling analyses of psychodrama theory. Now his efforts will be made available to a wider audience. With this volume his ingenious and highly original work will not only help create a sounder conceptual basis for psychodrama therapy, it will also establish Kellermann as one of a precious handful of significant thinkers on the foundations of psychodrama. My greatest wish is that aspects of his work will ignite many productive conversations and controversies, and that these will help to spawn a wave of creativity, a wave upon which psychodrama will ride into its second century of unique contributions to human life.

Jonathan D. Moreno, Ph.D.

Introduction

Dramatic impersonation has existed almost as long as civilization. Role playing, play acting, and other techniques borrowed from the theatre share the common goal of presenting the everyday lives of people in a dramatic manner. It is not surprising, therefore, that these techniques have been harnessed as part of the healing process and put to use in psychotherapy. J.L. Moreno (1889–1974) pioneered this application of dramatic elements in a therapeutic method he called psychodrama. Much has happened since the laying of that foundation. Today, psychodrama is quite solidly established as a viable alternative to other treatment approaches, and it has developed into a systematic treatment approach with established strategies and techniques, much to the credit of Zerka T. Moreno, whose contributions to the field were outstanding.

Psychodrama is based on the assumption that people are role players who pass through various stages of life.

> All the world's a stage,
> And all the men and women merely players;
> They have their exits
> and their entrances,
> And one man in his time
> plays many parts,
> His act being seven ages.

This quotation from Shakespeare's 'As You Like It,' (II.vii) embodies the essence of psychodrama. Recently, the idea that people are role players has received attention from developmental, social, and clinical psychologists who, as a result, have formulated comprehensive theories of the human life-cycle and of individual means of adjustment. They have reached the conclusion that, as people move across time, each new stage in life is a kind of turning-point which presents either an opportunity for growth or a potential personal crisis. In any case, the complexities of life demand an extraordinary capacity for adaptive working-through and adjustment.

In psychodrama, participants are invited to re-enact significant experiences and to present their subjective worlds with the aid of a group. Every aspect of life can thus be re-enacted, from infancy to old age: the coming and leaving of children; a baby crying; parents quarreling; adolescents dating; a couple discussing marriage or divorce; an old man dying in a hospital bed; a young woman contemplating abortion; a car accident; a soldier being killed in battle;

a woman who was raped now searching for revenge; an alcoholic talking with an empty bottle of liquor. Psychodramatic scenes portray predictable developmental life events or sudden crises, inner conflicts or entangling relationships. The re-enactments are as different from each other as are the lives of the people who present them. But despite these differences, all psychodramas share the one common element that makes them therapeutic: the presentation of personal truth in the protected world of make-believe as a way to master and cope vicariously with stressful life events in a creative and adaptive manner.

Often, people cope with situational stress in a highly fixated manner, loading another burden on their shoulders at every difficulty, as described in the following anecdote (adapted from Witztum, Hart, & Friedman, 1988):

Once upon a time, there was a man who set out for a journey, carrying a large bag on his shoulders. As he travelled along, the bag became heavier and heavier because, whenever he experienced a misfortune, he had the peculiar custom of putting a souvenir into his bag. The further he went, the more he felt the painful weight of the bag on his shoulders. One day he arrived at a cross-road where he saw a group of street-actors improvising a play. He decided to take a rest, while watching the rehearsal. One of the actors, who had seen the burdened man, started to imitate and mock him. The actor walked around and picked things up, working harder and harder to carry the bag, until he finally fell down exhausted. When the traveller recognized himself, he looked at his bag and started to cry silently. The actors approached him and asked him why he was so sad. The traveller said that he had come a long way with his bag but that he had no more strength to carry it. As he spoke, he took out a souvenir from his bag and told the story connected to that object, whereupon the actors, who had become full of inspiration, immediately enacted it in a dramatic fashion. Soon the traveller himself was emotionally involved in the play, enacting the protagonist role of his life's drama. When all the man's souvenirs had been presented, the actors suggested that he build a statue of the objects as a monument to all the difficulties he had encountered on his journey. The man did this and as he was looking at the statue, he realized that he could leave it there forever, symbolizing his own personal freedom. He bid the actors farewell and continued his journey, feeling peculiarly light, as if he had unloaded some heavy burden from his shoulders.

Ever since the first psychodrama session in which I participated nearly two decades ago, I have been impressed by the spontaneous moments of change which occur—moments that produce a kind of mysterious healing for which there appears to be no satisfactory explanation. Much of what happens in a psychodrama session evades easy schematization, making the work elusive and strange, yet at the same time exciting and familiar. From the beginning, I had an irresistible desire to find out what it was about psychodrama that made it such an effective instrument. As a result of this curiosity, I began to observe sessions systematically, interviewed literally hundreds of participants to get their points of view on the process, studied the literature carefully, surveyed the empirical research done, and drew conclusions from my own experience.

Focusing alternatively on different aspects of the process, I published some of the results from these investigations in various articles and in a Ph.D. Thesis at the University of Stockholm. This present book is a further development and a revision of that early work. It is an attempt to present a systematic analysis of the essential therapeutic ingredients in psychodrama. By delineating the variables at work in this method and by proposing more uniform definitions to some central psychodramatic concepts, I hope to improve the general standard of practice and research, and to reduce some of the confusion which surrounds the theory of psychodramatic technique. While the practical applications of psychodrama have been described in detail, comparatively little has been written about its therapeutic factors, and our understanding of what it is in the psychodramatic process that is truly helpful has remained rather limited. It is my hope that this book will be a step towards bridging this gap in our understanding.

This book is written for students in training and for practitioners who want to deepen their understanding of psychodrama. It may also be useful to individual, family, and group therapists who use action and drama therapy techniques in their practice, and for mental health professionals in general.

Many publications form an indispensable background to this book. A summary of these would be an exhaustive commentary on the basic process of psychodrama and would probably do disservice to formulations that are already renowned for their clarity. Excellent introductions and handbooks describing psychodrama have been written (or edited) by Blatner (1973; 1988), Corsini (1967), Fox (1987), Goldman & Morrison (1984), Greenberg (1974), Haskell (1975), Holmes & Karp (1991), Kahn (1964), Kipper (1986), Leveton (1977), Leutz (1974), Petzold (1978), Schutzenberger (1970), Starr (1977), Warner (1975), Williams (1989) and Yablonsky (1976), to name only the most important ones. Introductory and advanced readings on this subject should also include the original writings of J.L. and Zerka T. Moreno, and the essential papers on the subject which are presented in the references.

Chapter 1 of this book describes some of the difficulties involved in defining classic psychodrama and suggests a definition of psychodrama that applies to the work of the majority of practitioners, including those who are not purely Morenian. This definition is necessary and useful in that it makes possible the characterization of various applications and styles of psychodrama. Furthermore, some common guidelines of practice are discussed, including suggestions regarding the most favourable time and frequency of sessions, physical setting, and client, therapist, group, and auxiliary characteristics of protagonist-centered psychodrama. An actual psychodrama session is described with the kind permission of the protagonist and of the director, Zerka. T. Moreno. This is an extended version of the paper 'A Proposed Definition of Psychodrama' which was published in the *Journal of Group Psychotherapy, Psychodrama & Sociometry*, 1987, 40, 76–80. It is reprinted here with the permission of Helen Dwight Reid Educational Foundation (HELDREF); 1319 Eighteenth Street, N.W., Washington, D.C. 20036–1802, USA.

Chapter 2 is an attempt to develop a solid foundation upon which psychodrama techniques can be properly based. Moreno's theories are validated from a metascientific point of view and the governing assumptions of psychodrama are examined from a human and a natural science perspective. Integrative solutions in psychodrama suggest that these two perspectives may cross-pollinate one another. This is a reprint of the paper 'An Essay on the Metascience of Psychodrama' which was published in the *Journal of Group Psychotherapy, Psychodrama & Sociometry*, 1991, 44, 19–32, used here with the permission of HELDREF Publications.

Chapter 3 describes the professional roles assumed by psychodramatists and the skills required in each role. Psychodramatists, as analysts, are required to convey empathic understanding; as directors of drama they are required to create aesthetic theatre productions; as therapists they are required to heal mental suffering; and as group leaders they are required to manage the group process. Finally, as human beings and through the impact of their own personalities, they are expected to have a constructive influence on the psychodramatic process.

Chapter 4 discusses the influence of charismatic leadership and personality on the process of psychodrama, with the eventual conclusion that while a charismatic situation is inevitable in the initial stages of treatment, it is detrimental to an independent growth process in the long run. This chapter also contains some general guidelines for leadership in psychodrama. This is a reprint of the paper 'Charismatic Leadership in Psychodrama,' first published in the *Journal of Group Psychotherapy, Psychodrama & Sociometry*, 1985, 38, 84–95, reprinted here with the permission of HELDREF Publications.

Chapter 5 presents a model for understanding the therapeutic aspects of psychodrama and contains a summary of my doctoral dissertation, published at the University of Stockholm in 1986. It is emphasized that any understanding of how psychodrama is therapeutic requires an assessment of a multivariate field including not only the single aspects discussed in the following chapters, but various aspects working together with one another.

Chapter 6 discusses the therapeutic value of catharsis and emotional abreaction, arriving at the conclusion that the re-living of original traumatic events and the release of constricted emotions are insufficient to produce therapeutic progress. A phase of cognitive integration must complement the emotional abreaction. This is a revision of a paper entitled 'The Place of Catharsis in Psychodrama,' published in the *Journal of Group Psychotherapy, Psychodrama &*

Sociometry, 1984, 37, 1–13. It is used here with the permission of HELDREF Publications.

Chapter 7 explores the significance of action-insight in psychodrama. Action-insight produces a kind of intensive re-collection which leads to more profound learning experiences than does mere cognitive awareness, and makes it easier to translate the insights obtained into actual behavior outside the therapeutic setting.

Chapter 8 focuses on the interpersonal relationships which develop among the participants of a psychodrama group. This chapter deals with the question of the possibility of a real relationship that lacks the distorting characteristics of transference. It concludes that the use of therapeutic assistants ('auxiliaries') as the objects of transference, facilitates the development of authentic tele relations. This chapter is a revised version of a paper entitled 'Transference, Countertransference, and Tele,' first published in *Group Psychotherapy, Psychodrama & Sociometry*, 1979, 32, 38–55. It is used here with the permission of HELDREF Publications.

Chapter 9 emphasizes the importance of imagination and 'as- if' in psychodrama. Here the main discussion centers around the question of authenticity within the framework of role-playing. It is concluded that psychodrama allows people to use the world of make-believe and imagination in the same manner as the child uses play-acting: in order to resolve, in a symbolic form, those concerns which cause intrapsychic stress. This is a translation and revision of a paper entitled 'Psychodrama eine 'Als-Ob' Erfahrung' published in *Integrative Therapie*, 1982, 8, 13–23. It is used here with the permission of Junfermann-Verlag, Paderborn.

Chapter 10 explores the various uses of the concept of 'acting out' in psychodrama and in psychoanalysis. While this concept has a positive connotation in psychodrama and a negative one in psychoanalysis, the present chapter shows that there is really no contradiction between the two approaches. This is a revised version of a paper entitled 'Acting Out in Psychodrama and in Psychoanalytic Group Psychotherapy,' published in *Group Analysis*, 1984, 17, 195–203; reprinted here with permission.

Chapter 11 presents some preliminary ideas about the 'magic' or non-specific aspects of healing in psychodrama.

Chapter 12 presents the counter-therapeutic manifestations of resistance and describes some of its common functions. The chapter includes a description of a broad spectrum of techniques useful in handling resistances, either through analysis or manipulation. This is a modified version of the paper 'Widerstand im Psychodrama,' first published in Petzold, H. (Ed.) *Widerstand: Ein strittiges Konzept in der Psychotherapie*. Paderborn: Junfermann-Verlag, 1981, p. 385–405. A translation was published in the *Journal of Group Psychotherapy, Psychodrama & Sociometry*, 1983, 36, 30–43. It is reprinted here with the permission of the previous publishers.

Chapter 13 discusses the concept of closure in psychodrama and gives examples of useful termination strategies. This is a revised version of the paper 'Closure in Psychodrama,' published in the *Journal of Group Psychotherapy, Psychodrama & Sociometry*, 1988, 41, 21–29. Reprinted with permission of HEL-DREF Publications.

Chapter 14 describes the basic procedure of processing in psychodrama and discusses some of its problematic issues. As a training aid, processing may focus upon personal, professional, or group-related issues. If the difficulties in management are resolved, processing may become a powerful learning experience which give participants an opportunity to make sense out of the complex processes activated in psychodrama. A processing checklist is added as a systematic aid in evaluating the professional skills of psychodramatists.

CHAPTER 1

Definition

The term psychodrama is complex and multifaceted and a review of the literature shows little agreement on its definition. The term is loosely used to connote, among other things, clinical role playing, behavioural rehearsal, action analysis, creative dramatics, drama therapy, improvisatory theatre, and even spontaneous happening. Simplistic definitions of psychodrama, such as the 'science which explores the "truth" by dramatic methods' (Moreno, 1972, p.a), or the 'theory, philosophy, and methodology of J.L. Moreno' (Fine, 1979, p.428), are inadequate. By the same token, stating that psychodrama cannot be clearly defined because of its reliance on personal experience is unacceptable.

A brief and precise definition of psychodrama is important for a number of reasons. First, when conducting empirical research on the process or outcome of psychodrama, an exact definition is necessary in order to distinguish this approach from others. Second, when introducing psychodrama to clients and to society at large, a brief definition is necessary to help clarify what one may, or may not, expect. Third, a commonly agreed definition would facilitate discussion between practitioners of diverse persuasions.

Unfortunately, psychodrama has evolved to the point where not all those who call themselves psychodramatists can accept all others who claim the title. Not only are there basic theoretical conflicts, there are also wide variations in therapeutic goals and methods. The purpose of this chapter is to clarify the problem of definition, to discuss some of the reasons for this problem, and to suggest a comprehensive definition that might be agreed upon by a majority of investigators and practitioners. Furthermore, some practical guidelines will be suggested regarding when, where, for whom, by whom, and with whom to employ classical psychodrama.

I believe that there are six main reasons for the difficulty in defining psychodrama. These loosely fall under the headings of history, triadic system, eclecticism, application, structure and theory.

History

The problem of definition has its origin in the terminology of J.L. Moreno. While original, Moreno's definitions of psychodrama are often inconsistent and contradictory, especially when referring to psychodrama's goals. For example, Moreno variously defined psychodrama as a theology with religious postulations (Moreno, 1920), a dramatic art form with aesthetic ideals (Moreno, 1923), a political system with social values (Moreno, 1953), a science with research ambitions (Moreno, 1953), a method of psychotherapy with curative goals, and a philosophy of life. Even when taking the various phases of the early development of psychodrama into consideration, nothing close to a consistent psychodramatic paradigm remains. I suggest that psychodrama should be defined not as a theology, a dramatic art form, a political system, a science, or a way of life, but as a specific method of psychotherapy, a treatment approach to psychological problems.

Triadic System

A second source of confusion lies in Moreno's frequently quoted 'triadic system,' consisting of sociometry, group psychotherapy, and psychodrama. It may be questioned whether sociometry and group psychotherapy are inherent parts of the psychodramatic system, or are separate methods that may or may not be employed, according to the orientation of the practitioner. It is my position that while sociometry and group psychotherapy often represent valuable elements in psychodrama therapy, they are not inherent parts of it and should therefore be conceptually separated from psychodrama proper.

Eclecticism

A third obstacle to defining psychodrama arises from its eclectic character and its similarities to treatment approaches such as fixed role therapy (Kelly, 1955), social model learning (Bandura, 1971), gestalt therapy (Perls, Hefferline, & Goodman, 1973), encounter group (Schutz, 1971), drama therapy (Jennings, 1986; Landy, 1986), and other related action methods. While many of these approaches may include one or another element of psychodrama, in my view none of them encompasses the entire system of psychodrama as described below, and cannot thus be defined as psychodrama.

Application

Fourth, many practitioners fail to distinguish between therapeutic and non-therapeutic applications of the psychodramatic approach. Therapeutic applications involve professionally trained clinicians who attempt to treat more or less disturbed clients. In contrast, non-therapeutic applications include experimental activities for healthy people who participate for personal growth, as a pastime, for training, or for some other reason. While psychotherapy may be dramatically entertaining, psychodrama cannot be characterized simply as theatre. No matter how much we extend the applications of role-playing methods in various settings, psychodrama is definitely a form of treatment. Thus other role playing methods, while helpful to the participants—the use of action methods in a strictly industrial setting, for example—should be differentiated from classical psychodrama proper and be given another name, such as role training. When drama is used to improve a social situation, it should be called sociodrama or community theatre. Finally, when used within an educational setting, a descriptive term such as creative dramatics seems suitable.

Structure

A fifth reason for the difficulty in defining psychodrama is as a result of its emphasis on spontaneous experience and unrehearsed action and its general similarity to play. The fact that each psychodrama session differs so much from every other makes it difficult to generalize about the usual course of such therapy. To me, however, psychodrama does have a unity and structure which define its boundaries in terms of time, place and content. While optimal freedom of expression is given to protagonists in psychodrama, a certain process is followed, with established strategies of interventions and phases of development. Thus, playing in general, while emotionally rewarding, cannot be characterized as psychodrama, because of its lack of the necessary structure (as described below).

Theory

The fact that most definitions of psychodrama include some reference to theory is a sixth and final cause for disagreement. The terminology of psychodrama remains obscure, and practitioners lack a coherent theory to aid in their struggle for conceptual (co-)existence. In my opinion, psychodrama should be defined in a way that does not assume a specific theoretical orientation. Such a definition should not rest upon the intentions of the therapy or what is achieved, but rather upon a procedural description of what is actually done.

Procedural (or 'operational') definitions, required in empirical research, may be either narrow or wide (Kipper, 1978). A narrow definition of psychodrama, for example, requires the enactment of at least one scene or the use of at least one technique from the psychodramatic repertoire. A wide definition requires the enactment of at least three scenes, and the use of more than one technique. Such operational definitions may be supplemented by a description of the psychodramatic process. In my opinion, psychodrama should be given a wide definition, requiring the enactment of a number of scenes and the use of several action techniques in one single session.

A Comprehensive Definition of Psychodrama

With the above-mentioned issues as a point of departure, I propose the following as a comprehensive definition of psychodrama:

Psychodrama is a method of psychotherapy in which clients are encouraged to continue and complete their actions through dramatization, role playing, and dramatic self-presentation. Both verbal and nonverbal communications are utilized. A number of scenes are enacted, depicting, for example, memories of specific happenings in the past, unfinished situations, inner dramas, fantasies, dreams, preparations for future risk-taking situations, or unrehearsed expressions of mental states in the here and now. These scenes either approximate real-life situations or are externalizations of inner mental processes. If required, other roles may be taken by group members or by inanimate objects. Many techniques are employed, such as role reversal, doubling, mirroring, concretizing, maximizing and soliloquy. Usually the phases of warm up, action, working through, closure and sharing can be identified.

The main advantage of this definition is that it leaves open the option for a clear division of the various applications and styles of therapeutic practice according to the following dimensions:

1. Context—individual, group, family, or milieu.

2. Focus—person, group, or theme centred.

3. Location—in situ, stage, school, hospital, clinic.

4. Adherence—Morenian, Freudian, Adlerian, Rogerian.

5. Underlying theory—psychodramatic, psychoanalytic, behavioural, existential, humanistic.

6. Therapeutic goal—symptom reduction, crisis intervention, conflict resolution, personality change.

7. Therapist's intervention—directive, supportive, confrontational, reconstructive, expressive, interpretative.

8. Therapeutic factors emphasized—emotional release, cognitive insight, interpersonal feedback, behavioural learning.

9. Time and frequency of sessions—periodic, continual, single session, marathon, time-limited.

10. Population treated—age, sex, diagnosis, etc.

These applications can be regarded as variables which influence the process and outcome of psychodrama, each by itself and all together, and are parallel to the six widely accepted requirements in the design of psychotherapeutic research (Fiske, Luborsky, Parloff, Hunt, Orne, Reiser, & Tuma, 1970).

While there is a great variety of applications of psychodrama, it is possible to suggest some common guidelines of practice in terms of the most favourable time and frequency of sessions ('when?'), physical setting ('where?'), client characteristics ('for whom?'), therapist characteristics ('by whom?') and group and auxiliary characteristics ('with whom?') for classical, protagonist-centered psychodrama. Likewise, despite the tremendous variations, it is possible to make some generalizations about the outcome of psychodrama.

Time and Frequency of Sessions (When?)

A single psychodrama session may last from one to four hours, with the average (and optimal) time being two and a half hours. This includes a period of about half an hour for the warm-up phase, approximately one and a half hours for the psychodramatic enactment, and the remainder of the session for the sharing phase. An additional half hour is sometimes required for a pre- or post-session processing or group discussion period. It is my experience that if less time than this is available, any emotional processes begun will remain incomplete. Conversely, longer sessions without intermissions result in fatigue and lack of concentration among the participants.

Psychodrama may be conducted once a week, during intensive weekend workshops, or in weeklong seminars with up to three sessions a day. Most practitioners agree that intensive workshops speed up the therapeutic process because of the acceleration of self-disclosure, affective involvement and group cohesion. Once-a-week sessions proceed at a slower pace, but the continuity, gradual unfolding and repetitive working through of central issues may help participants to integrate better gains made in psychodrama into their daily lives.

In an attempt to investigate the most favourable pacing of psychodrama sessions, Hall (1977) compared the difference in outcome between an intensive weekend psychodrama experience and six spaced (once-a-week) sessions with female nursing students. The results showed that while the intensive weekend workshop significantly reduced feelings of anxiety, depression and distress among the students, no significant effects were noted for the spaced session group.

In my own practice, I have found it most favourable to combine the once-a-week sessions with occasional intensive workshops a few times a year. Experience has proven that such scheduling of sessions is advantageous, not only because it readily fits in with the weekly schedules of participants, but because, in the terminology of Mahler (1968), it seems to combine the advantages of weekly 'continual rapprochement' with intensive and periodic 'symbiotic regressions'. It is my experience that both of these processes are productive for the development of individuation in the group.

In most research on the outcome of psychotherapy, it is generally assumed that time is an important factor. Insufficient exposure to treatment is often given as a reason to explain negative treatment results. However, experience—corroborated by recent findings on short-term and time-limited psychotherapies—suggests that extended exposure to psychodrama is a relatively unimportant factor influencing outcome. A review of the research indicates that positive results may be obtained from comparatively short exposures to psychodrama (Kellermann, 1987a).

Psychodrama may, therefore, be characterized as a brief method of psychotherapy, sharing many of the common technical characteristics of crisis-oriented, focused, single-session therapies described by Butcher & Koss (1978). A single session psychodrama is of relatively short duration, with limited goals, the action being focused on a specific, basic and concrete issue. Many psychodramatic case studies presented in the literature describe such a form of single session therapy. Having said that, however, I agree with Kipper (1983) that 'such one-session case reports may unintentionally convey the message that "it takes one psychodrama to do the job." It is important to be cognizant of that possibility and make certain that readers will not falsely understand it in this way' (p.125).

The Physical Setting (Where?)

Psychodrama may take place in any open space which permits physical movement and provides privacy with no distractions. The use of Moreno's classical round stage with raised platform and balcony is rare today. It is more common to work in a moderately sized room, equipped with wall-to-wall rugs, a few mattresses, pillows, comfortable chairs and flexible lighting.

Psychological interventions are very sensitive to the setting within which they are delivered. According to Moreno & Moreno (1969), 'the configuration of space as a part of the therapeutic process is of utmost importance' (p.14). The atmosphere created by any given setting will influence the emotional state of the group. For example, a large and spacious room may evoke feelings of freedom, optimism and joy, while a smaller room without windows may give some people the feeling of being locked up. For years I worked in a municipal bomb-shelter in Jerusalem which invoked a paradoxical mixture of stuffiness, suffocation and underground repression together with safety and freedom of expression. In contrast, when working at a resort in Norway, I felt literally 'on the top of the mountain,' inspired by the fabulous view and powerful nature all around. While the bomb-shelter induced fantasies of destruction and defence, the mountain resort inspired vision and growth for me and for the participants.

Client Characteristics (For Whom?)

Psychodrama does not have one single target population. While most participants are between 20 and 50, some are below and above those ages. Younger and older participants are mostly treated in groups which are homogeneous in age, such as children's, adolescent or old age groups. Participants may be of either sex, although it seems to be an internationally recognized phenomenon, in psychodrama and in other methods of psychotherapy, that most participants are women. The reason for this female predominance is still unclear, but it does influence the norms and attitudes of the method at large; and I agree with Davies (1976) that psychodrama 'has a natural appeal to the extroverted' (p.204). Regarding intelligence, psychodrama may be used not only with highly intelligent and well educated people, but also with retarded and less educated people who may find psychodrama's broad spectrum of non-verbal techniques an excellent instrument for communication. There seems to be no relation between suitability to psychodrama and ethnic or socio- economic status, according to Kipper (1978). The same also seems to be true for religion, which, in my experience, has proven an insignificant criterion for the selection of clients for psychodrama.

The question, 'Who participates in psychodrama?' is thus readily answered. The question, 'For whom is psychodrama the treatment of choice?' is more difficult to answer. From one point of view, all people can benefit from psychodrama at various times in their life cycles, particularly when in emotional distress. From another point of view, there is a category of people for whom psychodrama is the treatment of choice—and yet there is no way to identify these people. It cannot be done along the lines of symptoms, syndromes or diagnostic categories. A helpful indication may be the person's coping ability or ego strength. But there is little consensus in this area. Goldman & Morrison (1984) recommend psychodrama for patients with all kinds of diagnoses: situational depression, severe behavioural disorders, chemical dependency, schizophrenia, manic depressive illness, psychotic disorders and eating disorders. 'We see [in psychodrama] literally everything that might be covered in the *Diagnostic and Statistical Manual of Mental Disorders, III*' (p.3).

This claim (implied also by J.L. Moreno), that psychodrama is the treatment of choice for all mental disorders, is greatly exaggerated. It is my experience that, while a wide variety of people may benefit from psychodrama, others are simply unsuited either to psychodrama itself, or to the setting in which it is conducted. Still others are best treated in conjunction with individual, group, family or pharmacological therapies. This point of view is similar to that of Polansky & Harkins (1969) who maintain that psychodrama should be regarded 'neither as a panacea nor as a nullity but as a mode of treatment which can be helpful to a substantial proportion of patients a large proportion of the time—which is about all one can say about any of the psychotherapies' (p.74).

Naturally, psychodrama can be helpful only to those individuals who are able and motivated to participate in the rather complex psychic rituals which characterize this approach. The ability, for example, to participate in the imaginary process of role playing without losing touch with outer reality seems to be a minimal requirement for participation. Furthermore, participants must be able to experience surges of feelings without a loss of impulse control, have at least some capacity to establish interpersonal relations, have a minimal tolerance for anxiety and frustration (ego strength), some psychological-mindedness, and a capacity for adaptive regression in the service of the ego. 'One could probably make a long list of so-called "inappropriate' patients since the crucial variable is not so much the specific diagnostic category, although this is partly a factor, as whether the patient can participate as an actor or member of the audience in a beneficial way and without interfering with the procedure' (Wolson, 1974, p.327).

There are those for whom psychodrama may be considered inappropriate. Extremely low-functioning chronic patients needing some form of constant rehabilitation are generally unsuited to psychodrama. These disordered individuals may profit from structured action techniques, role training exercises and a supportive group (Ossorio & Fine, 1959), but are generally unable to integrate the corrective emotional experiences of classical psychodrama. Furthermore, according to the literature of psychodrama and group psychotherapy, acute psychotic, paranoid, suicidal, manic, brain-damaged, sociopathic, and depressive patients, as well as 'as-if' characters, are poor candidates for outpatient psychodrama group therapy (Gonen, 1971; Wolson, 1974; Petzold, 1979; Yalom, 1975). Histrionic, narcissistic, borderline and related personality disorders, while they may benefit from psychodrama, require a special setting and a specially trained staff of auxiliaries. According to Sacks (1976a), candidates with physical disabilities, such as heart conditions, that make exertion or intense emotion dangerous, should be automatically ruled out. Sacks also suggests that patients who are too narcissistic to wait for their turn in a classical psychodrama may do better in a free interaction group.

Many types of people have been successfully treated with psychodrama, including prisoners, alcoholics, drug abusers, stutterers, disturbed children and families and people in crisis. The successful use of psychodrama therapy with adolescents, autistic children, hard-core offenders, anorexics, the sexually abused, alcoholics, and those dying of cancer was described by Holmes & Karp (1991). According to Leutz (1985a), psychodrama is indicated as treatment for disturbed human relations and interactions of more or less normal people as well as of neurotics, psychotics, narcissistic and borderline patients. 'Psychodrama helps the normal client to solve actual conflicts; the neurotic patient to uncover infantile conflicts; the psychotic patient to regain reality by means of concrete action; and the narcissistic and borderline patient in the process of separation and individuation' (p.246). Furthermore, psychodrama has been reported to be favourably used with some cases of psychosomatic disorders (Leutz, 1985a).

It is my belief that people with relatively strong egos who react in a nonadaptive manner to environmental stress are especially amenable to psychodrama. However, since most reports of failure or success are more anecdotal than experimental, we still have incomplete empirical evidence of the indications and contraindications of psychodrama therapy. My review of the 23 controlled outcome research reports published between 1952 and 1985 is so limited in scope that any generalization of its findings must be very tenuous. My report does indicate, however, that psychodrama is a valid alternative to other therapeutic approaches, especially in promoting behaviour change in adjustment, antisocial and related disorders (Kellermann, 1987a).

In sum, psychodrama may be helpful to a wide variety of people, cutting across diagnostic categories, individual and social problem areas, and a spectrum of behavioural disorders.

Therapist Characteristics (By Whom?)

The influence of therapists' characteristics on the process of therapy has traditionally received little attention in the literature, with the possible exception of the expressed expectation that therapists be experienced, competent and well trained. Psychoanalysts, who emphasize the detrimental influence of counter-transference, have even physically removed the persona of the therapist from the action and confined him or her to a place outside the purview of the patient. Lately, however, various therapist characteristics have been demonstrated to have a significant influence on the therapeutic process.

What are these potentially influential characteristics? Areas in which therapists may vary include proclivity for personal distance, activity, flexibility, or preference for goal-limited therapy (Wogan & Norcross, 1983); leadership style (Scheidlinger, 1982), self-disclosure (Dies, 1977; Curtis, 1982) and type of relations established with clients. Research has also been conducted on the effects of the therapist's feelings, interest, prejudices, expectations, and assertive behaviour on the therapeutic process (Janzen, & Myers, 1981). All of these studies conclude that the personal characteristics, clinical experience, and professional activities of therapists profoundly influence their techniques and attitudes, and affect the process and outcome of therapy.

The professional roles of the psychodramatist have been regarded as central to the psychotherapeutic process (see Chapter 3) from the very beginning, and the effects of the therapist's personality as a potent variable in therapy are obvious (see Chapter 4). Any research on the process and the outcome of psychodrama which does not include the multiple personality characteristics of the psychodramatist is incomplete.

Group and Auxiliary Characteristics (With Whom?)

According to Moreno, every participant in psychodrama is a potential therapeutic agent to the others. The group becomes a social microcosm which provides the setting in which new interpersonal relations may emerge. It is therefore crucial to organize the psychodrama group in such a way that a therapeutic atmosphere can develop. Some guidelines of organization for group psychotherapy, such as those recommended by Yalom (1975) and others, may be applicable to psychodrama as well.

A criterion for group selection which emphasizes cohesiveness as a primary factor of composition is ego strength. If the participants have equal ego strength, they generally develop some positive interpersonal 'chemistry,' or 'common language,' which greatly improves the positive outcome of psychodrama. Such interpersonal sensitivity, or 'tele' as it was called by Moreno (1953), is 'the factor responsible for the increased rate of interaction between members of a group' (p.312). Other criteria, such as sex, age and occupation may be allowed to vary widely, because mixed and heterogeneous sex and age groups permit a more extensive and realistic type of interpersonal sharing and learning than do homogeneous groups. Optimally, group members should be selected to represent a variety of life stages and personalities in order to fill the variety of desired roles, to empathize in doubling and to give multifaceted sharing after the psychodrama.

The size of a psychodrama group varies considerably. It can include as few as five members and as many as over a hundred, but most practitioners consider 10 to 15 participants to be the optimal number. A group of this size has enough participants to take the various roles required, yet is small enough for the psychodramatist to attend to the emerging interpersonal issues evolving between group members. In larger groups, the active participation of individual members declines, and the groups have difficulty building cohesiveness.

There are those who do profit immensely from participation in larger groups and open demonstration sessions. The presence of a large audience invokes for some a sense of being before a general public (Sacks, 1976a). This lends a sense of importance to what occurs on stage and for many protagonists the ensuing 'public' self-exposure is remarkably effective in relieving guilt and shame. With more disturbed participants, however, smaller and more intimate groups are recommended.

The Outcome of Psychodrama
Some professionals who have never experienced psychodrama for any substantial amount of time are afraid of psychodrama as a therapeutic method. Many tend to overdramatize its process and emphasize its presumed dangers. Others exaggerate its virtues in a naive, superficial manner which violates the most elementary precepts of social psychology. Both groups are unaware of the relatively recent attempts that have been made to investigate scientifically psychodrama's therapeutic potentials (Kipper, 1978; 1989; Schramski & Feldman, 1984; Kellermann, 1987; D'Amato & Dean, 1988; Schneider-Duker, 1991). Such controlled studies have shown that, employed by reasonably trained professionals with awareness of its limits, psychodrama can make a contribution either on its own or as an adjunct to any of the manifold branches of psychotherapy, whether these be behaviouristic, psychoanalytic, or existential-humanistic.

Because of the technical difficulty of studying the outcome of psychodrama in a scientific manner—so many variables are involved and it is impossible to control them all—most accounts of the effectiveness of psychodrama have been 'quasi-naturalistic,' or anecdotal. The conclusions from these studies, as well as the evaluations of participants of psychodrama, have been largely positive. At their worst, negative responses have included characterizations of psychodrama as boring, a waste of time, or of too short duration. Almost no negative side effects have been reported.

The follow-up studies, because they have been few in number, do not clearly indicate the ability of participants to apply the dramatic changes which occur during intensive psychodrama workshops to their life outside the group. Nonetheless, it is my experience that the effects of psychodrama may be felt long after the end of therapy. This is in agreement with Polansky & Harkins' (1969) conclusion that 'the psychodramatic situation may be exploited to bring powerful intrapsychic forces into play. When these can be harnessed, striking results may be achieved with some patients in the direction of eventual cure' (p.87).

Illustration of a Psychodrama Session

The following illustration is based on a session conducted with a group of over 50 students-in-training who participated in a psychodrama workshop with Zerka T. Moreno. The session lasted about one and a half hours and was videotaped. What follows is an edited version of the protagonist's description of the session, having watched it on video.

Who Shall Drive My Green Car?

Bill, the protagonist, was a 29-year-old man who was chosen by Zerka Moreno out of seven group members who had volunteered to work. He was well warmed up and presented his theme in the following manner: 'I have a little boy who is driving my car. I don't want it to be like that anymore. I want to meet the part in me which allows that little boy to drive the car. I want to drive it myself.'

Zerka asked Bill about the car: 'How does it look? What kind of a car is it? Who drives it?' Bill explained that the car was green with four seats: 'Two persons sit in the car, one is driving and the other is sitting in the back seat, representing two parts of myself: Small Bill and Big Bill. Small Bill drives the car while Big Bill sits in the back seat.' Zerka: 'Let's see that!'

SCENE 1: THE GREEN CAR

The scene is set with four chairs to portray the car: two chairs for the front seat and two chairs for the back seat. An auxiliary is chosen to play the role of Small Bill in the front seat while Bill himself sits in the back seat. The auxiliary is put in role by Bill, who shows him how to play Small Bill. Bill (as Big Bill) then sits in the back seat and expresses his wish to drive the car. But Small Bill refuses, arguing that he will not let Big Bill drive the car. Despite his desperate efforts to persuade Small Big to yield his seat to him, Big Bill fails to move Small Bill from his position.

Zerka urges Big Bill to be strong and the entire group tries to motivate Big Bill to stand up for himself and take his place in the car but Bill is stuck, seemingly overwhelmed and paralyzed by fear and unable to move in any direction.

Zerka suggests that Big Bill reverse roles with Small Bill in order to show Bill how to take the driver's seat. Zerka: 'You are strong, you know the love you want from your father. You are the one who remembers and knows.' But in the role of Small Bill, standing on his knees in front of the auxiliary playing Big Bill, Bill still is unable to come up with an idea and he remains immobile and silent.

ZERKA: Who do you want to meet behind all this?

BILL: My father.

ZERKA: OK, let's find out what it is that Small Bill did not get as a child.

SCENE 2: SMALL BILL IN BEDROOM

In the second scene, the protagonist—now at the age of eight—is lying in his bed in his room on an autumn evening, crying silently. He cannot fall asleep, being frightened and lonely and disturbed by the noise coming from a party which is taking place in the living room.

ZERKA: Why are you crying?

BILL: I am afraid of the darkness.

ZERKA: Who can be out there in the darkness?

BILL: My uncle Walter...

ZERKA: Let's meet uncle Walter.

The same person who played Small Bill in the first scene is chosen to play Walter and put in role by Bill. Bill (as Walter) explains that uncle Walter was a kind of paternal chief in their family, a huge man with a strong voice, a stiff foot and a glass-eye which especially frightened Bill.

BILL (as Walter): I am not always angry even though my voice sounds that way. I can see something in you, Bill, that I have never been able to take care of myself.

ZERKA: Walter, what do you want to tell Bill?

BILL (as Walter): Take care of yourself, Bill. You have opportunities I never had.

ZERKA: Now be the scared Bill lying in bed.

They reverse roles.

BILL: You are ugly, uncle Walter.

ZERKA: You don't have to be afraid of him, even though he has a glass eye…

WALTER: You don't have to be afraid of me. I know I am ugly but you are not ugly. Your dad told me what a good boy you are. I wish I could be like you, Bill.

BILL: Yes, I could perhaps use something from you, too.

WALTER: You see, Bill, this thing about my eye was an accident…I got a fishhook in my eye.

BILL: Does dad know you are here?

WALTER: No. Do you want me to go to the kitchen and tell him?

BILL; No. I can go to the kitchen myself!

ZERKA: Mother and father do not understand that a child has the right to be afraid. Say goodbye to Walter, we are going to change the scene.

They say goodbye to each other and Walter leaves.

ZERKA: Walter has been here, the one you are most afraid of. Now we must look into what makes Mum and Dad not accept the fact that you are afraid. Who are you going to meet?

BILL: Dad.

An auxiliary playing father is introduced. Bill explains that his father was a worker who laboured in so much noise that he became deaf in one ear.

ZERKA *(to the auxiliary playing Father)*: You have a son lying in his room, scared.

BILL: No, I met him in the kitchen.

ZERKA: Show us.

SCENE 3: BILL WITH FATHER.

First Bill instructs the auxiliary how to play Bill's father. Bill (as father) come in to the kitchen to get alcohol while the auxiliary (as Bill) is sitting in front of the stove, quivering.

AUXILIARY *(as Bill)*: Walter was here. I am scared and I can't sleep.

BILL *(as father)*: Yes, you are afraid Bill. I don't know how to take care of you. Shall I get mum?

BILL: No, I want you to be here!

BILL *(as father)*: But we have a party, and…you can't just be sitting here! Father carries Bill into the bedroom.

ZERKA *(to father)*: You won't get anywhere with your son if you are treating him like that. Bill, go out of the role as father and show us, as yourself, what kind of a father you need. Here, at least, you can make father who you want him to be. But remember, Small Bill inside of you is a human being with thoughts, ideas, and feelings. He has the right to be heard.

The scene from the kitchen is repeated, but this time in an ideal version. After giving the instruction to an auxiliary on how to play 'Ideal Father,' Bill becomes eight-year-old Bill in the kitchen while the auxiliary takes the role of Ideal Father.

FATHER: Bill, what do you do here in the kitchen?

BILL: I am so afraid. Walter was here.

FATHER: Are you so afraid? *(Father embraces his son and Bill breaks into tears in his father's arms.)*

BILL: I am so afraid that you will be angry with me!

FATHER: We shall be together now. Shall we go to your bed, so we can speak a little together?

FATHER *(at the bed-side)*: You have such a small bed, Bill, and I have such a big belly. *(They lie together in bed, talking playfully for a while. Bill is happy and content and falls asleep in his father's arms.)*

ZERKA: Now we have two possibilities: you can either show how you take care of the small one within yourself, or how you take care of your little son. I suggest we do the first scene once again.

SCENE 4. BACK TO THE BEGINNING

The scene is set as was the first scene, with Big Bill and Small Bill sitting in the car.

ZERKA: Now show us how you wish to bring the Little-One along with you into life. *(Talking to Big Bill)* You must show us how the Little-One can help you to be productive in life.

BILL *(Partly to the group and partly to Small Bill)*: He is the best playmate I have, really. But you are smart, too. So from now on I shall decide the speed of the car. I shall drive it, but I'll let you come with me, always, if you want to!

Bill changes places with Small Bill and shows the group how he drives the car himself with Small Bill in the back-seat.

The session is closed with sharing.

Discussion

This session clearly dealt with assertiveness in relation to outside and inside authorities. For the protagonist, to drive his car meant to be in charge of his own life and to stand up for himself. The green colour of the car symbolized growth, especially significant since his development had been arrested. But the session also addressed a conflict between the weak and strong parts of the protagonist, and the need to find a proper intra-psychic balance between them.

Bill had grown up as the youngest child in his family and, as such, had been given the role of the 'small one' who was expected to sit in the 'back seat'. This role was reinforced by Bill's fear of his uncle, the paternal chief of the family, and by the lack of support from Bill's father. Thus, in a certain sense, Bill still felt like a child dominated by frightening inner authority figures. And, although Bill was growing older and becoming 'Big Bill,' 'Small Bill' was still steering Bill's life. This left Bill 'sitting in the back,' immobilized by fear.

In his psychodrama, Bill was helped to confront the frightening figures from his childhood and to reverse roles with them. This helped him to understand what had hindered him from growing up as a man, and, in the light of this understanding, to take a step towards becoming his own authority.

This 'imaginary' or 'figurative' psychodrama (see Chapter 9) enabled the protagonist to present his inner world in the protected disguise of make-believe, to express pent-up feelings of fear and rejection, and to achieve significant action-insight. For the protagonist himself, the most significant part of the psychodrama was to receive support from his father and thus to internalize a more positive paternal figure. In Bill's own words: 'For me, this was the essence of my psychodrama. To a little son, a father is as close as he can get to God. A God must be aware of his role, and be willing to walk the road together with his son: from God to master of an apprentice, from teacher to separation, from separation to friend. But when Dad is not there, the son is left with a negative role model and insufficient masculine training. Father will be a weak role model. And that is what emerged in my psychodrama. Nobody had taught me how to drive the car. By seeing this pattern, something could slowly change. I started to learn how to drive myself and become a man in my own right. This made it possible for Big Bill and Small Bill to swap places in the last scene of the drama.'

Conclusion

I have here defined psychodrama as a certain kind of psychotherapy: a method of healing which uses action methods. Such a delineation, however, does not imply that psychodrama should be used only for the purpose of removing symptoms and for mediating disturbed patterns of behaviour. As illustrated in the above example, psychodrama is also a method used for promoting personality growth and development; its effects extend from the limited objective of helping to control symptoms to the liberation of the rich potentials of human growth and creativity. This introduces a new, or at least a wider dimension into the field of psychotherapy; a dimension that deals, on the one hand, with the problems of coping behaviour of the so-called 'normal' person and, on the other, with immaturity associated with inhibited growth. In the latter manifestation, psychodrama aims at a resolution of blocks in psychosocial development in order that the individual may aspire to more complete and spontaneous self-actualization, more productive attitudes towards life, and more gratifying relationships with others.

CHAPTER 2

Theory

Psychodrama seems to be known more for its applications than for its theories. According to reviews of the literature, there are comparatively few people developing psychodrama theory and there is little going on in systematic research. Instead, we find a large number of practitioners using techniques without any firm theoretical basis. Farson (1978) pointed out that most human-istic psychologists are anti-theoretical. This, I believe, also holds true for psy-chodramatists in general. It seems to me that psychodramatists have a preference for spontaneous action, emotional experience and the release of feelings at the expense of healthy skepticism, critical questioning and solid research. As a result, the theories upon which psychodrama is based have not been sufficiently expanded, revised or tested, and remain a hodgepodge of unrelated thoughts, unintegrated by any one systematic framework.

In Chapter 1 of this book I proposed a 'theory-free,' procedural definition of psychodrama. I did this not because I believe that psychodrama should be viewed in a pragmatic fashion as a collection of unsystematic treatment inter-ventions, but in order to unite practitioners of diverse persuasions within one common framework. It is hoped that this framework will be sufficiently broad to include a wide range of theoretical views of psychodrama. Kipper's (1988) response that 'a procedure (a method) requires a rationale, a model, or a theoretical foundation of its own' (p.165), goes without saying. But, from what I can see, such a theoretical foundation has not yet been developed. I agree with Boria (1989) that 'the theoretical structure of psychodrama is not more than a framework or a "skeleton" of a body still to be built' (p.167). This is, according to Polansky & Harkins (1969), one of the reasons why psychodrama has not gained more popularity: 'Most therapists prefer a method of treatment grounded on a reasonably well-developed general theory of personality, such as the psychoanalytic' (p.74).

We must make a commitment to theory if we want psychodrama to grow. Psychodrama theory should provide the practitioner with a framework within which to view the protagonist and with a rationale for each intervention. Such a theory would be evaluated continually, and revised according to ongoing observations.

Several practitioners justify their practice with the help of theories adapted from psychoanalysis, social psychology, Gestalt psychology, transactional analysis, self/ego-psychology, behavioural learning, eclecticism, existential philosophy, interpersonal approaches or humanistic psychology. But most psychodramatists still refer to the classical formulations of J.L. Moreno when asked to provide a rationale for their work. 'Psychodrama's scientific roots are buried deep in Moreno's philosophies of spontaneity, creativity, the moment, and theories of role and interaction' (Yablonsky & Enneis, 1956, p.149). It is my feeling that, although Moreno's theories are useful to explain many clinical situations, they fail to provide a sufficiently uniform and comprehensive theoretical structure for psychodrama therapy. Moreno was a creative inventor in his own way, but he never paid enough attention to the consistent validation of his system. In a desperate effort to create one unified theory of the universe, he attempted to bring together mutually exclusive viewpoints which were often based on contradictory assumptions.

The purpose of this chapter is to study Moreno's theories from a meta-scientific point of view by examining the governing assumptions of psychodrama when regarded as natural and/or as human science, and by discussing the possibility for integrative solutions. My hope is that this examination will pave the way for the development of a consistent theoretical basis for the practice of psychodrama, based upon the existing tenets of Morenean concepts.

A Metascientific Frame of Reference

Many writers, in and out of psychology, have dealt with the ways theories are used in science (Kuhn, 1970; Radnitzky, 1970; Hempel, 1965; Lesche, 1962). The present study has grown out of the suggestions of those writers employing 'metascience,' or 'philosophy of science' as a way of structuring and understanding theories, helping to describe them on a meta-level.

Schematically, the levels of observation are illustrated in Table 2.1 with examples from psychodrama.

Table 2.1. A Metascientific Frame of Reference.

Meta-theory	Meta-science	human/natural science
Theory	Theory of person, Theory of psychotherapy	spontaneity theory catharsis theory
Practice	Therapeutic practice	role playing

According to a division proposed by Dilthey (1944), there are two highly influential 'schools' of metascience: the natural sciences and the human sciences,

Table 2.2. The Governing Factors of Psychodrama as Natural and as Human Science.

Metascience	PD As Natural Science	PD As Human Science
Therapeutic Practice		
	Behavioral Psychodrama	Existential Psychodrama
Norms:	mental health	awareness of existence
Values:	normal behaviour	emancipation, experience
Goals:	symptom removal adjustment	spontaneity self-actualization
Diagnosis:	relevant	irrelevant
Respondents:	patients	individuals
Interventions:	therapeutic	dramatic self-presentation
Theoretic Assumptions		
Phenomena of Interest	overt behaviour in a role player	covert behaviour in a co-producing actor
Image of Person:	biological organism mechanical being	intentional person spontaneous being
Ideal of Person:	adapted	authentic
Ideal of Science:	'quasi-naturalistic'	humanistic
Ideal of Knowledge:	neo-behaviourism causal explanations description of regu- larities	intentional contexts understanding of acts historical biography
Ontology:	materialistic monism	idealistic monism
Epistemology:	determinism	non-determinism
Research-guiding Interests	logical empiricism	hermeneutic-dialectic
Status of research- Objects	subject-object	subject-subject

each reflecting a unique perspective toward the social world. The natural science approach is characterized as being empirical, positivistic, reductionistic, objective, analytic, quantitative, deterministic, concerned with prediction and largely operating with the assumptions of an independent observer. The human science approach is concerned with meaning, description, qualitative differences, the process of explication, investigating intentional relations, articulating the phenomena of human consciousness and behaviour within the context of a broadened conception of nature, and assuming the privileged position of the life-world, the primacy of relations and the presence of an involved scientist (Giorgi, 1970).

Corresponding to these two schools of metascience, the metatheory of psychodrama will be divided into one natural and one human science part, with the natural science approach illustrated by 'behavioural' psychodrama and the human science approach by 'existential' (or phenomenological) psychodrama. The reason for this division is not to create two separate systems, but to determine the fundamental viewpoints and governing assumptions that guide the thinking in each tradition of scientific practice.

One might argue that it is impossible to separate psychodrama in such a dualistic manner and that this separation may introduce an artificial, unnecessary and perhaps damaging split which would distort the integral psychodramatic system. I agree on the desirability of integration, which is shown by the illustration of 'integral psychodrama,' but insist on the temporary differentiation for heuristic purposes.

An overview of the governing factors in psychodramatic theory is presented in Table 2.2.

Therapeutic Practice

Behavioural psychodrama (Sturm, 1965) is based on medical thinking, the goal being to cure illness, remove symptoms, change behaviour, or promote social adjustment. Mental health is equated with 'normal' behaviour and diagnosis is relevant and necessary. The main function of the psychodramatist is technical: to prescribe for patients specific technical interventions so that they may achieve predetermined goals. Some traces of this thinking may be found in Moreno's writings, such as: 'Psychodrama puts the patient on a stage where he can work out his problems with the aid of a few therapeutic actors. It is a method of diagnosis as well as a method of treatment' (Moreno, 1937/1972, p.177). However, in spite of this quasi-medical language, psychodrama most often adopts a more humanistic approach to personality change.

In existential psychodrama, there is no conception of health, normality, or pathology, and diagnosis is therefore irrelevant and unnecessary. Psychodrama is not 'therapy' in the medical sense of the word, but an emotional experience within the framework of an interpersonal encounter with spiritual values of its own. This experience may or may not make the participants more aware of themselves or more balanced. In any case, the goal is not to produce 'cure,' but simply to become as spontaneous and creative as possible within the boundaries of each individual's personal limitations. A generous definition, it seems. But in order to differentiate this activity from dramatic entertainment and from spontaneous play in general, I still prefer to define existential psychodrama broadly as a kind of psychotherapy.

Integral psychodrama may be achieved through adapting the goals of technique to the needs of the respondents. The value conflict between health in behavioural psychodrama and awareness in existential psychodrama may perhaps be solved by the application of Maslow's hierarchical system of values. Behavioural psychodrama is used with patients who demand satisfaction of more fundamental needs, such as symptom removal. Existential psychodrama is used with anyone who is motivated to liberate him or herself from false self-conceptions and unrealistic perceptions of others. These protagonists have already satisfied their basic needs and may therefore strive for more self-actualization and spontaneity.

Theoretical Assumptions

Phenomena of Interest

The subject matter of investigation in behavioural psychodrama is the overt behaviour-acts of a role player, eschewing all reference to internal, mental life phenomena. Examples of Moreno's behavioural thinking include the emphasis on action-theory, action-language and motor events in psychodrama, as well as the focus on 'behavioural psychodrama' (Moreno, 1963) and the general depreciation of the psychoanalytic theory of the unconscious.

But Moreno never adopted an extreme and pure behaviouristic theory of the world. In reality, Moreno also investigated covert mental processes, subjective experiences, impulses, and psychic energies in a more existential manner.

The subjective, covert consciousness of an intentional person is brought into the field of investigation in existential psychodrama. In their paper on *Existentialism, Daseinanalyse, and Psychodrama*, Moreno & Moreno (1959) stated that 'the full involvement of the actor in the act is a regular procedure, and emphasis is continually placed upon a subjectivistic frame of reference to the extreme' (p.215). In line with this thinking, Jonathan Moreno (1974) characterized psychodrama as a form of phenomenological psychotherapy.

It should be mentioned that psychodrama does not only study the overt behaviour and covert consciousness of one individual, but also the whole realm of interpersonal relations. According to Marineau (1989), the territory of psychodrama as it appears in Moreno's book *The Words of the Father* (1920) is 'the family, the group, the world, the universe—the place where the person is expressing himself at any given moment' (p.108).

Moreno & Moreno (1959) acknowledged the two paradoxical principles operating in the therapeutic investigation: 'one is the utterly subjective and existentialistic situation of the subject; the other is the objective requirements of the scientific method. The question is to reconcile the two extreme positions' (p.216). The fundamental rift between those who emphasize subjective, inner experience and those who stress objectivity and rationalism may be repaired by a synthesis of the two points of view. Such a synthesis is attempted in integrative psychodrama.

Integrative psychodrama is best understood within Moreno's role theory, which takes both overt and covert phenomena into consideration. The role, according to Moreno (1937/1972) is 'a unit of synthetic experience into which private, social, and cultural elements have emerged' (p.184). Psychodramatic role theory was inspired by the functionalism of William James and John Dewey and by the social psychology of Mead (1934), who wrote: 'In social psychology we get at the social process from the inside as well as from the outside. Social psychology is behaviouristic in the sense of starting off with an observable activity—the dynamic, on-going social process, and the social acts which are its component elements. But it is not behaviouristic in the sense of ignoring the inner experience of the individual' (p.7).

Image and Ideal of a Person

When discussing the ideal of a person in Moreno's theory, I will consider his basic concept of spontaneity, defined as 'the variable degree of adequate response to a situation of variable degree of novelty' (Moreno, 1953, p.722). This definition is clearly behaviouristic and emphasizes normal, adequate, and optimally adaptive behaviour.

However, Moreno's definition of spontaneity has been frequently criticized for inconsistency, for example by Aulicino (1954).

So far as I can see, and according to the works of Bergson (1928) and Peirce (1931) who are quoted frequently in Moreno's writing, the concept of spontaneity is an existential phenomenon. Spontaneity in existential psychodrama would be defined as an uninhibited, immediate, and first response, impossible to quantify or measure. In line with this understanding, the image and ideal of a person in psychodrama is explicitly humanistic, viewing human beings as intentional and authentic, striving for genuine expression from within. Human beings should be considered as a whole, as living and as becoming, in and out of the world, in a particular situation and in a personal encounter with other people, doing something which expresses something significant in their life.

But Moreno (1951) did not take an either-or position because he felt that 'man is more than a psychological, social, or biological being' (p.201). This view of a person led Bischof (1964) to classify Moreno's personality theory as a biosocial interaction theory: a theory postulating that human beings have developing functions taking form through constant interaction between the biological organism and the social environment, and that this complex duality remains dynamic in every way.

Thus the image and ideal of a person in integral psychodrama is explicitly holistic, attempting to give a complete picture of human beings rather than a partial one. Holism, according to Farson (1978), 'considers the person as a complex dynamic system in interaction with a continually expanding physical, social, and temporal context' (p.27).

Ideals of Science and Knowledge

On the one hand, Moreno's investigations had a natural science ideal of logical-deductive reasoning with experimental research and the aim of objectivity. On the other hand, Moreno was an existentialist, deeply involved in phenomenological philosophy and metaphysical speculations following the ideals of subjectivity.

An example of the natural science ideal in Moreno's writings is to be found in Moreno's (1953) advocacy of sociometric empirical research on spontaneity: 'Sociometry has taken the concept of spontaneity from the metaphysical and philosophical level and brought it to empirical test' (p.39). This position is incompatible with a pure humanistic ideal of science. However, Moreno's research was never pure natural science. When he spoke of 'empirical tests,' these tests did not meet the general requirements of experimental or quasi-experimental research.

In reality, Moreno's humanistic bias shows through in most of his writing as, for example, in his studies of the 'encounter'. According to Moreno (1960b), 'The clinical encounter is the primary method for studying the personality of another person, and the data derived therefrom provide the criteria on which all other possible data should be evaluated' (p.145). Moreno's humanistic studies emphasize the hidden spiritual dimensions of reality and the intuitive, mystical sources of truth that cannot be investigated by the experimental approach. Moreno (1953) felt that the scientific-technological civilization denigrated humanistic values and threatened human survival, and that objective methods of knowing neglected the creative dimensions of experience.

Moreno himself said that his own research had neither subjectivity nor objectivity as ideals, but rather 'quasi-objectivity' (Moreno & Moreno, 1959, p.215). A better understanding between phenomenologists, existentialists, and empirical scientists could, Moreno believed, be successfully reached in sociometric theory. This would demonstrate that 'objective' and 'subjective' validation did not exclude one another but could be construed as a continuum.

From a historical perspective, Moreno was influenced by existentialist philosophy in Europe until 1925 when he moved to the United States. At that time he observed that 'a psychology of action is more akin to the Americans' (Moreno, 1972, p.11) and became influenced by the pragmatism of C.S. Peirce, W. James, and J. Dewey and by the empirical behaviourism which was then dominating the academic community in America. But he never took an either-or position.

An integrative approach to psychodrama research would take the position that no truly rigorous science can be accomplished until we analyze the pure phenomenal data themselves, free from any pre-suppositions. Thus, in attempting to resolve the subjective-objective and the internal-external dichotomies, both sources of knowledge would be considered: interiority, introspection and involvement of the subject and subjective experience which are the materials of the humanist, and exteriority, empirical data collected through the senses which are the materials of the natural scientist.

Ontology

I would assume that most psychodramatists agree with the common-sense view of ontology that body and mind interact and that both behavioural and existential events must be emphasized in psychodrama. However, some psychodramatists probably have a preference for the behavioural side, adopting a materialistic monism (there is only body), whereas others have a preference for the existential side, adopting an idealistic monism (there is only mind).

This has more than theoretical relevance. Because, if we believe that we *are* our bodies, that we are 'some-body', then we may emphasize physical expressions in therapy, concretizing feelings and using bioenergetic techniques. If, on the other hand, we emphasize the 'mind,' then we may emphasize mental imagery and cognitive insight.

Neither of these ontological positions reflects Moreno's view as well as did the pluralist solution of William James (1909). This view assumed that 'mind and body are but two of many aspects of reality and that there may be a continuum of cosmic consciousness behind the material world' (Knight, 1950, p.72).

Integral psychodrama is perhaps most compatible with the monistic double-aspect view of Spinoza, who argued that mind and body are but two aspects of a single underlying reality. What appears to be mind from one perspective appears as body from another. This may be illustrated by the use of psychodramatic action techniques that emphasize the expression of the whole person (mind and body).

Epistemology

Epistemology is concerned with the question of how we know, the relationship between body and mind, the problem of cause and effect, and with determinism. The methodological dichotomy which was introduced by Dilthey (1944) suggested that natural sciences are concerned with *explanation* while human sciences are concerned with *understanding*.

Behavioural psychodrama is based on determinism, demanding scientific explanation of behavioural events in terms of independent variables. Similarly, psychoanalytic psychodrama is based on determinism in so far as it attempts to explain a person's behaviour in terms of antecedent events.

Existential psychodrama is non-deterministic in its attempt to understand human motives and intentions. Existential psychodramatists prefer to ask *how* a person is acting in a descriptive manner, rather than *why* a person is behaving in a certain way. Since the realities of existence are probable rather than absolute, existential psychodrama cannot answer the question 'why' which appears to require ultimate and absolute causes, such as those assumed by psychoanalysis.

Moreno criticized Freud for relying too much on psychic determinism and not leaving enough room for spontaneity; he criticized Bergson for going to the other extreme. Within his spontaneity theory, Moreno (1972) tried to create a functional, operational determinism where 'in the development of a person, there can be original moments, truly creative and decisive beginnings without any horror vacui, that is, a fear that there is no comfortable past behind it from which it springs' (p.103). These moments, according to Moreno (1951) 'operate in a totally different dimension from the past-present-future continuum and are not submitted to causality and determinism' (p.208).

Integrative psychodrama attempts to encompass both positions. On the one hand, memories of past events are presented in psychodrama in order to gain insight into how those events formed the present behaviour. On the other, present (and future) experiences are externalized in order to perceive more fully the immediate existence of here and now.

Research-Guiding Interests

If the main motive in research is to gain information about objective processes, a logical-empirical approach to psychodrama should be taken. If the motive is emancipatory self-understanding, a descriptive, phenomenological and/or a process-oriented (hermeneutic-dialectic) research approach should be taken.

Behavioural psychodrama is oriented towards hard facts, quantitative studies, and controlled outcome research. Existential psychodrama is oriented towards qualitative studies, process research, and single case studies (n=1). Integral psychodrama makes a point of combining both qualitative and quantitative methods of research in any single study.

Moreno himself acknowledged the difficulties inherent in validating research on psychodrama (Bischof, 1964): 'The question as to the validity of psychodrama has aroused considerable controversy in the course of the years. There have been two opinions. One emphasizes that the usual measures of reliability and validity do not seem to be particularly appropriate for psychodrama. If each person acts out his life honestly, the data are perfectly reliable and valid. The second opinion is that the current methods of measuring validity can be applied. The two opinions do not exclude one another. The two methods of validation, ('existential' and 'scientific') can be combined' (Moreno, 1968, p.3).

Status of Research-Objects

In psychodrama research based on the natural science model, research-objects must be approached with neutrality in order for the observations be 'objective'. But for all its 'objectivity,' natural science is unable to provide a context within which people and their interactions 'make sense'.

Moreno (1953) took a decidedly opposite, subjective, humanistic position on the status of research-objects, similar to the Malinowsky tradition in anthropology, field work sociologists, symbolic interactionists and more recently ethnomethodologists in sociology: 'Social sciences like psychology, sociology, and anthropology require that their objects be given 'research status' and a certain degree of scientific authority in order to raise their level from a pseudo-objective discipline to a science which operates on the highest level of its material dynamics. It accomplishes this aim by considering the research objects not only as objects, but also as research actors, not only as objects of observation and manipulation, but as co-scientists and co- producers in the experimental design they are going to set up' (p.64).

A basic starting point of this qualitative paradigm in conceptualizing the social world is to understand situations from the perspective of the participants in the situation. In order to understand the world, the investigator must go out into the world, live among the people as they live, learn their language and participate in their rituals and routines. Basing research on the principle of role reversal, the investigator must be a part of and, at the same time, apart from, the phenomena of interest. Integrative psychodrama attempts to comprise both closeness and distance, both laboratory research and field- and action-research, both observation and participation, both passive interpretation and active involvement.

Integration

I have discussed some natural and human science aspects of psychodrama as they appear in Moreno's writings and suggested an outline of integrative psychodrama. But is it possible to justify such an integrative approach?

According to Giorgi (1970), the attempt to integrate is often more 'a sign of wishful thinking than an actual integration of viewpoints and the synthesis is a simple juxtaposition of opposition in a side-by-side manner rather than one integral scientific approach. Fundamental views in natural science are contradictory to the views in human science. This makes a combination difficult, if not impossible, to justify. To deny contradictions in order to facilitate integration is of course a distorted position' (p.54).

Moreno did not deny that contradictions existed but, rather than think in black and white dichotomies, persisted in his wish to find integrative solutions. Recognizing the paradoxical nature of human experience, Moreno appreciated that opposites do co-exist and in fact define each other. Neither side gives the whole picture and both together are more complete than either alone. Jonathan Moreno (1974), Leutz (1976; 1977) Petzold (1980), Buer (1989) and Marineau (1989) considered Moreno's work to be a successful synthesis of opposite viewpoints.

Moreno refused to compartmentalize reality, wanting to achieve synthesis at all cost. He had a preference for combining contraries into unities and struggled to discover similarities rather than differences between opposite conceptions; 'I attempted a synthesis, not only for science's sake but also in order to maintain my own mental equilibrium' (Moreno, 1951, p.205).

Moreno's integrative effort was predated by Stern (1938) who felt that psychology must preserve the correlation between part and whole, figure and ground, analysis and totality, methods of explanation and methods of understanding. Like Moreno, Stern was critical of one-sided approaches, rejecting behaviourism because it closed off introspection, opposing psychoanalysis because it closed off the study of behavioural phenomena, and turning away from experimental psychology because it closed off experiential data.

We have a tendency to conceptualize phenomena in a dualistic manner, and thus many theories are described in terms of dichotomies and oppositional forces. Maslow (1968) emphasizes the importance of giving up this habit. 'Difficult though it may be, we must learn to think holistically rather than atomistically. All these 'opposites' are in fact hierarchically-integrated, especially in healthier people, and one of the proper goals of therapy is to move from dichotomizing and splitting toward integration of seemingly irreconcilable opposites' (p.174).

It is my position that psychodrama should strive towards such an integration. In the process of achieving this goal, psychodrama does not have to represent either an integration or a separation. I would rather see it as an ongoing developmental movement in which the natural and human aspects continually separate and differentiate while the whole theory individuates. Thus, in a way similar to the separation-individuation process of the human self (Mahler, 1968), a unified theory of psychodrama would develop. In the dialectic tradition of Hegel, this movement might be described as suggesting a thesis, contradicting it with an antithesis, and finally reaching a synthesis. According to Kuhn's (1970) theory of paradigmatic shifts, integral psychodrama would develop like a pendulum swinging from one side to the other, from qualitative to quantitative studies, from subjective to objective, from mind to body, and from theology to science, not being allowed to swing too far to either side. The middle ground of blending aspects of both approaches would represent the optimal position.

Conclusion

While most psychodramatists have focused almost exclusively on technical problems, the time has come to direct our interest towards the examination of theoretical issues as well. Much work remains to be done in the field of theory building, including studies on such central concepts as dreams, conflict, stress, regression, fixation, human development, learning, memory, perception, cognition, thinking, emotion, motivation and psychopathology. Furthermore, revisions of Moreno's theories of role-playing and role-taking, spontaneity-creativity, sociometry and sociatry, the 'cosmic' man and social atom and network, as well as a discussion of the political relevancy of his book *Who Shall Survive?* would be important. I hope that the present chapter will be of some help in making such future work more integrative.

CHAPTER 3

The Psychodramatist

In many ways, practicing psychodrama is a taxing job. It demands complex skills and personal qualities not developed in most people. For one thing, mastering the cast of characters involved in the psychodrama is in itself a monumental task. Furthermore, the practitioner must continually shift focus, from empathizing to staging to problem-solving to leading the group, while providing a clear sense of personal presence. Weiner (1967) emphasized the need for the psychodramatist to be a qualified and skilled professional within such diverse fields as psychiatry, sociology, medicine, biology, anthropology, education, society, and group process. Practicing psychodrama combines several of the more difficult accomplishments of the individual psychotherapist, psychoanalyst, group therapist, behaviour therapist, and theatre artist. While the simultaneous and natural occurrence of a high standard of proficiency in these skills in the same person is unusual a dedicated psychodramatist will strive to obtain excellence in them all.

The job of the psychodramatist has been insufficiently discussed in the previous literature, and therefore the purpose of this chapter is to give a basic description of the professional skills which are required of a psychodramatist. Such a description is important for several reasons. Obviously, it is indispensable as a basis for planning, executing, and evaluating psychodrama training programs, as a guideline for processing the work of students, and especially as an aid for establishing standards of certification. It is also important to take into account various therapist-related variables when conducting empirical research (Orlinsky and Howard, 1978; Lieberman, Yalom, & Miles, 1973), e.g. measuring type and skilfulness of therapist behaviour when evaluating outcome (Schaffer, 1983). Finally, a job-description may offer dedicated practitioners new ideas of how to improve their professional expertise.

The person in charge of a psychodrama session is variously called 'director of psychodrama,' 'psychodrama therapist,' 'psychodrama leader,' or simply 'practitioner of psychodrama'. In the following discussion, the uniform and neutral title 'psychodramatist' will be used.

The Professional Roles of the Psychodramatist

All psychodramatists enact a few specific and sometimes overlapping roles. Moreno (1972) described these as the roles of producer, of therapist/counsellor, and of analyst. I have revised the meaning of these roles and have added a fourth role which I feel is intrinsic to psychodrama, namely that of the group leader. Table 3.1 gives an overview of these roles and their functions, skills and ideals, which together comprise the professional demands on the psychodramatist.

Table 3.1. The Professional Roles of a Psychodramatist.

Roles	Functions	Skills	Ideals
Analyst	Empathizer	Understanding	Hermeneutic
Producer	Theatre-director	Staging	Aesthetic
Therapist	Agent Of Change	Influencing	Healing
Group Leader	Manager	Leadership	Social

Psychodramatists fulfil four interrelated and highly complex tasks. First, as analysts they are responsible for making themselves fully and accurately aware of the protagonists' condition. This includes understanding both personal and interpersonal phenomena in order to attribute meaning to experience and increase awareness of self. Second, as producers, psychodramatists are theatre directors translating the material presented into action which is emotionally stimulating and aesthetically pleasant. Third, as therapists, they are agents of change who influence their protagonists in ways that facilitates healing. Fourth, as group leaders, they foster a constructive work group climate which facilitates the development of a supportive social network. The overlapping and interlacing of these various roles forms the basis of the psychodramatist's professional identity.

Drawing on my own experience and on frequent observations of several other psychodramatists, I will discuss the modes of activity and professional skills that characterize these four roles and mention some of the controversies involved in their enactment, thus presenting a model of practice which any practitioner may strive to achieve.

1. Analyst

As analysts, psychodramatists are empathic listeners attempting to understand both personal and interpersonal phenomena. The primary task of this role is to gain a detailed understanding of the participants' feelings, thoughts, behaviour, and attitudes from a genetic, topographic, dynamic, economic, structural, adaptive and/or psychosocial point of view (Rapaport, 1960). According to Moreno (1937/1972), 'the director is the research leader—behind his new mask of the director the old masks of the observer, of the analyst, of the participant group member and of the actor are hidden, but still functioning' (p.247).

A proper term for analytic activity in psychodrama would be 'action-analysis,' rather than psycho-analysis or socio-analysis (Haskell, 1975), because this analysis covers not only inner psychic phenomena, or outer social phenomena, but the full range of communicative action of the whole person. As action-analysts, psychodramatists attempt to give meaning to present behaviour either in terms of past experiences (repetitive action), or in terms of counter-action, abreaction, and communicative action (see Chapter 10).

The possession of empathic skills is a necessary precondition for functioning in the psychodramatic role of analyst. According to Rogers (1957), it is also one of the necessary and sufficient conditions for bringing about personality change. Empathic skills include the ability to perceive the complexities of the emotional fabric in people accurately and can be developed by a combination of theoretical knowledge and life experience, as well as by exposure to psychodrama as protagonist and to psychoanalysis as analysand. Moreover, professional supervision may help to shed light on possible 'blind spots' and counter-transference issues which might otherwise contaminate or impair empathy.

The Five Stages of Action-Analysis

I believe that five stages of action can be distinguished in the psychodramatist's process of gaining knowledge of the protagonist.

(1) First, psychodramatists perceive what has been actually communicated by the protagonist, either verbally or nonverbally (object perception). This implies the capacity to be receptive to the immediate sensory (e.g. visual and auditory) material which is presented. Some psychodramatists in this phase become 'doubles' to the protagonist, a process that is called 'pacing' (Buchanan & Little, 1983) in NLP and in which psychodramatists try to match the verbal and non-verbal behaviours of the protagonist by giving special attention to eye-movement patterns, breathing, body posture, changes in facial muscles and colouring. The criteria of good object perception are clarity and precision; the result, an objective awareness of the protagonist. While this sounds simple, experience shows that our attention is very selective and that we frequently perceive only what we want to perceive.

(2) Second, psychodramatists identify emotionally with the protagonist while at the same time maintaining a separate identity. This involves an intuitive feeling on the part of the psychodramatist and implies a capacity to be simultaneously close and detached. The criteria of good empathic induction are responsiveness and sensitivity; the result, a subjective awareness of the protagonist.

(3) Third, psychodramatists comprehend the underlying messages and latent meanings of what is manifestly communicated by the protagonist. This does not involve extraordinary powers of perception, but rather an ability to listen with 'evenly suspended attention' to the 'hidden melody' of the unconscious. In the words of Palmer (1969): 'It takes a great listener to hear what is actually said, a greater one to hear what was not said but what comes to light in the speaking. To focus purely on the positivity of what a text explicitly says is to do an injustice to the hermeneutic task. It is necessary to go behind the text to find what the text did not, and perhaps could not, say' (p.234).

(4) Fourth, psychodramatists communicate back to the protagonist, in a meaningful way, what has been understood. This requires a capacity to know when the right moment has come to verbalize one's understanding or to suggest an intervention as a consequence of that understanding. Considerable sensitivity and appropriate timing are required in order not to force a premature interpretation on the protagonist.

(5) Fifth, psychodramatists seek verification from the protagonist of their understanding and, if mistaken, must be able to correct it. While theoretical preconceptions provide psychodramatists with concepts and models which guide their understanding, such previous knowledge is oppressive if used as a universal truth which protagonists are then persuaded to adopt. According to Singer (1970), 'While clients seem remarkably willing to understand that at best we know little, they seem rightfully unwilling to forgive us our intentions of having them prove us right in our theoretical preconceptions' (p.390).

In order for this not to happen, it is wise to approach the protagonist with 'socratic ignorance,' a philosophical attitude based on sceptical inquiry and critical questioning which minimize predetermined responses and shatter pretensions and presuppositions of knowledge. When entering the personal world of a protagonist with this attitude, the psychodramatist is like a stranger visiting for the first time; he or she must inquire about everything perceived.

2. Producer

As producers or stage managers, psychodramatists create dramatic art in order for the session to be an aesthetic experience. According to Moreno (1972), psychodramatists are engineers of coordination and production, and have to be on the alert to turn every clue which the protagonist offers into dramatic action.

In their capacity as stage managers, psychodramatists' task is to create a stimulating work of dramatic art. This work requires the psychodramatist to have specific directing skills, to help the protagonist set the scene, to control the placing of the actors on stage, to correct the personification of auxiliaries, to handle the warm-up, rhythm, and timing of the action, to give the stage the right atmosphere through lighting and physical set-up, and to be able to suggest possible ways of concretization which translate a situation into symbolic presentation. Furthermore, psychodramatists are expected to induce spontaneity in the session through their own enthusiasm, imagination and willingness to approach each session as a new adventure. According to Karp (1988), 'the director must have true sense of play, fun, and freshness and embody the humour in life as well as the pathos' (p.49). 'Like a playwright, the therapist guides dialogues, opens and resolves conflict. Like a sculptor, he or she shapes space. Like the conductor of an orchestra, he or she blends the contribution of many sources' (Riebel, 1990, p.129). Competence in these skills can be acquired from creative dramatics, drama therapy, role playing, improvisation and other forms of action methods based on drama.

The producer role makes it possible for psychodramatists to employ creatively a large inventory of psychodramatic techniques, and not only to use them in the classical way, but also to simplify and invent new uses for them. Like painters, sculptors, musicians, writers, dancers, actors, poets and other artists who use techniques as vehicles of expression and then expand them beyond their ordinary range, creative psychodramatists try to discover original ways of using their instruments. Directing intuitively rather than according to preordained rules, psychodramatists are often unconscious of how and why they do what they do, using what some artists call 'secret sources of inspiration,' a kind of creative activity which is beyond the reach of words.

Such refinement of specific skills presupposes the psychodramatists' knowledge of classical theatre production (both as director and as actor). According to terminology used in the theatre, the psychodramatist should be able to blend the Stanislavsky approach of emotional involvement and identification with the Brechtian approach of distancing and objectification. These two positions reflect the experiential and the observational tasks of the psychodramatist as producer. While each practitioner is inclined more towards one or the other of these extremes, both positions are important and it is essential to find a proper balance between them.

A suitable illustration of the psychodramatic role of producer is the famous Swedish theatre director Ingmar Bergman. Bergman's universe is ruled by the twin forces of fertile curiosity and creative energy. His art is bound up with an ability to establish a close and creative personal contact with his actors. This ability emanates in turn from his conviction that, in the final analysis, it will be the actor and the actor alone who must bring the text to life in the hearts of the audience. Observing Bergman at work, one cannot stay unimpressed by the intensity with which he follows every word and every move with an alert, almost childish excitement. It seems that he completely forgets himself when he directs, and becomes one with the other person. His great talent is that he hears notes that others don't hear, not even the actors themselves, and can give cues to bring out those notes. Without giving many instructions, he is able to create an atmosphere that empowers the actors and brings out the best in them (Marker & Marker, 1982).

Another illustration is that of the master director of illusion, Federico Fellini. Fellini is the expert in capturing the vibrations of a dream, a fantasy, or something that exists in another dimension. Similarly, skilful stage-managers are able to turn the psychodramatic stage into a place where anything, including the 'impossible,' can happen. They are passionately romantic and almost allergic to realism because realism ignores the spirit of the person and does not provide access to the sacred, ritualistic, transcendental and cosmic dimensions of experience. Meshing fact and fiction, they produce a kind of aesthetic truth in which the universals of time and space are dissolved. Tricks that cheat death, instruments that foretell the future, devices that help remember the past, and magic shops are some of the techniques psychodramatists use to produce dramatic art. Everybody knows that sculptures do not talk, that God makes no bargains, that empty chairs do not speak back and that walls between people are invisible. But skilful psychodramatists are able to lead protagonists across the border that separates the real outer world from the fantasy world of imagination. Before their natural suspicion is aroused, protagonists find themselves in a boundless place where the experience of reality is expanded and, for a short while, protagonists become more than mortal. When emphasizing the living spirit of inanimate objects in this way, psychodramatists produce unpredictable moments of change which conventional theories cannot sufficiently explain. During these moments, psychodramatists look like magicians, with extraordinary and amazing powers at their disposal (see Chapter 11).

3. Therapist

As therapists, psychodramatists function as agents of change who influence their protagonists in ways which facilitate healing. According to Moreno (1972), the ultimate responsibility for the therapeutic value of the total production rests upon the shoulders of the psychodramatist.

In their capacity as therapists, psychodramatists perform numerous healing interventions in order to alleviate suffering and bring protagonists one step further on their therapeutic journeys. This work requires psychodramatists to have extensive knowledge of normal and abnormal psychology, psychiatry and psychotherapy, to be able to apply psychodrama to a variety of protagonists who may need symptom reduction, crisis intervention, conflict resolution, and/or personality-change and be able to put into operation various therapeutic factors, such as emotional release, cognitive understanding, interpersonal feedback, and/or behavioural learning. Psychodramatists are required to employ psychodramatic techniques competently and put in action psychodramatic processes. They must facilitate the revival of past scenes and their associated affects, handle the many resistances which constantly evolve during psychodramatic explorations (see Chapter 12), and be able to choose between various therapeutic interventions according to the demands of specific situations. Finally, they are expected to justify their practice with a consistent theory—a rationale for why they, for example, choose to follow up on certain clues while they leave other clues unexplored.

The repertoire of the psychodramatist encompasses both nonverbal and verbal therapeutic interventions. Therapeutic interventions are intentional acts of influence calculated to produce a therapeutic (preventive, stabilizing, reparative, developing, or supportive) impact; they are possible responses to what a protagonist says or does. As such, therapeutic interventions suggest a framework for help-intended communication in psychodrama.

This communication may take many forms. Nonverbal interventions include, for example, the therapeutic use of physical distance, vocalization, eye-contact, body posture and the intentional use of silence as a means to stimulate imaginary processes. Whatever meaning one gives to nonverbal interventions, they are powerful influences and should therefore be used with great care and sensitivity. One of the most forceful nonverbal interventions in psychodrama is physical touch. It has various meanings for different protagonists. For some, touch may be experienced as an invitation to regress to a childlike state in which one receives parental caring and nourishment. Occasionally, such contact may provide a mysterious kind of healing energy which in itself helps the protagonist regain emotional balance. For others, physical touch may be felt as an intrusion of privacy or as a sexual seduction. One of the major challenges facing psychodramatists is to find the optimal physical distance for the protagonist to make progress. The nonverbal aspects of psychodrama are further discussed by Fine (1959).

Like nonverbal interventions, verbal interventions must be carefully gauged. The following verbal interventions are often used in psychodrama and will be described here: confrontation, clarification, interpretation, catharsis, acceptance, suggestion, advice, teaching, and self-disclosure (Bibring, 1954; Greenson, 1967; Goodman & Dooley, 1976).

> *Confrontation* refers to those statements which focus on the obvious, central, or significant issue to be explored. For example, when confronting a protagonist with a feeling, the psychodramatist focuses on this feeling and thus paves the way to its continued exploration. A confrontation may also be seen as an intervention which puts protagonists on the spot, not letting them avoid a difficult issue. According to Moreno (1972), attacking and shocking clients is at times just as permissible as laughing and joking with them. But confrontations should be used only within a safe and supportive relationship, in which the sense of security may enhance the protagonist's ability to experience painful emotions. The ideal blend of support and confrontation may be illustrated by the image of the psychodramatist who with one

arm embraces the protagonist and with the other holds a mirror in front of him or her.

Clarification refers to those questions which aim to clarify what was just communicated in order to receive a more detailed description of a situation.

Interpretations are those verbal explanations which demonstrate the source, the history, or the cause of an experience in order to provide a cognitive framework for that experience. It should be emphasized, however, that 'interpretation and insight-giving in psychodrama is of a different nature from the verbal types of psychotherapy' (Z. Moreno, 1965, p.82). In contrast to some classical psychoanalysts who give verbal interpretations, psycho-dramatists convey new insights through the person of the double, in role reversal, or with other action-techniques, thus emphasizing the gradual process of self-awareness evolving within the protagonist during the action (action-insight). (Action-insight is discussed in more detail in Chapter 7).

Catharsis refers to the efforts by the psychodramatist to encourage the release of pent-up feelings. Its specific function in psychodrama is not only to facilitate emotional abreaction but also to integrate the expressed feelings. (Catharsis is discussed in more detail in Chapter 6).

Acceptance refers to the unconditionally positive attitudes which the psy-chodramatist shows towards the protagonist during the session. It provides the necessary non-judgmental framework within which protagonists can present themselves without fear of critique and disapproval. The therapist communicates to the patient: 'I believe in you, in your abilities and in your intrinsic worth. I accept you as you are and there is nothing despicable in you. I am here for you and I ask no gratitude in return, nor do I ask you to love me, respect me or admire me.'

Suggestion refers to the infusion of an altered state of mind in the protagonist and may evoke a kind of trance similar to that which occurs in hypnosis. Suggestions may be used in order to evoke memories, fantasies and dreams or as an invitation to regress to an earlier state of functioning. Suggestions may evoke imaginations so vivid that all sorts of wild ideas emerge; the protagonist knows what is going on without realizing fully what is happening.

Advice and *teaching* comprise didactic instructions which provide the protagonist with information or guidance. While most protagonists dislike being told what to do, others find concrete advice very helpful. When attempting to reinforce desired behaviour or minimize undesired behaviour, psychodramatists use praise and encouragement rather than negative critique or disapproval.

Self-disclosure refers to the sharing, by psychodramatists, of their own immediate and past experiences, feelings, and thoughts. The decidedly transparent posture taken by many psychodramatists emphasizes the real as well as the transference aspects of the therapist-client relationship.

One of the difficulties regarding the therapeutic function of psychodramatists concerns their use and misuse of manipulation. The word manipulation has two meanings. On the one hand, it means to treat something with skill—for example, the skilful channeling of protagonists' own emotional, intellectual, and adaptive assets into reasonably gratifying directions. As such, manipulation is certainly a necessary intervention in psychodrama. But if, by manipulation, one understands the authoritarian enforcement which occurs when the protagonist is caused to do something against his or her will and in the absence of genuine mutuality, then it is an improper intervention and detrimental to any sound therapy; it may have a damaging long-term effect on the protagonist's autonomy and independence.

4. Group leader

As group leaders, psychodramatists are managers of group process who attempt to foster a constructive work group climate (Bion, 1961) and a supportive social network. According to Moreno (1937/1972), 'the director is himself a symbol of balanced action, orchestrating, integrating, synthesizing, melting all the participants into a group' (p.247).

In their capacity as group leaders, psychodramatists are concerned with interpersonal relations and believe that problems are best solved in a social context rather than in a private setting. Psychodramatists are required to be able to (1) organize the group structure; (time, composition, meeting place, and remuneration procedures), (2) establish group norms regarding, for example, confidentiality, decision making, physical contact, social inter-action outside the group, and interpersonal responsibilities, (3) build cohesion in the group, regulate group tension level, and foster interest in the goals of the group, (4) encourage active participation by all group members, facilitate interaction and communication between them, and clarify the evolving relations through the use of action methods or verbal interpretations. Finally, psychodramatists are required to be able to (5) remove the obstacles to the development of a social atmosphere which is built on cooperation, for example by dealing with competition in a way which will be a corrective learning experience for the group.

Psychodramatists are aided in their role as group leaders by knowledge of social psychology, group dynamics, group composition, group processes, stages in the development of groups, therapeutic factors in group psychotherapy, and various methods of group psychotherapy, including the psychoanalytic, humanistic-existential and task-oriented. The ability to use various methods of total group observation and interpretation, such as Sociometry (Moreno, 1953),

Focal Conflict Theory (Whitaker & Lieberman, 1964), FIRO: a Three-Dimensional Theory of Interpersonal Behaviour, (Schutz, 1966), and SYMLOG: a System for Multiple Level Observation of Groups (Bales & Cohen 1979), and to discern the various stages of group development (Lacoursiere, 1980), further enhances the ability of the psychodramatist as group leader.

Which is the ideal type of group leader in psychodrama? Lieberman, et. al. (1973) described four leadership functions: emotional stimulation, caring, meaning attribution, and executive function*. Several types of leadership styles emerged from these four dimensions, such as the Energizer, the Provider, the Social Engineer, the Impersonal, the Laissez-Faire, and the Manager. One common type of psychodramatist was described as an 'Aggressive Energizer,' (highly zealous, eccentric, charismatic, emotionally stimulating, supportive and attacking). Another investigation of the personality of psychodramatists was conducted by Buchanan & Taylor (1986) who found that most psychodramatists were extroverted, intuitive emotional perceivers. In spite of these preliminary conclusions, it is my impression that leadership style in psychodrama varies according to the personal orientation and idiosyncrasy of the practitioner. The ideal type of group leader in psychodrama is the one who has found the optimal balance between the four psychodramatist roles and his or her own personality, and who is able to shift leadership style according the demands of each situation.

Psychodramatists disagree on how much to control their protagonists and groups. Some leaders direct with merciless authority, taking a sometimes despotic control of the action, while others are so considerate that they scarcely make their leadership known. Psychodrama leaders must be able at times to 'take charge,' of a session and respond to what he or she knows the group really needs rather than appealing for permission, apologizing for taking initiative, asking 'democratic questions' or taking at face value what the participants may claim they 'want'. Like dancers, psychodramatists can either lead or follow the protagonist. When leading, the psychodramatist is initiating action with authority, directing with purpose and determination. When following, the psychodramatist is attentive and responsive to the protagonist, who makes the decisions and leads the way. However, there is a third, ideal leadership position

---

* These four types correspond to the four professional roles of the psychodramatist described [in brackets]:

(1) Emotional Stimulation (challenging, confronting, activity; intrusive modeling by personal risk-taking and high self- disclosure), [Producer]

(2) Caring (offering support, affection, praise, protection, warmth, acceptance, genuineness, concern), [Therapist]

(3) Meaning Attribution (explaining, clarifying, interpreting, providing a cognitive framework for change; translating feelings and experiences into ideas), [Analyst]

(4) Executive Function (setting limits, rules, norms, goals; managing time; pacing, stopping, interceding, suggesting procedures). [Group Leader]

in psychodrama in which the psychodramatist and protagonist work together with equal status as a genuine team, sharing decision-making and joining in a mutual relationship of give-and-take. In this ideal position, psychodramatic group leaders are required to be sensitive to the protagonist's feelings, while on occasion taking a firm and positive stand on crucial issues. In the words of Leutz (1974), 'the psychodrama is really therapeutic only when the director 'swings with' the protagonist' (p.86).

Conclusion.

In this chapter I have described the four professional roles and the patterns of behaviour which make up the psychodramatist's professional identity.

A minimum level of skilfulness in each role is a precondition for practicing psychodrama and is, I believe, a reasonable requirement for certification. However, while dedicated practitioners strive to obtain a high standard of excellence in all roles, each is probably more talented in one role than in others. For example, someone may be more gifted as a stage-master than as an analyst. Furthermore, 'only a megalomaniac would presume he has all strands of the individual and group processes under observation, much less under precise control' (Polansky & Harkins, 1969, p.75). In cases such as this, psychodramatists will benefit from working together with other practitioners of diverse talents who complement and enrich one another.

While little systematic investigation of psychodramatists' actual role performance has been reported, I believe that practitioners occasionally struggle with various difficulties in their efforts to perform the required tasks. From the point of view of role theory, these difficulties may be characterized as: (1) intra-role conflicts; (2) inter-role conflicts; (3) intra- personal role conflicts; or (4) inter-personal role conflicts.

(1) Intra-role conflict is a discrepancy between the role and the person, between the requirements of the role and the inner value system of the person. For example, a non-assertive person may have difficulty assuming the role of group leader.

(2) Inter-role conflict is an opposition between two or more different roles in the same person. Every presented psychodramatic role may be in conflict with the other roles the psychodramatist must play. For example, the altruistic therapist role may be difficult to combine with the more egotistic producer role which requires a certain amount of dramatic (and perhaps exhibitionistic) skill.

(3) Intrapersonal role conflict is a contradiction between one's own definition of a role and the expectations of others. For example, a behavioural psychodramatist may perform the role of analyst in a way which is unacceptable to colleagues trained in the psychoanalytic tradition.

(4) Interpersonal role conflict is a discrepancy between practitioners who play different roles. For example, psychodramatists who feel more comfortable with the rational analyst role may have difficulties working together with psychodramatists who are more irrational and impulsive and who emphasize the creative role of producer.

During the course of their training and during their professional careers, psychodramatists attempt to come to terms with these conflicts. But it is misleading to talk about psychodramatists merely in terms of role performance and skilfulness. What matters is not only what they do professionally, but also who they are personally, as human beings. Professional skills and personality are closely knit, and as Moreno & Moreno (1959) pointed out, 'it is extremely difficult, if not impossible, to separate the skill from the personality of the therapist. Here skill and personality are, at least in the act of performance, inseparably one. It may be said bluntly: the personality of the therapist is the skill' (p.39). Hence, it is not enough merely to perform the professional tasks: to empathize, influence, dramatize, and lead the group. The psychodramatist must also be a significant other person who encounters the protagonist as a human being. Through the impact of their own personalities, psychodramatists are expected to have a constructive influence on the psychodramatic process.*

In summary: psychodramatists are required not only to find the optimal blend between the roles of analyst, producer, therapist and group leader, but to perform these tasks in a way which is in harmony with their own personalities. If psychodramatists approach their task with due respect for other human beings; if they can listen to and understand the underlying messages of the protagonist; if they can inspire emotional involvement and spontaneity; if they can help the protagonist to remove some of the obstacles for personality change; if they can facilitate the development of constructive relationships in the group; if they can combine the foregoing requirements with their own personal short-comings...if they can do all of these things, then they will have done a job which is as good as can be expected.

A Training Exercise Evaluating Role Performance

Four empty chairs are put on the stage. Each chair is described as representing one of the above mentioned roles and the participants are invited, while sitting on the chairs, to give a short soliloquy of their experiences with each role. This gives an opportunity to investigate how psychodramatists in training (and certified practitioners and trainers) relate to the different roles—with which

---

* *A processing checklist, constructed to aid in evaluating the professional skills of psychodrama directors, is presented in on page 68. This checklist may be complemented with the rating scale measuring important personality characteristics of group psychotherapists in training which was presented by Bowers, Gaurone and Mines (1984).*

roles they are more and less comfortable, where lie their strengths and weaknesses in task performance, what specific needs they have for more training or personal growth, and what are the potential conflicts for them between roles.

For example, one student director described his performance in the following manner. As an analyst, he felt as he were on the top of a mountain, wanting to have a better overview, or as if he were an owl, needing more knowledge but having difficulties integrating head and body. As a producer, he felt like a tap which could be opened or closed or like a bubbling stream, sometimes stumbling on blocks which stopped his creativity. As a therapist, he felt as if he were walking on a path, not knowing where it ended, or as if he were a parent, speculating on how much to give without expecting anything in return from his children. As a group leader, finally, it disturbed him that he was not able to see the individual trees because of the great forest. He also felt like the captain of a ship on which his sailors constantly threatened to mutiny.

I tried this exercise with considerable success at the Norwegian School of Psychodrama (Directors of Training: Eva Røine and Monica Westberg). The exercise was experienced by participants as a constructive aid in teaching and a promising evaluation tool of director performance. Furthermore, the four roles demonstrated high content and construct validity, with surprising agreement between protagonists on task performance in each role and between students and trainers on the students' self-evaluations. The exercise was concluded with specific assignments for each student, indicating delineation of areas in need of improvement.

CHAPTER 4

Charismatic Leadership

> The Rebbe of Kotzk prayed to God: 'Master of the Universe, send us our Messiah, for we have no more strength to suffer. Show me a sign, O God. Otherwise…otherwise…I rebel against Thee. If Thou dost not keep Thy Covenant, then neither will I keep that Promise, and it is all over, we are through being Thy chosen people, Thy peculiar treasure.'

In times of personal misfortune, people search for a messiah or some other all-powerful authority to give them support and guidance. Today the prestigious heritage of the messiah is represented in our culture by the priest, the physician, or the psychotherapist, to whom we attribute magical powers and a certain godliness. Some charismatic and forceful members of these professions are more likely than others to be assigned the role of messiah. While most of these authorities refrain from doing more than interpreting the patient's idealization of them as transference manifestations, there are a few who use their personal powers to influence patients, thereby playing the role of the ideal authority in a less than positive manner.

An authority figure of the latter type was J.L. Moreno, who, much like a guru, would enrich the 'magic' powers of psychodrama with his own charismatic personality. He sometimes deliberately played the role of the loving father in order to reinforce or subdue the parental image, or to introduce himself as an ideal parental substitute. An entire generation of psychodramatists continued this tradition using Moreno as a role model. Some even went so far as to recommend that 'the good psychodrama director must, like Moreno himself, have certain charismatic qualities' (Greenberg, 1974, p.20), and that 'acting omniscient and clairvoyant was part of the character of being a psychodrama director' (Yablonsky, 1976, p.9). This chapter will attempt to evaluate these recommendations. The following variables of leadership will be included in my discussion: (1) the personality of a charismatic leader; (2) individual followers and their idealization of the leader; (3) the obedient group; (4) the psychodramatic situation; and (5) the therapeutic value of charismatic leadership.

The Personality of a Charismatic Leader

Charisma is defined as that personal quality which gives an individual the capacity to elicit popular support for his or her leadership. While many features (e.g. beauty, charm, brilliance, wit, altruism) may also arouse love and admiration, charisma specifically refers to spiritual powers, personal strength, forceful character, and the ability to excite, stimulate, influence, persuade, fascinate, energize, and/or mesmerize others. According to Zaleznik (1974), charismatic persons all 'have the capacity to secure emotional ties of others to themselves' (p.233).

Charisma may be manifested, for example, in leaders' use of language (demagogic skills), in mime ('hypnotizing' eyes), and/or in their general appearance (assertiveness). Most charismatic leaders act as if they know what they are doing. They are strongly attached to a belief system, and they often see themselves as called to fulfil some historic mission. 'Without shame or hesitation, they set themselves up as the guides and leaders and gods of those who are in need of guidance, of leader-ship, and of a target for their reverence' (Kohut, 1978, p.826).

In group psychotherapy and psychodrama there are endless shades and degrees of charismatic leadership. While the status (and one hopes the competence) of leaders inevitably casts them in roles of authority (Singer, 1970), leaders may be described as more or less democratic, authoritarian, narcissistic, and empathic. As compared with democratic leaders, charismatic leaders are ideology- rather than reality-oriented, rely on personal appeal and power rather than on decision-making by consensus, demand adaptation rather than accepting different opinions, summon rather than delegate authority, and canalyze rather than coordinate power (Scheidlinger, 1982). But, as compared with the authoritarian personality described by Adorno, Frenkel-Brunswik, Levinson, and Sanford (1950), they may also be highly unconventional, unprejudiced, tolerant and without the desire to dominate and control the lives of others. One such charismatic, nonauthoritarian leader was described by Lieberman, Yalom and Miles (1973) as 'expressing considerable warmth, acceptance, genuineness, and caring for other human beings' (p.29).

Many charismatic leaders might be conceived of as narcissistic personalities with a very high emotional investment in themselves. They are often preoccupied with fantasies of unlimited success, power, or brilliance and with feelings of self-importance and grandiosity. Some of them are inclined towards exhibitionism, and their relationships alternate between the extremes of overidealization and devaluation of others (Kohut, 1978).

While many charismatic leaders have little empathy with the inner lives of others, some of them appear to show genuine concern for the well-being of their followers. Perhaps Freud (1961/1931) thought of these leaders when he wrote: 'People belonging to this type impress others as being 'personalities;' they are especially suited to act as support for others, to take on the role of leaders and to give a fresh stimulus to cultural development' (p.218).

Although charisma rests on the extraordinary powers of the charismatic leader, it would be a mistake to assume that it could exist without a minimum of voluntary obedience on the part of the followers. This particular interdependence between the leader and the led has been investigated and discussed in sociology (Weber, 1953; Parsons, 1967), social psychology (Hollander, 1967), sociometry (Jennings, 1950), group dynamics (Lippit & White, 1958), group psychotherapy (Scheidlinger, 1982; Berman, 1982), small-group research (Hare, 1976), psychiatry (Rioch, 1971; Deutsch, 1980), and psychoanalysis (Fromm, 1941; Schiffer, 1973).

Individual Followers and Their Idealization of the Leaders

There are many reasons why people idealize authorities. Individuals under stress, for example, will idealize any psychotherapist who gives them reason to believe that he or she can help them to relieve their suffering. Lonely, oppressed, depressed, and insecure individuals tend to regress to childhood states of dependency and helplessness when they encounter people who try to be of assistance. Everybody finds it a relief to have someone strong and secure to turn to for consolation and support.

Idealization is to a large extent a survival of infantile fantasies that stem from the magical powers projected by the child upon the parents. For example, rescue fantasies may be attributed to a mother or protective powers may be attributed to a father. The therapist, seen as a parental figure who is all-understanding and tolerant, thus serves as an object of identification and an ego ideal in the same manner and for the same reasons that the parents once did.

Obedient Groups

Not only individuals but also groups of all sizes provide a fertile ground for the idealization of a leader and the infantilization of group members.

Belonging to a group seems to encourage people to give up their personal responsibility and transfer it to the leader (Fromm, 1965/1941). According to Freud (1955/1921), 'a group is an obedient herd, which could never live without a master. It has such a thirst for obedience that it submits instinctively to anyone who appoints himself its master' (p.81).

One reason for this is that the group offers collective identity, explicit ideology, solidarity, cohesion, and some form of messianic hope which has a great appeal to individuals. Further, the group has the potential to satisfy interpersonal needs for inclusion (feeling that 'I belong'), control (feeling that 'I trust'), and affection (feeling that 'I love') (Schutz, 1966). This last need, the need to love, is emphasized by Newman (1983), who describes the effects of 'superstar' charisma through the analogy of the Pied Piper:

When the charismatic leader pipes his tune, the feeling aroused in us goes far beyond listening and agreeing. It becomes adoration. I have heard people say, 'I never listen to the words he says, I just adore'. This is a feeling especially associated with love-sick adolescents. In my day it was called 'having a crush' on someone. It is proverbially known to be blind, inarguable, beyond discussing. (p.205)

The need to love is often accompanied in groups by the need to be dependent. Groups that act as if they have no powers of their own are described by Bion (1961) as Basic Assumption Dependency groups. The essential aim of the basic assumption dependency group is to attain security through and have its members protected by one individual. It assumes that this is why the group met. The members act as if they knew nothing, as if they are inadequate and immature creatures. Their behaviour implies that the leader, by contrast, is omnipotent and omniscient (Rioch, 1970, p.59).

Such dependent groups are similar to religious sects or extremist political groups in their aim to escape personal freedom and responsibility (Fromm, 1965/1941).

In summary: it seems that, whether we like it or not, whether we try to induce it or to prevent it, at one time or another individuals and groups have the need to submit in shared admiration for their therapist.

The Psychodramatic Situation

While there are many styles of leadership in psychodrama, the classical style has several charismatic features. Such leadership demands that the director have the ability to preside over a session in a fairly godlike fashion. According to Polansky and Harkins (1969), directors must possess interpersonal energy, moment-to-moment inventiveness, and occasional controlled flamboyance in a measure not available to everyone. Leaders are trained to function in a variety of roles, including those of parent, wizard, hero, and god. For a few of these leaders, 'psychodrama offers a seductive lure of power and narcissistic gratification'(Sacks, 1976a, p.61).

For some charismatic directors, the use of psychodramatic techniques and procedures becomes less important than the use of their own personalities to activate, stimulate, and energize protagonists. These leaders' charisma may become the most powerful instrument for warming up protagonists and group members to spontaneous action. Aware of the regressive needs of protagonists, these directors arouse confidence by inducing a hypnotic-like state of suggestion in order to establish a close working relationship rapidly. In a surprisingly short time, this relationship may become one in which the director is attributed with extraordinary powers and the participants are admiring followers. Once this situation has been established, the director tries to offer a sort of re-parenting experience, where he or she functions as a substitute ideal parent.

The field of psychodrama provides fertile ground for such situations. Through the introduction of 'as-if' techniques, like 'magic shop' and 'auxiliary world,' and through the maximization of imagination, deliberate efforts are constantly being made to change the experience of everyday reality to a dream-like state of imaginative surplus reality (see Chapter 9). Despite the fact that protagonists are discouraged from transferring feelings onto the director (transferences when detected are carried off and discharged upon auxiliaries), and despite the director's effort to establish a transference-free (tele) relationship with protagonists (see Chapter 8), some directors remain the target of idealization, perhaps through a combination of their own will and that of the group members. For all that such techniques as role reversal, sharing, action socio-metry, processing, and direct encounter act to neutralize love-transference, protagonists will remain dependent as long as the director continues to play god.

The most outstanding example of charismatic leadership in psychodrama, according to accounts in the literature, seems to be that of J.L. Moreno. Yablon-sky (1976) narrated: 'All attention focused on Dr. Moreno, who appeared suddenly from the wings like a magician. He stood quietly in the center of the stage for several minutes, simply surveying the group. He had a happy-omnipotent look on his beaming face...Although he stood silently on the stage for two to three minutes, his presence seemed to produce emotional waves' (p.8).

According to Kobler (1974 / 1962), 'Moreno's personality combines the verve and flamboyance of a master showman, which he indeed is, with the roguish charm of a Viennese bon vivant, which he once was. Massive and broad-browed, he wears his dandy hair in the Bohemian artist's style of yesteryear, longish and curling over the ear. His blue eyes are heavy-lidded, giving him an expression at once somnolent and watchful. His language, embellished by a lilting Austrian accent, tends to be epigrammatic, poetic, paradoxical' (p.36).

Blatner (1966) noted that Moreno had an amazing 'healing touch:' 'I have heard the term 'charismatic' applied in speaking of Dr. Moreno, and at times, I feel this is consistent with my observation of him in relation to groups' (p.129).

Naturally, people reacted in different ways to Moreno, and not everyone was mesmerized by his personality. However, as many people did find him charismatic, he is a suitable illustration for the present discussion. As an idealized leader, Moreno provided a role model for generations of psychodramatists and still plays an important part in the dynamics of the psychodramatic community. Like a shaman, Moreno was a typical outsider, who achieved his status in the ritual realm in compensation for his exclusion from authority in the psychiatric establishment. According to his wife, Zerka T. Moreno (1976), 'to the psychiatric fraternity, he was a problem; his views of man and his interpersonal and intergroup relations flew in the face of all that was being taught. He was just too controversial, too personally difficult to accept; a maverick, a loner, a narcissistic leader, charismatic but aloof, gregarious but selective, lovable but eccentric, unlovable and appealing' (p.132).

At the institute bearing his name, Moreno was called simply 'The Doctor,' thus being assigned the magic healing power of the physician. But instead of correcting these fantasies about himself, Moreno emphasized the element of imagination and thus (perhaps unintentionally) encouraged everyone to set him up as a target for their admiration. In this way it is probable that Moreno also satisfied his own narcissistic wish to play god. A study of Moreno's work makes us question whether his preoccupations with psychodrama, sociometry, and group psychotherapy, and with the issues of god, moment, encounter, spontaneity-creativity, role-playing, etc., were largely autobiographical and the result of his own introspection rather than based on professional experience. It seems to me that a narcissistic theme—albeit an often productive one—runs through his theoretical work like a red thread. As was true of Freud, Moreno preferred to be surrounded by followers rather than peers. But he was more than a teacher to most of his students; he was a father-figure to look up to and be loved by; a kind of 'godfather' who talked to his students as if they were his offspring. While some resented being talked to like this and rejected seeing him as a father figure, others chose to be adopted as his children. No professional boundaries were maintained with Moreno's patients; likewise, friends, relatives, employees, and colleagues were treated as patients in psychodrama. They were all brought together to form a cohesive, psychologically inbred group of which he was the leader. The devotion of Moreno's followers and his own dedication to the 'cause' almost led to the development of a psychotherapeutic cult. However, 'as his followers became men and women with powers of their own, Moreno often pushed them away, or they left him' (Fine, 1979, p.436).

The Therapeutic Value of Charismatic Leadership

Given the impressive capacity that charismatic psychodramatists seem to have for bringing about change in their protagonists, one might assume that the development of such charismatic powers could perhaps be very useful to all practitioners. On the other hand, if such change is solely the result of suggestion, then perhaps psychodrama directors should instead concentrate on learning how to avoid using charisma in their professional capacity. The use of charisma for the purpose of influencing behaviour raises not only methodological questions about the most effective way of doing this but also profound ethical questions. Most of us have strong reservations about charismatic leaders who misuse their power to dominate people, although we may feel differently about leaders who use it to try and improve the situation of others.

Elements of charisma may be found in many psychotherapeutic approaches, for example in supportive, time-limited, and various kinds of group psychotherapy as well as in those approaches based on patients' hopes and expectations

(Frank, 1973). The value of these approaches, however, is very difficult to evaluate because so many variables are involved—suggestibility, placebo effect, persuasion, spontaneous remission, faith healing, magic expectations, doctor-patient relationship, fame and popularity of the therapist—and because so many varieties of charisma are possible (e.g. demagoguery, appearance, confidence, integrity).

Advocates of the use of charisma claim that the immediate relief experienced by an individual influenced by a powerful personality is proof enough of its validity. However, critics claim that any improvement achieved under these circumstances is only temporary, and that as soon as the supportive agency disappears and the charismatic influence wears off, the problems tend to return. Cures of this type are sometimes characterized as 'transference cures' since the patients thus helped are said to be merely responding to a powerful and protective (parental) authority. According to Berman (1982), 'such cures...may end at some point with bitter disappointment, with a sense of being betrayed by 'a god that failed' (p.198).

Liberman, et al (1973) have presented perhaps the most systematic data about the effects of a charismatic leader upon a group. Their study showed that such leaders were both very influential and able to evoke change and also had the most casualties in terms of dropouts from the group. In a discussion of therapeutic progress in relation to the therapist's personality, Wolberg (1977) concludes: 'During early phases of therapy there is often an immediate and dramatic relief of symptoms brought about by such positive factors as the placebo influence, emotional catharsis, idealized relationship, suggestion, and group dynamics. There is some attitude and behavior change but little or no reconstructive personality change' (p.56).

It would therefore seem that if charismatic leadership in psychodrama is at all useful, it is in the initial warm-up phase and in the early dependency phase of treatment, when the development of group cohesion is a paramount issue and individuals need the leader as an ego ideal and object of identification. Thereafter, leaders must be able (and willing) to allow individuals to move on towards autonomy (Rutan & Rice, 1981). When this does not happen, the patient's ability to perceive reality is obstructed, thereby causing damage in the therapeutic process. Learning to see who the therapist really is is one of the unavoidable steps in the clients' acquisition of a greater capacity for reality testing and for achieving autonomy. The distortion of reality inherent in idealization leaves the patient a child, unable to grow up. Sooner or later, patients will realize that they have been cheated by a leader who has not challenged their flattering idealizations. When this happens, those who have been deceived are justifiably angry and disillusioned (Greben, 1983).

In the long run, charismatic influence is detrimental to independent growth processes. Thus, charismatic psychodrama directors, who offer themselves as substitute 'good' parents, actually prevent maturation by encouraging messianic expectations. Psychodramatists who rely on magic and faith healing and who promise miracles if their followers will only submit to their dominance 'are definitely anti-therapeutic' (Liff, 1975, p.121).

It should be noted that the charismatic situation is as potentially harmful to leaders themselves as it is to their patients. A charismatic leader stands in danger of beginning to cultivate actively and consistently the role of magician (see Chapter 11). And once having been drawn into meeting idealized expectations, it is difficult to change one's role.

In addition to this danger, the countertransference possibilities in such a situation are boundless and very subtle. The most obvious danger in this area is that the leader will fail to perceive that the idealization is a transference and will begin to accept it as reality. Such leaders 'feed their own self- esteem at their patient's expense...and since the line between 'reparative' and 'destructive' is so thin...there are only 'bad' narcissistic therapists' (Volkan, 1980, p.150). Finally, such therapy runs the danger of deteriorating into a folie-a-deux, where both leader and patient are trapped in a closed system that encourages mutual exploitation and corruption. It is in cases such as this that psychotherapy is misused to produce cults. According to Temerlin and Temerlin (1982), this cult mentality may be observed in many psychotherapeutic approaches—humanistic, experiential, and psychoanalytical—in which 'the leader does not consider patients' idealization to be a transference, to be understood as part of treatment, but uses it to encourage submission, obedience, and adoration. Patients become true believers with totalistic patterns of thought, increased dependence, and paranoia' (p.131). While psychodrama never became a cult in this sense—despite the influence of charismatics such as Moreno—Gonen (1971) observed certain 'cultish aspects' (p.199) which he believed had retarded psychodrama's entrance into the mainstream of psychiatry.

Leadership Guidelines
In conclusion, the following general guidelines are suggested for all types of leadership in psychodrama:

   (1) that leadership be based not only on irrational personality factors (e.g. demagogic skills) but also on rational (professional) competence;

   (2) that leaders endeavour to reduce the inequality between themselves and their clients and not to increase their own power;

   (3) that leadership be evaluated and criticized regularly;

   (4) that leaders be sensitive to their followers' temporary need to idealize and become dependent;

(5) that leaders be able to work through the feelings of disappointment which arise in individuals and groups when their dependency needs are not satisfied; and

(6) that leaders have the capacity to make adequate assessment of their own assets and defects and not rely upon the power attributed to them.

The psychodrama director is an ordinary person with an extraordinary, demanding job. He or she is not a magician but a reasonably spontaneous and creative individual, generally with more than an average amount of integrity. Being oneself, with one's human limitations, role repertoire, and authenticity, seems to be a basic requirement. It is therefore possible to function as a psychodrama director without acting omnipotent.

CHAPTER 5

Therapeutic Aspects

What is helpful, or 'therapeutic' in psychodrama? When asked this question, one participant emphasized the experience of being accepted as she really is. Another talked about finally understanding 'how it all started' and felt that, through this self-awareness, she had developed a kind of freedom which changed her ability to choose what to do with her life. Despite these and other enthusiastic responses, comparatively little has been written about the thera- peutic aspects of psychodrama. Our understanding of what it is in the psycho- dramatic process that is truly helpful has, thus far, remained rather limited. Yet perhaps it is not necessary for the healing aspects of psychodrama to remain obscure.

Therapeutic Aspects

A therapeutic aspect (or factor) may be defined as an element that causes a therapeutic effect. Thus, therapeutic aspects are 'agents of change,' 'curative factors' or 'growth mechanisms' that contribute to a positive outcome in psy- chotherapy. Such aspects are, of course, closely related both to processes within the patient and to interventions of the therapist; thus we are presented with a complex mass of data, suggesting a variety of elements that influence the outcome of therapy, both individually and all together.

In spite of this complexity, therapists from various schools emphasize those 'basic' factors which they believe are most effective in their particular form of psychotherapy. For example, psychoanalysts emphasize the importance of re- constructive self-understanding or 'insight' to produce lasting personality change. From a social-learning-theory perspective, change is produced through the mediation of cognitive processes or schemata (Bandura, 1977). Person-cen- tred practitioners believe that the qualities of the therapist, especially positive regard, accurate empathy, and congruence, are of crucial importance. Behaviour therapists insist that therapeutic change may be understood only within the conceptual framework of learning through reward and punishment. According to some hypnotherapists, none of the above factors can compare in importance to the therapeutic paradoxes that the therapist invokes in order to create a change of the second degree (Watzlawick, Weakland & Fish, 1974). Finally, many authors notice the influence of 'non-specific' or 'extra-therapeutic' healing aids which occur not only in psychotherapy, but also in nonprofessional relationships, or 'by themselves,' as in the placebo effect.

Although the above psychotherapies emphasize one specific therapeutic aspect, other writers have tried to present a list of several aspects that are important in psychotherapeutic healing and that may be conceptualized as 'common denominators' of various psychotherapeutic approaches. For example, Frank (1961) suggested that psychotherapy provides new opportunities for learning at both cognitive and experiential levels, enhances hope of relief, provides success experiences, helps to overcome alienation from fellows, arouses emotions, and provides new information and alternative solutions about the 'cause' of a problem. According to Bandura (1977), all effective psychological treatments alter a component of an individual's self-schema, namely perceived self-efficacy. Bandura outlined four sources of information with different degrees of potency for producing change: verbal persuasion, emotional arousal, vicarious experiences, and performance accomplishments. Sundberg & Tyler (1962) suggested that psychotherapy strengthens the patient's motivation to do the right thing, reduces emotional pressure by facilitating catharsis, releases the potential for growth, changes habits, modifies the cognitive structure, gives self-knowledge, and facilitates interpersonal relations. Marmor (1962) suggested that psychotherapy releases tension through catharsis, provides cognitive learning, operant conditioning, and opportunities for identification with the therapist, and that psychotherapy gives an experience of repeated reality testing. Finally, Lazarus (1973), in his multimodal system of 'Basic Id,' suggested seven interactive modalities that influence change: behaviour, affect, sensation, imagery, cognition, interpersonal relations, and drugs.

Psychodrama utilizes a multiform of therapeutic healing aids, and Blatner's statement (1973) that it 'should be viewed most realistically as functioning within an eclectic approach to the helping relationship' (p.120), seems most justified. In the individual treatment of each protagonist, several different aspects may be flexibly applied with various therapeutic goals, such as role training, symptom reduction, crisis intervention, general self awareness, conflict resolution, or personality change. In the words of Fine (1979), 'if simple behavioural training methods are not sufficient to reach the patient's goals, a more psychodynamic or psychosocial depth therapy is required' (p.448).

A large body of literature has been published on therapeutic factors in group psychotherapy (e.g. Bloch & Crouch, 1985). Until the mid 1950s, the literature consisted mainly of impressionistic accounts by therapists of what they thought to be the important aspects of their own practice. Corsini & Rosenberg (1955) attempted to establish a general classification of such accounts by reviewing 300 articles on group psychotherapy. They found nine major classes of therapeutic factors, which could be subsumed into three broader categories: (1) emotional: acceptance, altruism, and transference; (2) cognitive: spectator therapy, universalization, and intellectualization; (3) actional: reality testing, ventilation, and interaction.

The 1960s saw the beginning of systematic research in this area, the most common methodological approach being to ask members of psychotherapy groups what aspects they found most helpful in their group experiences (Dickoff & Lakin, 1963; Butler & Fuhriman, 1983). From this research literature, Yalom (1975) abstracted a list of 12 curative factors which he termed: self-understanding (insight), interpersonal learning (input and output), universality, instillation of hope, altruism, recapitulation of primary family group (family re-enactment), catharsis, cohesiveness, identification, guidance, and existential issues. In a study carried out by Yalom, Tinklenberg, and Gilula (Yalom, 1975) on a relatively small subject population, it was found that interpersonal learning, together with catharsis, cohesiveness, and insight, were the factors most valued by the subjects. A great number of similar studies were carried out with different types of groups and participants during the following years with very similar results, indicating that participants in group psychotherapy seem universally to value these basic aspects of the process.

In an attempt to investigate whether these factors were also regarded as helpful by participants in psychodrama, I conducted two studies (Kellermann, 1985b; 1987c) with different questionnaires distributed among a fairly large population of former protagonists of psychodrama. These studies showed that emotional abreaction, cognitive insight, and interpersonal relationships were again perceived to be more helpful than other aspects of the therapeutic process. Although there are limitations to how much can be learned from self-reports, the consistent results from these studies indicate that, at least from the point of view of group members, catharsis, insight, and interpersonal relations are therapeutic factors central to psychodramatic group psychotherapy.

Because of the questionable nature of self-evaluations, results from such studies are inconclusive unless complemented by theoretical reports from experienced practitioners of psychodrama, who may offer a more comprehensive picture. If asked, I believe that J.L. Moreno would mention some or all of his primary concepts of personality theory—social atom, tele, warming up, role playing, spontaneity, creativity and cultural conserves (Bischof, 1964)—as explanations for the therapeutic powers of psychodrama. When asked a similar question, Zerka Moreno (personal communication) mentioned the following therapeutic aspects of psychodrama: the 'real' relationship factor (tele), the self-disclosure and genuineness of the therapist, the self-revelation in an accepting group (existential validation), catharsis of integration, and action-insight. In simple words, Zerka Moreno (personal communication) called psychodrama 'a non-punitive laboratory for learning how to live'. When Leutz (1985b) attempted to answer the question of 'what is effective in psychodrama,' she focused on its special setting (the scene), on the medium of spontaneous play, on the function of the auxiliary, and on the psychodramatic techniques (double, mirror, role reversal) which, according to her, are theoretically derived from the conditions of early human development. She added that 'by making a conflict tangible, concrete and visible, it becomes dispensable and thus the person can change' (Leutz, 1985b).

Blatner and Blatner (1988) summarizes the psychological foundations of psychodrama thus: 'The utilization of the innate tendency to play may be extended beyond therapy with children and adapted for the treatment of adolescents and adults. Activity and the use of techniques that increase the vividness of the experience add to the empowerment of the patient. Including a skill-building orientation addresses deeper attitudes while sustaining the cognitive elements of the therapeutic alliance. Developing channels of self expression helps generate healthy sublimations for previously uncultivated emotional needs. Emphasizing the future and applying methods for developing the capacity to create a more vigourous ego ideal is another important aspect of therapy. In all of these, the patients are helped to make more functional bridges between their subjective experiences and objective assessments of reality' (p.88). The therapeutic process of psychodrama, according to these accounts, covers a wide range of human experiences, including emotional, cognitive, interpersonal and behavioural learning.

The therapeutic aspects listed above constitute important efforts to 'cut through' varied psychotherapeutic experiences and develop a conceptual framework that explains why psychodrama leads to change. However, in striving for simplicity, these lists have frequently lacked some crucial aspects, such as the almost mysterious or magical 'non-specific healing aids'. If, however, we want to comprehend fully the nature and function of psychodrama therapy, no healing aids—natural or supernatural—should be disregarded.

While therapeutic factors are complex and multifaceted, I believe it is possible, without too much simplification, to divide them into the following seven broad categories:

(1) therapist skills (competence, personality);

(2) emotional abreaction (catharsis, release of stored-up affect);

(3) cognitive insight (self-understanding, awareness, integration, perceptual restructuring);

(4) interpersonal relationships (learning through encounter, tele, and transference-countertransference explorations);

(5) behavioural/actional learning (learning new behaviour through reward and punishment, acting out);

(6) imaginary simulation ('as if' behaviour, play, symbolic presentations, make-believe);

(7) non-specific healing aids (global secondary factors).

Assuming that these categories represent a comprehensive summary of major therapeutic factors, it is now our task to identify their manifestations in the process of psychodrama therapy. Taken together, these factors suggest a model for understanding the complex therapeutic process of psychodrama.

Figure 5.1 illustrates the aspects of psychodrama which facilitate therapeutic progress (developing from left to right) and the resistance which operates counter to this progress. The relevant psychodramatic concepts are discussed in the following chapters (chapter numbers are written in brackets).

Figure 5.1. A Model of the Therapeutic Aspects in Psychodrama.

```
T              EMOTIONAL       catharsis (6)  →      R
H                                                     E     c
E   S          COGNITIVE       action-insight (7)  → S     l
R   K                                                 I     o
A   I    →     INTERPERSONAL   tele (8)  →           S     s
P   L                                                 T     u
I   L          IMAGINARY       as-if (9)  →          A     r
S                                                     N     e
T   (3)        BEHAVIORAL      acting out (10)  →    C     (13)
                                                      E
               NON-SPECIFIC    magic (11)  →               (12)
```

There is, of course, a danger in a model of this sort, as it may introduce an arbitrary division of aspects which in reality are inseparably interconnected with one another—for example, emotional and cognitive elements. The model is, accordingly, suggested here only for heuristic reasons, to help identify the various elements in the process of psychodrama therapy. It is evident that any understanding of how psychodrama is therapeutic will require an assessment of a multivariable field including not only single elements, but various aspects together, such as catharsis together with tele.

This omniform view is in agreement with that of Appelbaum (1988), who emphasized the importance of thinking in multivariate terms when conceptualizing change: 'In conceptualizing change we are merely at the primitive stage of delineating variables, one symptom of which is the creation and use of many different words that mean the same thing. We are far from successfully integrating delineated variables through the use of higher order abstractions. Thus, it is easy to talk in terms of one means of change as paramount, with depreciation or ignoring of other means of change. In a better world we would recognize...that understanding change requires an accounting for all of the variables, and that refined integration would put them in rank order of influence on the process of change' (p.207).

Thus, in the same way that emotional problems may be caused by a combination of factors (e.g. conflicts from childhood, developmental arrest, disturbed relations, repression, inhibition, or inadequate habitual learning), the pathway to healing must also take different routes and be explained according to widely different points of view. Furthermore, one must recognize that all healing processes may differ for different people, with different therapists, in the context of different settings, and also for different matches between patient, therapist, and group. One patient may make progress through action-insight while another may find the warm and authentic inter-personal relation to be more helpful. For still others, a corrective emotional experience may be the central determinant of personality change.

To make the picture even more complicated, the relative importance of therapeutic factors may change during the process of therapy: at the beginning of the group catharsis may be more important than action-insight, while at the end of the group the rankings may be reversed. A short description of the therapeutic process of psychodrama will be given here.

Classical psychodrama, according to Moreno (1972), consists of three stages: the warm-up, action, and sharing phases of the session. A fourth stage of analysis was suggested by Moreno and is today replaced by what I here will call the 'processing' phase, which is further described in Chapter 14. These stages include the following, traditional phases of virtually all methods of psychotherapy. After the initial contract of treatment and some brief or extended personality assessment of the patient, the therapist attempts to focus on some problematic issues which will be addressed in therapy. Resistances against starting therapy are analyzed and/or neutralized and some form of verbal or non-verbal communication of the inner world of the patient is initiated. The actual process of treatment was described by Freud (1914) as 'remembering, repeating, and working through,' indicating a gradual process of re-integration of past and unconscious material within the therapeutic setting. Jung (1967) preferred to describe this process as following the four phases of (1) confession, (2) explanation, (3) education, and (4) transformation.

The process of psychodrama therapy is similar to these descriptions, including a phase of emotional warm-up to a re-enactment of a past event in the here-and-now. In the middle phase of action, the protagonist is helped to achieve catharsis, to gain action-insight and act-fulfilment. While the entire process of psychodrama is important, the middle phase of action is assumed to be the most influential for the protagonist because, according to Strupp (1972), in the middle of therapy, the patient is most susceptible to external stimuli and most open to change. This is the high-point of the session, according to the Hollander Psychodrama Curve (Hollander, 1969). Thereafter follows a phase of winding down, of working through, integration and re-learning. The protagonist is finally helped to return to the outer world of day-to-day realities with the phase of closure and group sharing.

Petzold (1978), in his 'tetradic system of integrative therapy,' gave a compre-hensive summary of the process of psychodrama in terms of four phases: 'in the first (diagnostic-anamnestic) phase of remembering, emotional processes are stimulated; in the second (psycho-cathartic) phase of repeating, emotions are explored and expressed; in the third (integration) phase of working through, emotions are cognitively integrated; and in the fourth (new orientation) phase of change, behaviour is tested in action' (p.83).

Let us consider the following example of a psychodrama session from the perspective of therapeutic aspects.

Trust or Distrust?
Eva, a divorced, middle-aged woman was chosen as the protagonist by the group. She had hitherto been fairly secretive and often complained that she had difficulties trusting the group. Despite her general apprehension, she had played a few auxiliary roles in other people's psychodramas with great flair and usually gave honest and emotional sharing.

During the warm-up phase, Eva mentioned that she had a lot of pent-up aggression towards her step-father who had treated her badly for many years. Eva's biological father had died when she was a child and her mother had re-married when Eva was ten years old. In the first scene, the step-father (played by Tom) was presented as a silent, hardworking farmer who totally dominated the home. Eva had longed for a loving father but felt with her new step-father that he had disliked her from the beginning. He demanded her to work both in the house and on the farm and punished her severely if she did not do what he asked of her. Eva portrayed in a family sculpture how her mother (played by Jill) had slowly became more distant, leaving Eva isolated and lonely without anyone to lean on for support.

As the drama proceeded, Eva presented a number of scenes from her childhood which forced her to depend only on herself and which gradually increased her mistrust of people in general. When role-reversing with her mother and step-father, Eva repeatedly expressed feelings of indifference, cold-ness and egocentrism. In a particularly moving scene from her adolescence, Eva reconstructed an event in which her stepfather had forbidden her to enter the house after she had come home too late at night. When her mother finally let her in, her step-father had spanked her in a humiliating manner, leaving Eva furious with degradation and despair. Eva was torn between a burning desire for love and a growing resentment with humankind and she cried loudly in grief.

Two group members were chosen to represent these contradictory view-points and to maximize Eva's conflict. This provoked Eva to express her hate in words, to curse her parents in a primitive, cleansing manner. She seemed to explode in anger as if feelings which she had kept in for a long time were released. This emotional outburst, however, left her even more drained and empty than before and she began to feel the pain of not receiving her desired parental love. In this context, Eva suddenly remembered a scene five years earlier when she had taken care of her mother who was dying of cancer. The director suggested that she present this scene in action and Eva rapidly set the scene (a hospital bedroom) and instructed Jill to play her dying mother. Eva felt obligated to nurse her mother, but her hate prevented her from doing this willingly. As the director urged her to take a last farewell from her mother, Eva refused, stating that 'I cannot say good-bye! I cannot forgive her and let her go!' She explained that she had never been a part of her mother and so there was nothing to separate from. The director asked what she would need in order to take farewell from her mother and she answered: 'To be part of a safe place, a safe sea- shore to land on.' The director therefore suggested, as a closure scene, that she construct such a safe, symbolic sea-shore to land on, perhaps representing a 'good mother'. Eva, however, stopped cooperating and became uncommunicative, as if withdrawing from the outer world. The director observed her regressed state and said to the group that Eva needed to be taken care of without having to take responsibility for the care-taking; she wanted to be met as a needing child and not as an adult. The director asked those group-members who honestly felt close to Eva to come and hold her and nurse her. Eva responded willingly but passively to the caring of the group and, gradually, let herself relax, crying softly. Then she opened her eyes and looked around the room, facing the group members who were gathered around her with a warm and relieved smile on her face.

In the sharing portion of Eva's psychodrama, it became clear that the choice of the auxiliaries had been very significant. Tom, who had played the role of the step-father, talked about how he had left his own children in a boarding school when they were young. Jill, who thought she had cancer, said she had played the part of the dying mother with greatest difficulty. Other group members talked about separations from their parents, of wanting to be taken care of and accepted unconditionally, and conflicting needs of giving and taking. This psychodrama had undoubtedly touched upon universal issues of existence which everyone had dealt with in their own lives. A lesson verbalized by the director was that it is easier to separate (internally and externally) from important people in our lives if the relation has been 'cleansed' from noxious content and thus finished in terms of emotional residues.

Almost a year later, I asked Eva for her permission to include a description of her psychodrama in this book and on the same occasion I asked her what—if anything—she had found helpful in this session. As we recapitulated the various scenes in the psychodrama, Eva said that, for her, nothing was as important as the experience of presenting herself honestly to the group and trusting them to accept her as she was. She emphasized, however, that this was only the beginning and that she viewed the psychodrama, not as a 'one-session-therapy' but as a developmental process with continuity.

This vignette shows how unresolved infantile needs may be reactivated in psychodrama and symbolically satisfied by the group. Because of her traumatic life-history, Eva's need to have persons around her whom she could confide in and completely trust had heretofore not been satisfied. By her deep involvement in sessions with other protagonists, and as a result of her own psychodrama session, she experienced a new learning which contradicted what she had earlier learned in life.

Conclusion
Despite the difficulties in determining the therapeutic aspects of psychodrama, the above example illustrates how psychodrama helps to secure therapeutic effects primarily through a multitude of influences, including the inter-personal (tele), emotional (catharsis), cognitive (action-insight), imaginary (as-if), behavioural (acting-out), and non-specific (magic) agencies. The ultimate results of these combined forces may be widely different and include a relief from tension, a restoration of homeostasis, or a recapturing of a sense of mastery, which in themselves may restore adaptive defences and produce symptomatic cure. It is my hope that the following chapters will provide a deeper understanding of these therapeutic ingredients.

CHAPTER 6

Catharsis

One of the more controversial issues in the literature on psychotherapy concerns the comparative advantages and disadvantages of catharsis. Unfortunately, the arguments for and against are more often impassioned than impressive and we are provided with little systematic treatment of this subject from either a theoretical or an empirical perspective. The object of this chapter is to review the concept and the therapeutic value of catharsis and to reassess its status within the framework of psychodrama.

Historical Development

Catharsis has played an important role in psychotherapy for almost a hundred years (Weiner, 1977). Yet the use of the term goes back to long before the advent of psychotherapy. Aristotle, in his Poetics, used the term to describe the release of feelings in spectators who watched a tragedy. He believed that tragedy functioned 'through the arousal of pity and terror to achieve a proper *catharsis*, or purification, of the same emotions' (Aristotle, 1941, p.1460). Since Aristotle's days, the word 'catharsis' has been interpreted in many different ways. The accepted modern opinion is that catharsis is a medical term signifying an emotional purge in a patient. It is possible that this medical interpretation assumes a cleansing *from* emotions, as if they were noxious things to be gotten rid of. And indeed, in the centuries from Aristotle to the present, patients were cleansed of evil spirits, demons, and other detrimental powers by priests, exorcists, somnambulists, mesmerists, and hypnotists, all of whom believed that something evil or unclean was influencing the person from within and that this had to be driven out.

The medical interpretation of catharsis was powerfully reinforced in the late nineteenth century by Freud. Having studied hypnotism with Charcot, Freud provoked an emotional crisis in his hysterical patients and then guided the discharge of what he first re-conceptualized as repressed emotions, and later, as 'blocked libido' (Breuer & Freud, 1893).

In the early twentieth century, Moreno adapted the cathartic principles of Aristotle and the religious rituals of the Near East to the drama theories of Diderot, Lessing, and Goethe, and created the method of spontaneous drama (later developed into psycho-drama) in which protagonists were given the opportunity to liberate themselves from 'conserved' roles and written manuscripts.

As time passed, many cathartic psychotherapies developed, such as Character Analysis (Reich, 1929); Narcoanalysis (Horsley, 1943); Gestalt Therapy (Perls, 1969); Primal Therapy (Janov, 1970); and Bioenergetic Analysis (Lowen, 1975). The techniques differed, but the principle remained the same: to induce patients to purge themselves mentally of whatever morbid content was stored inside them. Common to these psychotherapies was the assumption that emotions 'build up' in a reservoir, like steam in a pressure cooker, if not expressed. This buildup caused internal pressure, or tension, which resulted in psychological malfunctioning. To regain a state of well-being, the patient had to drain off the emotional residue by expressing ('catharting') it. This theory is sometimes called the 'hydraulic model' (Bohart, 1980), and goes back to Freud's 'economic' point of view of the psyche as a repository of energies that requires periodic discharges (Blatner, 1985).

A review of the literature makes it clear that there is a confusing and overlapping mass of related terms used to describe catharsis, such as 'ventilation,' 'abreaction,' 'primal scream,' or the Reichian type of complete orgasm, total climax. Each therapeutic approach uses its own terminology, together with various rituals, to allow its patients to 'get things off their chests,' to 'cry themselves out,' or to 'blow off steam'. Yet some of these different but related phenomena—like acting out, peak-experience, act-completion, action-insight, AHA-experience, confession, salvation, regression, and need-satisfaction— which are sometimes designated as catharses, should not be designated as such. Blatner's (1985) differentiation of various components of catharsis, between catharsis of action, integration, and abreaction, catharsis of inclusion, and spiritual (or cosmic) catharsis, is also confusing and obscures the definition of catharsis. For catharsis refers, specifically and exclusively, to the release of stored up content through affective expression (observable surface changes in face, body, voice, and/or behaviour).

The Experience of Catharsis

The experience of catharsis may be illustrated by the psychodrama of Walter, a married man in his forties who complained of feeling tense and irritated most of the time. He had told the group that he suffered from frequent headaches and that he had difficulties relaxing at work. At times he looked as though he would explode, and it was clear to everyone that something was pressing him from within. When he was chosen as the protagonist, it came as no surprise that he wanted to work on his general state of anxiety. During the course of the interview, he mentioned that he hated working for his aggressive and domineering father-in-law, but that he felt too afraid and too guilty to face up to the situation and to quit his job. In one of the scenes, Walter presented a situation in which he was unjustly accused of stealing money from the firm in which he worked. In spite of his protests and explanations, his father-in-law (played by an auxiliary) insulted and denigrated him and threatened to go to the police.

The situation very rapidly lost its 'make-believe' quality and one could see that Walter was starting to lose control and that real anger was stirred up in him. Despite his efforts to keep calm and in control, something was 'breaking through' within his body, something which had been there for a long time, an old, dammed-up rage that was finally bubbling forth. It seemed as if Walter were re-experiencing all the scenes in his life when had been pushed around and he shouted 'I didn't do it! I didn't do it!' Suddenly his body went into spasm and the tears literally burst from his eyes, splattering his shirt and blinding him for a moment. Then everything turned upside down and he was truly crying for the first time in many years. When it was all over, Walter looked as if he had uncovered a secret, a simple truth which, until now, he had been unable to put into words or even into thoughts. But his body had always harboured the truth, reminding him of it through headaches and tension. After this session, Walter reported that his headaches had almost completely disappeared and that he felt much less tense and irritated at work. He felt that he had made a significant connection between his present tension and his frustrations as a child, an insight which helped him deal more effectively with present and future anxiety-provoking situations.

As with all affective expression, catharsis happens involuntarily and spontaneously, 'on the spur of the moment'. Here the word 'emotion' is taken literally—from the Latin *'e-movere'* meaning outward motion—conveying the idea of an outward expression of something inside. But catharsis differs from other affective expressions in its intensity, rawness, and primitiveness, as well as in its time-and-place distortion where here-and-now is mistaken for there-and-then. For example, weeping as a response to a recent loss is a normal grief reaction, while bursting into tears after a long period of withholding may be regarded as catharsis. Non-cathartic expressions of emotions (such as sadness) include also the resistive sobbing of someone who covers up anger, the manipulative crying of someone who wants to arouse attention, and the symptomatic whining of someone who is chronically depressed.

Catharsis differs from individual to individual in both quality and quantity. The intensity of liberation is highly relative and must be appreciated, not from an objective perspective, but from the perspective of each person's own experiential world. 'A seemingly mute expression of emotion may, for a highly constricted individual represent an event of considerable intensity, while an emotional storm for an impulsive individual may be a day-to-day regularity' (Yalom, 1975, p.84). While many participants in psychodrama stress the experience of being 'overwhelmed' by feelings, others enjoy it as a pleasurable experience, one of relief after having released pent-up emotions, or of sexual excitement which may occur as the by-product of emotional excitation. One woman exclaimed: 'It is like an orgasm! If you had it, it is blessed, it is a miracle!' This experience is similar also to the comforting relief felt after a verbal confession: 'Now everything will be all right. It has all come out in the open and there is no need to cover up anymore!'

It is not only patients who differ in their descriptions of catharsis and its effects. Three authoritative psychodramatists perceive the experience of catharsis as: 'a relief after an extreme state of tension, or an emotional culmination where resistances are gone' (Schutzenberger, 1970); 'an upheaval, a breaking up of constricted emotions and stiff structures' (Leutz, 1974); and 'the feeling that we are as we would like to be in our imagination' (Z. T. Moreno, 1971).

Yet despite the different perceptions, a common thread runs throughout experiences of catharsis. Catharsis refers to that emotional expression whereby something closed in, with a natural tendency to get out, is finally let out. Thus, catharsis may be understood as a 'label for completing (some or all of) a previously restrained or interrupted sequence of self-expression, that which would have occurred as a natural reaction to some experience had that experience not been thwarted' (Nichols & Efran, 1985, p.55). According to this view, catharsis is a kind of safety valve for reducing the tension within and between people, and it is therefore not surprising that most of us think of catharsis as something positive, a precious moment, an ideal state of being. In our world of common-sense, catharsis—and release in general—have a positive connotation. However, this in itself does not make catharsis therapeutic.

Catharsis as Cure?

The curative value of catharsis remains a controversial issue. Catharsis has traditionally been believed to be curative in cases of post-traumatic stress disorders, 'in which what has happened is only that the reaction to traumatic stimuli has failed to occur' (Freud, 1894, p.47). It is also considered valuable in the treatment of schizoid, avoidant, obsessive- compulsive, or passive-aggressive personality disorders in which affect is inhibited, and in the treatment of some somatoform disorders in which affect is repressed and somatized. But advocates of catharsis believe that almost all patients—neurotic, psychotic, ego-strong or ego-weak, inhibited or impulse-ridden—have stored up 'energies' and may therefore benefit from catharsis at least in some stage of their treatment. These proponents of catharsis claim that catharsis in and of itself can cure in a kind of automatic way, and argue that the immediate sense of well-being experienced after a powerful emotional release is proof enough of its validity. At the heart of this belief in catharsis is the sense that holding one's emotions in leads to feeling 'bottled up,' while letting them out leads to relief.

In the opposing camp, critics of catharsis either dispute its benefits or deny them completely. They argue that relief obtained through catharsis is only temporary, that tension tends to reappear after a period of time, and that general expression of an emotion does not necessarily reduce that emotion; for example, crying does not always reduce the experience of sadness. They also question whether emotional expression can, by itself, provide therapeutic change—whether, for example, the expression of anger solves any real, inter-personal conflicts.

Advocates of the therapeutic value of catharsis rely on a simplistic view of mental health as 'purity of the soul' and mental illness as 'pollution of the soul,' with catharsis as the intermediate agent of cleansing. They conceptualize a catharsis-cure in terms of opening a safety-valve for imprisoned aspects of the self to be released. According to this view, a healthy individual is one who is able to give free and spontaneous expression to emotions and who is constantly in a dynamic process of transformation. For advocates of catharsis, playing out evil in a legal framework not only provides a safety-valve for surplus anger, but also offers an opportunity for gaining emotional balance and self-control. Clients may vicariously express anger at their therapists, at other group members (auxiliaries), or at inanimate objects. For example, if protagonists have a lot of repressed anger, Goldman & Morrison (1984), recommend that they scream, beat the 'bataka,' or throw metal chairs against the wall. Whatever the instrument used, the reduction of tension may facilitate frustration tolerance and delay action until a satisfactory solution to the conflict is found.

Empirical research on the value of catharsis has focused mainly on the frustration-aggression hypothesis, as espoused by Dollard, Doeb, Miller, Mowerer, & Sears, (1939), who suggested that aggressive behaviour reduces the instigation to aggression Early research, for example by Feshback (1956), Berkowitz, Green, & Macanley (1962), Kahn (1966), Mallick & McCandless (1966), and Hokanson (1970), found little support for this theory, as have the more recent studies of Zumkley (1978), Bohart (1980), Warren & Kurlychek (1981), and Tavris (1982). All these authors demonstrated that the expression of anger, whether verbal or physical, does *not* automatically reduce anger; they did, however, conclude that interpersonal, behavioural, and/or cognitive factors were crucially related to whether catharsis was anger-reducing or not. With a mass of accumulated evidence from controlled research studies of children, Bandura & Walters (1965) concluded that far from producing cathartic reduction of aggression, direct or vicarious participation in aggressive behaviour within a permissive setting maintains the behaviour at its original level and may actually increase it. In an effort to balance these various views, Gould (1972) suggested that catharsis of aggression would benefit primarily individuals who are inhibited or otherwise unable to express their feelings. Impulsive personalities, such as chaotic adolescents who have difficulty postponing satisfaction, tolerating frustration, and delaying immediate expression (Willis, 1991), may be less amenable to cathartic treatments. This view is congruous with Yalom (1975), who said that 'many restricted individuals are benefited by experiencing and expressing strong affect. Others, with contrasting problems of impulse control and great emotional lability may, on the contrary, profit from acquiring an intellectual structuring and from reining in emotional expression' (p.103). Similarly, Butler & Fuhriman (1983) found that catharsis was ranked top in outpatient groups, while being less effective among hospitalized patients.

Theoretical studies within the framework of psychoanalytic thinking are also critical to the original catharsis hypothesis. For example, Kris (1952) says: 'We are no longer satisfied with the notion that repressed emotions lose their hold over our mental life when an outlet for them has been found' (p.45), and Binstock (1973) maintains that 'the role of catharsis in human affairs is a most restricted and humble one' (p.504). From a technical point of view, Bibring (1954), Dewald (1964), and Greenson (1967) emphasize that while catharsis has a rather limited curative role in psychoanalysis, it can give the patient a feeling of conviction regarding the reality of his or her unconscious processes. Finally, Slavson (1951) pointed out that 'the value of catharsis lies in the fact that it induces regression to stages in emotional development where arrest or fixation occurred' (p.39).

Within the field of group psychotherapy, Yalom (1975), in his comparative study of curative factors, concluded that 'the open expression of affect is without question vital to the group therapeutic process; in its absence a group would degenerate into a sterile academic exercise. Yet, it is only a part process and must be complemented by other factors' (p.84). His data is supported by the studies of Lieberman, Yalom, & Miles (1973) and Berzon, Pious, & Parson (1963), who found that pure ventilation, without the acquisition of skills for the future, was of no curative value. Similarly, in their review of catharsis in religious and magical healing rites, psychoanalysis, clinical hypnotherapy, group therapy, behaviour therapy, the social psychology of aggression and the treatment of war-neuroses, Nichols & Zax (1977) found that catharsis, alone, was never enough to bring about a psychotherapeutic cure.

Advocates of catharsis as the single curative factor, however, seem to pay little attention to such research data, and implicitly accept the therapeutic value of catharsis. They argue that what the critics repudiate is not 'real' catharsis, but some form of 'pseudo-expression of feelings' and maintain that patients who experience the 'real' thing, for example a 'primal experience,' will be immediately and permanently cured. Rose (1976) write that the critics have failed to get positive results with catharsis 'because what they have identified as feeling is simply not sufficiently intense' (p.80). Similarly, Scheff (1979) holds that it is the critics' failure to follow a procedure of repeated emotional discharge during a properly distanced re-experiencing of a traumatic scene that accounts for most of the difficulties they encounter, and not a lack of validity of cathartic therapy in itself. Some empirical evidence is put forward by Janov (1970), Karle, Corriere & Hart (1973), Nichols (1974), Nichols & Zax (1977), and by Scheff (1979). Within the framework of human potential encounter, Heider (1974) consider catharsis to be the 'most frequent and valued tool for entry into transcendental realms of experience' (p.30).

A common-sense approach to the value of catharsis would seem to take into account Gendlin's (1964) observation that 'major personality change involves some sort of intense feeling process occurring in the individual' (p.105). The notion that tension reduction leads to relief is also easily accepted by most people and there is little doubt that 'unloading' one's difficulties on someone else genuinely lightens the burden of conflict. Such release may help to break a vicious circle of frustration and repression which often characterizes neurotic individuals. One must emphasize, however, that the benefits from catharsis depend largely on the response persons receive when they express themselves. For example, when the expression of anger is met with retaliation, the experience may result in a new frustration rather than in relief. Thus, giving expression to what one has heretofore kept in, *in the right environment,* can become an important new experience which leads to therapeutic growth.

The Role of Catharsis in Psychodrama
One of the firmly noted assumptions in psychodrama is that the development of catharsis on the part of the protagonist is a major curative factor in the therapeutic endeavour, and as such is promoted. Regardless of when it happens—during the warm up, action, closure or sharing phase—it is often regarded as the 'peak' or culmination of the session and then viewed as the single, most significant event in that psychodrama. According to Ginn (1973), 'the entire arsenal of dramatic weaponry is marshalled for the achievement and maximization of the cathartic moment' (p.16). Polansky & Harkins (1969) were so impressed by the positive use of psychodrama for affect discharge that they 'began to think of psychodrama as perhaps the specific for treating affect inhibition' (p.79).

However, when the difficulty in determining the role of catharsis in personality change is taken into account, it seems monstrously overvalued in psychodrama. While catharsis may have substantial value in certain contexts, it does not merit treatment as an end in itself rather than a means to an end. In some circles, catharsis has become so cherished and romanticized that it has achieved functional autonomy. There is no doubt that emotional release is central to the psychodramatic process, but only in combination with other factors. Catharsis may set the stage for the change process by loosening up fixated positions, but sooner or later, the conflicts underlying these fixations must be dealt with, either through interaction with the outer world or in terms of one's own feelings.

Psychodramatists who provoke release for its own sake, without paying enough attention to resistance-analysis, working through, and integration, may be compared to the early 'id-analysts' in psychoanalysis who put all their efforts into uncovering the unconscious. This position may be farther contrasted with the later ego-psychologists who took ego- functions such as reality testing, adaptation, object-relations, defences, and integration into consideration in their psychotherapies, with less of an emphasis on cathartic release. Practitioners who strive for both release (id) and integration (ego), will be more effective than those who emphasize release alone. This view is congruent with that of Weiner (1974) who altered Freud's dictum: 'where id is, there shall ego be,' to 'where mind is, there shall body-mind be' (p.48).

Moreno (1923, 1940) enlarged the original etymological meaning of catharsis to include not only release and relief of emotions, but also integration and ordering; not only intense reliving of the past, but also genuine living in the here-and-now; not only a passive, verbal reflection, but also an active, non-verbal enactment; not only a private ritual, but also a communal, shared rite of healing; not only an intrapsychic tension-reduction, but also an inter-personal conflict-resolution; not only a medical purification, but also a religious and aesthetic experience. This understanding of catharsis reflects a considerable extension of that depicted above and presents, implicitly, a two-phase process of psychodrama: (1) release and relief (catharsis), and (2) integration and ordering (working through). In the words of Zerka Moreno (1965): 'restraint has to come after expression'.

The first phase of psychodrama includes both resistance-analysis and catharsis. Protagonists are not manipulated into expression, but helped to overcome those resistances which block their spontaneity. Thus, calling a breakdown of defences a 'break-through' is an error in technique. Catharsis is neither induced, nor inhibited, but allowed to emerge in its own time and in its own form. Only when communication is open and feelings flow are protagonists encouraged to maximize their expression, in order to 'let it all out!'

The specific function of catharsis in psychodrama is to facilitate self-expression and enhance spontaneity. Self-expression is more than mere affective liberation; it includes communication of perceived inner and outer reality, of self- and object-representations, of values, defences, body images, etc. Protagonists are encouraged to express themselves in any way they find suitable, ideally in an atmosphere free of disapproval or retaliation. But, as Cornyetz had already pointed out in 1947, 'the psychodramatist does not satisfy himself that the release took place for here is the starting point of the task of psychotherapy and not the finishing-point' (p.62).

The second phase of psychodrama includes integration of released feelings. Whatever was released must be re-integrated in order to prevent it from 'going up in smoke'. This integration may involve restoring order into an internal emotional chaos, new learning of coping strategies, working through of interpersonal relations, or transformation of partial feelings to complete feelings. In the words of Goldman & Morrison (1984), 'as we move from the core of our spiral with the climax, both insight and integration have begun. Throughout, it is essential that the protagonist be aware of feelings, thoughts and actions. The link between the affective and the cognitive is necessary for the protagonist to integrate the session, even though he/she may not be able to completely integrate everything at the close of the session' (p.32).

Conclusion

This chapter surveyed the concept of catharsis and discussed its curative value within psychodrama and within current thinking in psychotherapy. Catharsis was defined as an experience of release that occurs when a longstanding state of inner mobilization finds its outlet in action. Such a release is not curative in itself but can effect a change only in combination with other factors, such as sharing with a sympathetic group. Considering that catharsis is not the single, or even the most curative factor in psychodrama, it seems to be greatly overvalued by many practitioners.

CHAPTER 7

Action-insight

In the previous chapter I discussed the therapeutic value of catharsis and came to the conclusion that the emotional release would be completely ineffective if not accompanied by an appeal to reason and rationality and complemented with some cognitive *insight*.

Insight has traditionally been regarded as an important factor producing cure. Psychoanalysis and virtually all psychodynamically oriented psychotherapies have utilized self-awareness as a central aspect of the treatment process. According to participants in psychodrama, self-understanding is more helpful than other factors (Kellermann, 1985b). The process of gaining such understanding has been given different names or not even been mentioned by some. Yet, whether it is labelled as self-actualization, making the unconscious conscious, enlightenment, illumination or insight, most psychotherapies, including some cognitive-behavioural approaches (Bandura, 1977), will provide patients with an understanding of themselves and of their difficulties—how they arose and how they can be changed—whether psychoanalytical, cognitive, or existential-humanistic.

Self-understanding, however, does not automatically produce therapeutic effects. It has long been recognized that intellectual insight alone does not facilitate emotional or behavioural changes (Freud, 1910; 1937; Adler, 1930; Ferenczi & Rank, 1925; Alexander & French, 1946; Horney, 1950; Fromm-Reichmann, 1950; Sullivan, 1953; Hobbs, 1962; Gendlin, 1961; Singer, 1970; Janov, 1970; Kohut, 1984). The fact that clients gain a basic understanding of their problems and explore their childhoods does not guarantee that they either can or will do anything about them. Many patients have obtained a high degree of insight and yet have made no therapeutic progress (Thorne, 1973, p.865; Yalom, 1975, p.43). One cannot simply tell people what they suffer from and expect them to change. Nor does it help to explain the reasons for their problems in terms of some accepted theory of child development, even if the explanation is correct. 'If information alone could bring about therapeutic change, patients could get well by reading their psychiatric case summaries and psychological test reports' (Appelbaum, 1988, p.205).

In order for therapy to be successful, the process of self-discovery must be emotional rather than intellectual and should be accompanied by a meaningful learning experience. Patients must go beyond seeing the cause of their suffering in the past and experience the meaning of their feelings and actions in the present (Applebaum, 1988). The goal in reconstructive therapy is not to gain 'intellectual insight,' which basically is a defence mechanism, but to attain 'emotional insight,' the capacity to 'be in touch with the unconscious' (Rycroft, 1968) on a physical and emotional basis. It seems to me that there is no fundamental disagreement between psychoanalysis and psychodrama regarding the therapeutic value of such emotional insights. Psychodrama helps us become more aware of ourselves, of our feelings, dreams, life styles, inner lives, conflicts and motivations. It helps us to recognize what we are doing to ourselves and to others and to evaluate our behaviour in terms of our goals. It may also help us recollect the experiences of infancy and childhood that have been the forerunners and sometimes the sources of later mental disturbances. In the words of Maslow (1971), 'If the psychoanalytic literature has taught us nothing else, it has taught us that repression is not a good way of solving problems' (p.47). But self-understanding or insight is not a goal in itself in psychodrama. Often insight is no more than hindsight, and remains unintegrated unless supported by action and behavioural change (Wheelis, 1950). In psychodrama, the process of self-discovery must be complemented with an element of foresight—the enhancement of anticipatory awareness to be used in future coping behaviour (Rapoport, 1970). In order to emphasize that this process is achieved in action rather than as a result of verbal interpretation, Moreno preferred to describe the process of self-discovery in psychodrama as 'action-insight'.

Although 'action-insight' is one of the basic therapeutic aspects of psychodrama and a key concept in the theory of psychodramatic technique, it has remained largely neglected in the literature. The purpose of the present chapter is to define the concept and to discuss its applications within the framework of psychodrama therapy.

Action-insight

Action-insight is the result of various kinds of action learning. It may be defined as the integration of emotional, cognitive, imaginary, behavioural and interpersonal learning experiences. 'In psychodrama we speak of action insight, action learning, or action catharsis. It is an integrative process brought about by the synthesis of numerous techniques at the height of the protagonist's warm up' (Z. Moreno, 1965).

Action-insight cannot be attained through introspective analysis while lying on the couch. It is achieved only in action, while moving about, standing still, pushing and pulling, making sounds or gestures or pronouncing words; in other words, while communicating through action-language (see Chapter 10). Introspective analysis may be an important aspect of many therapies, but it is not a part of the psychodramatic process of gaining action-insight.

The 'in-sight' in action-insight specifically refers to the looking 'in;' the searching for inner truth and awareness of self, in contrast to grasping the outer world of the senses, the so called 'reality'. According to Blatner (1973), 'psycho-drama facilitates "acting-in": the applications of *action* methods to the explora-tion of the psychological aspects of human experience' (p.2).

Action-insight is experienced differently by different people. This is illus-trated by the following statements from participants who were asked about their personal experiences of action-insights in psychodrama: 'My mind became crystal clear and every detail of my self came into focus with extraordinary clarity as if the doors of perception were suddenly opened.' 'My body was open to every sensation and I knew what I was feeling.' 'I was aware of my needs and motives and I recognized the personal consequences of my actions.' 'Memories were brought to light and I felt that I was about to find something which had been hidden deep down within myself for a long time'. 'Disconnected elements within myself were united.' 'It was as if I finally was able to "make sense" of myself and my life.'

Action-insight may appear as a sudden flash of comprehension—'Eureka! I've got it!'—or as the gradual unfolding of discoveries over a long period of time. It is impossible, however, to determine who has had 'it' and who has not. Insight is not an 'either-or' phenomenon; 'either you have it or you don't!' It should rather be viewed as a process in which one becomes more and more aware and open to sensations all through life. It is also impossible to determine when one has 'got enough of it' as illustrated by the truism: 'Insight is something you think you have, until you get more of it.' Each passage of life may be a potential crisis or an opportunity for creative change which demands new ways of adjustment and understanding.

The experience of action-insight may be illustrated by a rebellious young woman who presented all the signs of late adolescence crisis; she dressed in provocative black clothes, shaved her head and started to use drugs. She was brought for treatment because of an intense mother-daughter conflict and unduly aggressive behaviour. In a psychodramatic session, she presented a situation in which she expressed hostility towards her mother (played by an auxiliary). In the midst of her rage, she suddenly became silent, her eyes filled with tears and she said soundlessly 'You knew what he did with me all the time and you did not stop him!' It became apparent that her father had sexually abused her for many years and that it was a well-kept secret in the family. Being able to confront her mother with this fact during the psychodrama opened up a flow of self awareness and she exclaimed: 'That's why I don't want to be a woman! That's why I hate men! That's why I shaved my head! That's the reason I hate you!' This kind of understanding did not explain her coping behaviour in a detached, analytical and reconstructive manner; 'I understood that my behaviour was a reaction to what my parents did to me...' Rather, it was experienced with intense emotional involvement while talking directly to her mother: 'I hate you! How could you do this to me? What kind of a mother are you?' While such an action-insight certainly did not lead to an immediate cure, it became a turning-point which paved the way for real therapeutic progress.

Action-insight is closely related to catharsis and can be described as a kind of cognitive release of an idea from the unconscious. The affective expression of catharsis is preceded, accompanied, or followed by a cognitive illumination where 'a spotlight is switched on, psychic content of the patient, thus far hidden in the dark, appears in the limelight of his consciousness' (Buxbaum, 1972, p.161). For example, a sudden expression of grief may be accompanied by the memory of an earlier separation. Catharsis experienced in full consciousness will facilitate the experiential remembering that leads to action-insight. 'Whenever something clicks, falls into place, each time a gestalt closes, there is the "Aha!" click, the shock of recognition' (Perls, 1969, p.236).

The Process of Achieving Action-insight

The steps involved in achieving action-insight are similar to those of a creative problem-solving process. According to Wallas (1926), such a problem-solving process tends to proceed along the following four stages: preparation, incubation, illumination and verification. These stages will be described as they appear in psychodrama and illustrated with a fictitious example. In the first stage, a situation is dramatized in which a problem is presented and facts are collected. (Skinny Joe dates girl. Bully makes fun of Joe. Girl leaves.) In the second stage, the problematic situation is explored and frustration is expressed; spontaneous and unconscious processes dominate and create unexpected connections. (Joe feels miserable, tries out some solutions, but fails.) In stage three, new insights are gained and a solution to the problem is found (Joe goes to body-building and assertiveness-training). In the final stage, the insight is tested against reality and possibly translated into action. (Joe confronts Bully and wins fight. Girl returns to strong Joe!) While this caricature illustration is far from a realistic description of an actual psychodrama, it does provide a general overview of the steps that are involved in achieving action-insight.

Non-interpretative Means of Developing Action-insight

Psychodramatic action-insights cannot be handed over from one person to another and cannot be given to the client by the therapist in the form of an interpretation. Though some psychoanalytic practitioners frequently analyze either individuals or the group-as-a-whole, most psychodramatists (trained in the classical Morenian tradition) refrain from giving interpretations. According to Zerka Moreno (1965), 'Psychodrama is actually the most interpretative method there is, but the director acts upon his interpretations in the construction of the scenes. Verbal interpretation may either be essential, or entirely omitted at the discretion of the director. Because his interpretation is in the act, it is frequently redundant. Even when interpretation is given, action is primary. There can be no interpretation without previous action' (Moreno, 1972, p.236–237).

Kipper (1986) differentiates between 'action' and 'verbal' forms of interpretations: 'Unlike verbal interpretations, which represent a component of conventional approaches to psychotherapy, action interpretations are unique to clinical role playing and psychodrama. The use of action interpretations is consistent with the fundamental premise of behaviour simulation-based therapies, namely that therapy is rendered through actional language. Thus, whenever a therapist wishes to introduce a point of interpretation, it, too, should take the form of a role playing enactment... To the impartial observer, action interpretations may appear as an indirect way of making the protagonist aware of the meaning of his or her behavior' (p.104).

The proper term for analytic activity in psychodrama would be 'action-analysis,' rather than psycho-analysis. In action-analysis, the psychodramatist tries to give meaning to present behaviour, either in terms of past experiences (repetitive action, e.g. transference), or in terms of counter-action (resistance), abreaction (catharsis), and/or communicative action (acting out) (see Chapter 10).

The goal of behavioural and psychoanalytic psychodrama is to explain the 'cause' of behaviour in a deterministic manner. The goal of existential psychodrama, however, is to attempt to understand human motives and intentions without any reference to reason. Existential psychodrama is non-deterministic, preferring to ask 'how' a person is acting in a descriptive manner rather than 'why' a person is behaving in a certain way. Interpreting a protagonist's presented material is often less effective than letting the hidden meanings evolve by themselves in action. For example, Evelyn, an obese woman who was unable to keep a diet, complained that her overeating had a disastrous effect upon her figure. In psychodrama, she presented a scene in which she argued with her husband. He had returned home tired, wanting to read the evening paper while she wanted to go out and visit friends. In the middle of this argument, she exclaimed: 'You don't satisfy my needs!' and she took out a big apple from her purse and started to eat it. She looked apologetically at the surprised group members and added: 'I eat when I am bored, when I am angry!' It was clear from her action in the scene that Evelyn's hunger and over-eating was an expression of frustration with her husband. This understanding evolved by itself in action in a self-evident fashion without the need for outside clarification or interpretation. Having reached this level of understanding, Evelyn proceeded, during the rest of the session, to explore her pattern of expressing, satisfying and postponing her real needs.

The development of action-insight is facilitated by means other than the giving of verbal interpretations. The most effective way to pave the way for action-insight is to establish a context which fosters spontaneity and resolves resistances. When people are allowed to express themselves freely, to talk and act as they want, to associate and act from within and to be true to themselves and honest with others, significant inner material will emerge spontaneously and transform personal truth and distant history into issues of immediate relevance.

In a paradoxical manner, action-insight is the result of both involvement and detachment. Though role playing stimulates emotional involvement, activating the experiential self-as-subject ('I am...'), many psychodramatic techniques also encourage reflection, detachment and the observational self-as-object ('looking at myself from the outside'). For example, in the technique of mirroring, protagonists are asked to look at themselves from the outside; in doubling, they listen to clarifying voices and in role reversal they see themselves from the other person's perspective. Only when they become emotionally involved in the actual role playing do protagonists come closer to their immediate and spontaneous experiences. 'Psychodrama tries, with the cooperation of the patient, to transfer the mind 'outside' of the individual and objectify it within a tangible, controllable universe... The protagonist is being prepared for an encounter with himself. After this phase of objectification is completed, the second phase begins; it is to resubjectify, reorganize, and reintegrate that which has been objectified' (Moreno, 1972, p.xxi).

Thus, as the emotional experience has been allowed to assume increasingly regressive expression, protagonists are encouraged to seek emotional distance from themselves and to observe and reflect upon what they have just experienced and expressed. The shift in emphasis between the experiencing part of the self on the one hand, and the observing part on the other, recurs as a central element in psychodrama and the aim is to achieve an harmonious balance between them.

To some extent all roads to self-awareness involve elements of learning. Psychodramatic action-insight develops as a result of (1) experiential learning; (2) learning through doing; and (3) non-cognitive learning.

1. Experiential Learning
The first and most obvious characteristic of action-insight is that it is based on an actual personal learning experience and not merely on verbal information. The learning gained through such an experience is passionate and involved, emphasizing the personal participation in the discovery and validation of knowledge (Polanyi, 1962).

For example, it would be meaningless to tell an overprotective mother to be less protective. However, if, in psychodrama, she is persuaded to reverse roles with her child, even for a short time, and to experience intensely how it feels to live under her own protective behaviour, she might change. Such a first-hand awareness may give the protagonist an experience which is sufficiently meaningful to produce a lasting impact.

Worthy of note in this context is the observation made by Rogers (1969) in his book 'Freedom to Learn,' that in order for learning to be meaningful, it must involve the whole person in a significant experience. Learning which involves only the mind, has no relevance for most people. 'When the toddler touches the warm radiator he learns for himself the meaning of a word, "hot"; he has learned a future caution in regard to all similar radiators; and he has taken in these learnings in a significant, involved way which will not soon be forgotten' (p.4). Psychodrama, in a similar way, tries to provide a significant learning experience, based on what Leutz (1985b) called a psychodramatic 'experience-of-evidence'.

Significant learning experiences which lead to action-insights are sometimes called 'corrective emotional experiences;' a term coined by Alexander (1946). The principle behind such an experience is that poor parenting in childhood may be altered by remedial 'good' parenting in adulthood (whether by a therapist, a substitute parent, an auxiliary or by the re-educated parent him- or herself), in order to 'set the record straight'. Moreno's dictum from 1923 that 'every true second time is the release from the first' (p.76), conveys a similar message of giving adults what they might have missed as children. Within the context of psychodramatic 'surplus reality,' situations are sometimes re-enacted in a more satisfying manner, leading to what is sometimes called a 're-parenting' of a deprived protagonist.

We may ask, however, if it is really possible to heal early deprivations through corrective experiences. According to Stone (1981), 'one cannot give to the elaborately organized personality of an adult what he missed as an infant or young child, in the original form in which the lack occurred, and expect it to repair the defective structuralized developments occasioned by its lack' (p.103). However, while it is impossible to correct mistakes from the past, it may be possible to supercede some of the negative learning from that time. By evoking an adaptive regression in the service of the ego to earlier stages of functioning, protagonists may be provided not only with an opportunity to re-experience the past in a new and satisfying manner, but also to un-learn some of the not-so-desirable attitudes, habits and patterns from the past. Thus, a person may continue to grow from the point at which development was arrested.

For example, Robert was a young, non-assertive man who had grown up with a very strict father. When he was a child, his father had enforced an almost military obedience in his only child. As a result, Robert had developed low self esteem and suffered from periods of severe anxiety attacks. His psychodrama was closed with a prolonged emotional experience with a 'good father' who held Robert in his arms while sitting in the rocking chair. Though perhaps not 'corrective' in the real sense of the word, Robert reported later that this experience gave him a sense of hope and achievement, evoking a profound sense of trust in the possibilities of life. Perhaps even more significant was the accepting group which encouraged Robert to express himself in any way he found suitable. As a result, Robert started to demonstrate more assertive behaviour both within and outside the group and was delighted when the negative responses which he had anticipated did not appear. By digesting Robert's past experiences and affirming his current ability, psychodrama succeeded in un-linking the present feelings from the past trauma and in providing Robert with a genuine new learning experience.

Using similar data, Kutter (1985) came to the conclusion that both insight and corrective emotional experience are important curative factors in group psychotherapy and that one without the other will not lead to permanent change.

2) Learning Through Doing

The second characteristic of psychodramatic action-insight is that it is based on learning through doing more than on talking, on practice more than on theory, and on overt behaviour more than on inner thinking.

Telling people what they are doing and what consequences they may expect from their actions is notoriously ineffective. People are especially unsusceptible to verbal persuasion when they are emotionally upset. 'Intense fear, burning anger, and passionate love are known to blind our perceptions and to make us unreceptive to what someone tells us is reasonable. We do not talk a paranoiac out of his delusions; we do not persuade the victim of phobias that he can, if he wants to, stop being afraid; we do not convince the addict that, with more will power, he can do without his drugs; and we seldom are able to give a depressed suicidal patient a reason for living' (Fox, 1972, p.191). Talking about swimming will not teach anyone how to swim; in order to learn how to swim, one must jump into the water and practice swimming. Similarly, interpersonal or beha-vioural skills cannot be learned through talking. They must be practiced in action, sometimes over a long period of time.

Many patients claim to have achieved some insights, yet when the necessary steps toward a real change are required, the patients characteristically hesitate and ask: 'But how do I change?' or 'So what do I do now?' This inability to translate self-awareness into action may be the result of resistance, anxiety, or lack of working through, but it may also be the result of insufficient learning through doing.

Understanding which has been achieved through practice, rather than through experimental thinking, is readily translated into overt action. Accord-ing to the action model of Schafer (1976), we don't 'have' such action-insights, we 'are' them, or we 'do' them; they are claimed, manifest behaviour rather than metapsychological constructs.

The following is a short illustration: William was a young man who had grown up with an unloving mother. In his psychodrama he presented many frustrating experiences from his childhood. It became clear that, as a result of these childhood experiences, William had developed a negative generalized concept of women. He felt that all women, not just his mother, were basically evil and selfish. Many years in individual verbal therapy had taught him that his maladaptive behaviour could be traced back to his mother, but he did not know what to do with this 'insight'. The psychodrama group, which included both men and women, became an experimental environment in which William was encouraged to work through his unresolved conflicts with women and 'unlearn' some of his undesirable previous patterns.

3) Non-cognitive Learning

The third characteristic of psychodramatic action-insight is that it is based on 'non-cognitive' learning. Cognitive learning, which takes place 'from the head up,' is unimportant in psychodrama. Getting protagonists to understand why they act as they do is not a goal for most psychodramatists. However, while cognitive understanding is considered a manifestation of resistance that prevents real change from taking place, non-cognitive, 'gut-level' learning, which involves processing at the bodily and perceptual-motor level, is a central part of the psychodramatic process. This process seems to rely more on the emotional and intuitive than on the intellectual and analytical modes of the mind.

Observing that change in experiential knowing was a common dimension in psychotherapy, Bohart & Wugalter (1991) suggested that such knowing occurs when a meaning sequence is not merely cognitively apprehended, but has come to be 'understood' at a more direct perceptual-motor level. It is only when things are so understood that they lead to meaningful therapeutic change. According to Greenberg (1974), 'The sensory stimulation of the psychodramas, together with the emotional catharsis brought on by spontaneity and tele can and do, according to Moreno, cause a restructuring of the protagonist's perceptual field (whether he is on the stage or in the audience) and bring insight or understanding to his problems by means of configurational learning' (p.19).

Non-cognitive learning often cannot be translated into words. It is based on mental and physical sensations which seem to belong to a preverbal, early phase of child development. Such learning, for example, occurred when a regressed protagonist who was overwhelmed by feelings of sadness and isolation suddenly felt less lonely as a result of physical comfort. The 'holding' action (Winnicott, 1965) which is based on the actual physical 'holding' of the infant in the adult's arms, provided the necessary care and nurturing for the protagonist's inner self to develop.

A further example. Thomas was a young man who, a few years earlier, had been witness to the drowning of a small child and had felt guilty every since. It was as if he had been responsible for the death of the child and he felt that his life was no longer worth living. Following the psychodramatic enactment of the traumatic scene, he was urged by the director to undo what had been done, and to rescue the baby (played by an auxiliary). Thomas pulled the baby out from the water, an act which was repeated in role reversal, with Thomas playing the role of the baby. When being rescued, Thomas started to cry like a child, screaming for help, as if he, himself, was drowning. The director instructed the auxiliary to save Thomas and take him out of the water. Having returned to his own role, Thomas was blinded with tears, begging and crying: 'I don't want to live anymore! Please leave me in the water. Let me die instead of you!' The auxiliary playing the child pulled him out of the water and sat beside him, still holding him in his arms and said: 'No, you must continue to live. You must live for both us. I was supposed to die, not you. You were not responsible for my death.' Thomas became quiet and looked at the floor for a long time. Then he raised his head with a different expression on his face. It was as if he finally had let the truth sink in and he realized that he had to go on living. Where common sense had let him down, the words of the child who spoke to him from death had a profound impact. A year later, though still mourning the child, Thomas reported that the session had liberated him from the worst part of his guilt feelings.

Conclusion

Action-insight occurs when a protagonist understands the roots of the conflict and recovers the memory of repressed experiences. The popular notion, however, that cure results from the sudden recall of a single traumatic event from the past, is untrue. The protagonist's troubles seldom stem from a single source, and psychotherapy is never simply an intellectual process. Therapeutic progress occurs as a result of a gradual increase in self-knowledge which is based on a non-cognitive, practical experience, accompanied by the emotional re-living of past events.

Insight and catharsis must work together: protagonists must both understand their feelings and feel what they understand. However, 'neither catharsis nor insight is a panacea. The emotional habits of a lifetime develop a functional autonomy no longer dependent on their original cause. Abreaction facilitates but does not guarantee insight, just as insight facilitates but does not guarantee reduction of symptoms' (Sacks, 1976b, p.42). Frequently, both insight and catharsis must be supplemented with specific role-training (for example assertiveness, relaxation and problem-solving training) to produce any substantial change.

Psychodramatists have traditionally favoured feelings at the expense of thoughts. Perhaps as a reaction to the psychoanalytic emphasis on introspection, many practitioners of psychodrama have come to devalue any cognitive understanding and to idealize emotions over intellect. Buhler (1979) quoted Kalen Hamman as saying that by 'having been trained to use our minds to help suppress our feelings, we tend to respond to "permission" to feel by trying to suppress our (and others') intellects' (p.10). A careful examination, however, of the conditions necessary for therapeutic progress leads to the reduction of the dichotomy between thinking and feeling, between insight and catharsis and between mind and body. Yet, what we consider as 'mind' is so intimately connected with what we call 'body' that one cannot be understood without the other. Every insight reverberates through the body, and, on the other hand, changes in our physical condition influence our whole mental attitude. Thus we need to be constantly reminded that 'thinking about oneself, as well as feeling, is a relevant basic human process' (Buhler, 1979, p.19). As I have already emphasized in Chapter 6, psychodrama attempts to provide a two-phase process which includes both emotional release and cognitive integration. 'Therapy is an *emotional and a corrective* experience. We must experience something strongly, *but we must also*, through our faculty of reason, understand the implications of that emotional experience' (Yalom, 1975, p.28).

CHAPTER 8

Tele

Thus far I have discussed the therapeutic value of catharsis and action-insight in psychodrama. Psychodramatists who emphasize the role of emotional release and the cognitive integration of that release tend to attach less importance to the possible benefits of interpersonal relations in psychotherapy. In some psychodrama groups, the exploration of relations is almost totally neglected. Most practitioners, however, regard the relations which develop between the members of the group and between therapist and patient as a potentially powerful curative force in psychodrama.

This latter position is consistent with Moreno's (1937) characterization of psychodrama as 'inter-personal therapy,' and as 'an invitation to a meeting, a meeting of two; eye to eye, face to face' (Moreno, 1914). If utilized properly, such meetings are believed to be essential for the process and outcome of psychodrama therapy, whether they occur during the actual sessions (between protagonist, auxiliaries, group members and the psychodramatist) or in open encounters, in the post-action sharing phase, or between actual sessions.

When asked to provide a rationale for their work, practitioners who focus on interpersonal relations to enhance the therapeutic effects of psychodrama justify their practice with the help of social psychology, interpersonal psychology, object relations theory, or transactional analysis. Although these schools employ widely different terminologies, they all stress the inter-relatedness of individual and environment and view behaviour and personality development as determined by the social interaction between people. According to Schecter (1973), human relatedness emerges as a result of 'social stimulation and reciprocal interaction, often playful and not necessarily tension reducing' (p.21). The theory of personality development suggested by Moreno (1953) resembles the above formulations insofar as it views the interaction between individual and environment as essential for the development of an inner world. According to Moreno (1953), human beings are born into a 'social atom,' a social network which continues to affect them throughout life. More specifically, Moreno contends that the personality of the child evolves from relationships with parents and other important persons with whom there is intimate contact. It is therefore impossible fully to comprehend clients without taking their social atoms into consideration.

The interpersonal theory of psychodrama was summarized by Fine (1979) as follows: 'Psychodrama is usually conducted in a group since the theory underlying psychodrama is socially interactive. The therapy group is a social network providing a supportive, protective climate in which the learner can test and expand his limits in the presence of the group's members and therapists. In psychodrama therapy, each patient is the therapeutic agent of the other. The group provides a setting for the development of new relationships. Tele replaces transference. Group members are taught to distinguish between spontaneous interpersonal interaction and habituated or maladaptive interpersonal behaviour. In the psychodrama group, honest, here-and-now relationships are established, examined, enhanced, and expanded. Here, a person can examine his intrapsychic world and distinguish between reality and fantasy' (p.442).

Interpersonal therapy is based on the assumption that people change and develop, not only as a result of merely being together, but through the active working through of inter-personal perceptions, feelings, conflicts, attitudes and communications with the 'generalized others' (Mead, 1934) in their social atoms. Such working through may involve an examination of the source of protagonists' interpersonal styles and a recognition that some patterns of interaction which originated in childhood affect interactions in the present. In dealing with unsatisfactory relations from the past, psychodrama aims to free people of psychological 'baggage,' which may then help them get on with the business of leading happier, more fulfilling and satisfactory lives in the present.

On the psychodramatic stage, protagonists are invited to present all the various people to whom they have been connected, and, if necessary, may re-write the dialogues and the roles these people played in their lives. In the process of this work, accounts may be settled with the people protagonists love and hate, from the present or the past. When all the persons who played important roles in their lives have had a chance to speak, and when they have exhausted their answers to these persons, the protagonists will search actively for their inner voices and unique personal truths. Finally, whatever conclusions they may draw from such an experience, protagonists come to recognize that they belong, primarily, to themselves and claim a unique place in their own inner universes.

Mental Representations

The concept of mental representation is indispensable for a proper understanding of the interpersonal aspects of psychodrama. A mental representation is a relatively permanent image of anything that was previously perceived, a kind of inner picture or memory image of ourselves (self representation), of others (object representation), or of the world at large (symbolic representation).

Mental representations also include the relations which existed between ourselves and others and the relations between these important other people. According to Blatner and Blatner (1988), 'the dynamism of internalized experience, memories, anticipated repeated traumatic events, symbolic reactions...are all part of this complex psychodramatic 'inner truth'... One way to correct these private fictions is to play them out in a context in which social validation can allow for at least symbolic fulfillment, followed by an opportunity to correct perceptions and resolve conflicts' (p.119). With the help of auxiliaries, the psychodramatic stage offers an extraordinarily powerful vehicle for the externalization of such internalized mental images; there, they are summoned to life and made to appear in a three-dimensional space. Sandler & Rosenblatt (1962) compared the representational world to a stage set within a theatre: 'The characters on the stage represent the child's various objects (important people), as well as the child himself. Needless to say, the child is usually the hero (the protagonist) of the piece. The theater, which contains a stage, would correspond to aspects of the ego, and the various functions such as scene shifting, raising or lowering the curtain, and all the machinery auxiliary to the actual stage production would correspond to those ego functions of which we are normally aware' (p.134).

In terms of mental representations, interpersonal conflicts can be traced to inner pictures of mighty parental figures who exercise a powerful and frightening influence over a helpless and inferior self. When such images are projected upon real people in the outer world, intense emotions of a childish origin arise and overshadow the actual relation given in the here-and-now. This is what psychoanalysts call 'transference;' the influence of the past on a present relation. In my view, important aspects of interpersonal events may be understood in terms of transferences, and this concept will therefore serve as an introduction to the subject in the present chapter.

Transference

Transference means literally to take something from one place to another. As indicated above, the concept is used in psychotherapy to describe the process of taking experiences from the past and putting them in a present situation. When a person is involved in a transference relationship, he or she distorts the perception of the present and confuses it with the past. The most common example is when a patient relates to the therapist as if the therapist were his or her father or mother.

Transferences occur not only towards therapists, but also towards all people and are of course frequent among the members of psychodrama groups. Here is a simple example. When Rachelle entered the group, she expressed hostility and irritation towards another female group member, Yvette, apparently without any sound reason. Before Yvette had had a chance to present herself,

Rachelle complained that she did not want to be in the same group as Yvette: 'I cannot stand her snobbishness, she thinks she is better than everyone else!' During the course of the following sessions, however, we learned that Yvette reminded Rachelle of her younger sister whom she had disliked since childhood and whom she secretly envied because of the sister's success in life. In a psychodramatic exploration of Rachelle's sibling rivalry, Yvette agreed to take the role of the sister and to play the role of a successful and coaxing woman. During this enactment, Yvette expanded in her role as the sister and, in role reversal, Rachelle discovered new dimensions of the behaviour of the sister which helped her not only to come to terms with her inferiority feelings towards her sister, but also to understand that Yvette was a different person. Rachelle and Yvette later became good friends.

Whatever the origin of transference processes, they initiate powerful, complicated and mysterious emotions which affect not only our perceptions of others, but also the manner in which we establish relations in groups, our choice of auxiliaries, and our feelings towards the psychodramatist in his or her role as group leader. For this reason, transferences should be dealt with in a sensitive and considerate way and, if possible, should be utilized as a source of information about the personality of clients.

Counter-transference

Much has been said about patients' tendency to view their therapists in various unrealistic ways. It is likewise true that the therapists, over time, are likely to experience a variety of emotions toward their patients, some more than others. However, when psychotherapists develop interpersonal distortions and preferences of their own and transfer earlier fantasies upon their patients, it is called 'counter-transference'. Two aspects of counter-transference can, according to Rycroft (1968), be distinguished:

On the one hand, counter-transference constitutes the therapist's own transference upon the patient. For example, a therapist who has difficulty handling his or her own feelings of anger might tend to inhibit a patient's expression of anger. In this sense, it is a disturbing element in treatment, a potential danger to true empathy; it amplifies the need for the continual analysis and supervision of the therapist. According to Dewald (1964), counter-transference in this sense has its origin in therapists' *unconscious* tendencies which cause them to react toward patients in a way which to a certain extent is inappropriate and which constitutes a displacement from earlier relations and experiences in their own lives.

On the other hand, if personal feelings are utilized as a basis for understanding patients, counter-transference can be an important tool in treatment. Counter-transference is in this case a therapist's proper emotional attitude toward the patient—a *conscious* reaction to the patient's behaviour. According to Heimann (1950), Little (1951), Gitelson (1973), Racker (1968) and others, therapists can use this latter kind of counter-transference as a type of clinical evidence, assuming that their own emotional responses are based on a correct understanding of the patients' personality organization.

The following is a personal example: I was the group leader in a psychodrama training group. One of the participants, Charles, who had previously told the group of his authoritarian and rejecting father, started during the second year of the group to rebel against me, accusing me of being unfair in my treatment of him. I felt frustrated by his repeated accusations and angry for being unjustly criticized. It was obvious that he had touched a sensitive spot in me and my immediate impulse was to shout back at Charles or to kick him out of the group. According to the first aspect of counter-transference, it seemed as if I was slowly developing a full-blown transference upon Charles who came to represent a frightening critical image for me.

But instead of responding with a defensive explanation of my innocence, or with some act of revenge, I used the second aspect of counter-transference—my knowledge of Charles—to help me become aware of the transference situation which had developed. The uncomfortable feelings that Charles had evoked in me were examined for what they revealed about him. If I had failed to be aware of this situation and let myself be affected by it, I would have run the risk of renewing the original script that helped to establish Charles' interpersonal problems in the first place, and the vicious circle would have been continued and perhaps even reinforced. Instead, I tried to show, through a psychodramatic re-enactment of some father-son situations, that Charles was repeating an earlier script with his father and that I had received a role in this drama. As a result of this exploration, in which another group member was chosen to play the role of the father, Charles was more inclined to develop a more trusting relation with me than before, and I came to view him in a less hostile manner.

According to the first, 'classical,' approach to counter-transference, it seems that my emotional response to Charles' rebellion was largely defensive, a 'vulnerable spot' which indicated a need on my part for continued psychotherapy or consultation. However, according to the second, 'totalistic' approach to counter-transference, my response originated not only as a result of my neurotic disposition but also as a result of Charles' interpersonal needs, such as his need to control and depreciate people and to evoke aggression and rejection in them: an interpersonal pattern of adjustment which had been developed in relation to his authoritarian father.

I would like to emphasize, however, that it is not always advisable to 'look behind the curtain' when a group member rebels against the leader. As Freud pointed out, 'sometimes a cigar is simply a cigar'. According to Williams (1989) 'a group member who is very angry with the director, for instance, may not agree to be diverted to the alleged 'origins' of the interaction, such as in a family-of-origin psychodrama. Such persons may, quite rightly, suspect a trick, or a power-play, or a subtle way of invalidating their perceptions and making out that they, rather than the interaction, are pathological and need to be examined. In such denials, madness lies for both parties, although only one (the group member) may appear to be mad' (p.193).

While experienced psychodramatists should be able to retain a certain degree of objectivity and neutrality, they cannot be completely free from some idiosyncrasies of their own. If they are not sufficiently aware of their inner emotional responses, any displacement will disturb the therapeutic process. However, the distorting effects of counter-transference in psychodrama are somewhat reduced by the use of auxiliaries and by the constant ability of the group to 'guard' the patient and to guide the therapist.

Counter-transference is not a phenomenon limited to the therapist-patient relationship. It may also occur among auxiliaries, and a minimum of group cohesion is an indispensable pre-requisite for a constructive development of the psychodramatic process. Moreno (1972) pointed out that 'if the auxiliary egos are troubled among themselves because of (1) unresolved problems of their own; (2) protest against the psychodrama director; (3) poor portrayal of the roles assigned to them; (4) lack of faith and negative attitude toward the method used; or (5) interpersonal conflicts among themselves, they create an atmosphere which reflects upon the therapeutic situation. It is obvious, therefore, that if transference and counter-transference phenomena dominate the relationship among the auxiliary therapists and toward the patients, the therapeutic progress will be greatly handicapped' (p.xviii).

Tele

Moreno & Moreno (1959), however, found the concepts of transference and counter-transference inadequate to describe interpersonal relations in psychodrama. With regard to transference, Moreno pointed out that the fictitious and distorted aspects were too much emphasized and that the reality aspects of a meeting which takes place in the here-and-now were overlooked or entirely forgotten. With regard to counter-transference, Moreno recognized the disturbing aspects of therapists' unconscious emotional predispositions, but maintained that they should not lead therapists to adopt a 'neutral,' but rather a 'transparent' attitude towards patients.

These conclusions were based on the observation by Moreno & Moreno (1959) that 'there is another process active at the same time as the patient unconsciously displaces fantasies on the therapist. A part of the patient is not drawn into regression, but rather perceives the therapist intuitively in the present as the therapist really is. Even though it does not seem so strong at the beginning of therapy, the transference is reduced and replaced with this real perception' (p.6). In order to describe such real interpersonal relationships with a concept other than transference and counter-transference, Moreno & Moreno

(1959) suggested the use of the word 'tele,' from Greek, meaning 'at a distance'. Literally, tele conveys the message that people are in contact and communicate with one another at a distance, and that they send emotional messages from afar.

This peculiar choice of word is no exception from the obscure psychodramatic terminology, which is largely influenced by classical Greek drama. A reason for choosing such an irregular concept as 'tele' may have been the lack of adequate terminology for the description of inter-personal phenomena, in contrast to the rich vocabulary which is used to describe individual and social phenomena. Thus, when Moreno wanted to describe the link between people, the factor which connected an individual to a group, and inter-personal phenomena such as separateness and connectedness, reciprocity, interaction, communication, and mutual empathy, he had to create a wholly new term which encompassed these processes. 'Tele' conveyed 'the simplest unit of feeling transmitted from one individual towards another' (Moreno, 1953, p.314). Unfortunately, however, Moreno included such a wide variety of interpersonal aspects in the meaning of tele, that the concept was obscured rather than clarified, and Moreno's students have been unable to unite around a common definition.

In my understanding, tele is best defined in terms of the reality dimension in interpersonal relationships, the 'insight into, appreciation of, and feeling for the actual makeup of another person' (Moreno & Moreno, 1959, p.6). It embraces not only the attractive, but also the repulsive aspects of relations between people, and carries with it an authentic meeting, or encounter, in which people take each other for what and whom they are. As such, it can be characterized as a kind of 'inter-personal chemistry'. In Moreno's (1951) words, 'tele is the fundamental factor underlying our [real] perceptions of others' (p.275). As opposed to transference, tele should be used to describe not a repetition of the past distorting the present, but a new response which is appropriate in the here and now.

Moreno's tele concept is deeply rooted in existentialist philosophy and can be further explained by Martin Buber's (1923) theory of 'I-Thou'. Put simply, this theory conveys the idea that 'I cannot be I except in relation to a Thou'. This I-Thou relation is unlike that which Buber calls an 'I-It' relation, in which the 'I' treats the other person as an object rather than as a subject. Tele assumes in this context the significance of an I-Thou relation, while transference can most nearly be characterized as an I-It relation.

It is my opinion that some of the different but related inter-personal phenomena—like empathy, rapport, mutual reciprocity, group cohesion, interpersonal sensitivity, preference and communication—which were designated by Moreno as tele, should not be designated as such. For tele refers, specifically and exclusively, to the non-repetitive, real-life based and authentic aspects of relations.

Empathy, the emotional entrance into the reality of another human being, is a necessary component of tele. But it was considered by Moreno as a one-way feeling of the therapist into the private world of the patient, as distinct from the mutual two-way feeling which sometimes occurs between group members in psychodrama. Especially in the technique of role reversal, there is, according to Moreno & Moreno (1959), a mutual exchange of empathy and appreciation, a kind of therapeutic love which, if it develops, is powerful healing agent in itself.

Accumulated research evidence—for example, from the Temple Study (Sloane, Staples, Cristol, Yorkston, & Whipple, 1975), the Menninger Project (Kernberg, Burstein, Coyne, Appelbaum, Horwitz, & Voth, 1972), the Tavistock Studies (Malan, 1976a, 1976b), and the Vanderbilt Psychotherapy Project (Strupp & Hadley, 1979)—has shown that the quality of patient-therapist interaction represents the fulcrum upon which therapeutic progress turns. The therapist's ability to empathize or 'reverse roles' with the patient in particular has been repeatedly demonstrated as an essential therapeutic ingredient in most methods of psychotherapy.

When considering the ways in which communications may be transmitted from psychotherapist to patient, Frank (1961) does not rule out the possibility of 'telepathy'. Some eminent psychodramatists—among them Zerka Moreno—have also expressed or hinted at their belief that not only empathy, but something akin to 'telepathy' operates between therapist and patient in psychodrama. Sometimes psychodramatists are so in tune with their patients that they almost seem to be reading their minds. While this extended definition of 'tele' (at a distance) and 'patheia' (healing) may be far-fetched, it does convey some of the inherent meaning of the original tele-concept of Moreno.

Real Reaction Versus Transference Reaction

In psychoanalytic terminology, the 'non-transferring' or real aspects of the relationship between patient and therapist are called a 'working alliance' (Greenson, 1967). A working alliance is very similar to tele, emphasizing a kind of mutual agreement and cooperation between two real persons without which there would be no collaboration.

PATIENT   THERAPIST

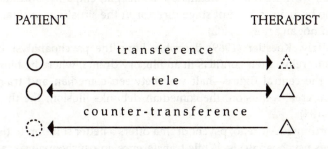

Figure 8.1. Variations of the Therapist-Patient Relationships

Figure 8.1 is an attempt to show, in a simple and schematic manner, the direction of interpersonal relations in transference, counter-transference, and tele.

We may question, however, if it is at all possible to differentiate between the two sides of the inter-personal coin; the one based on transference and the other based on tele. How can we distinguish the appropriate reactions from the inappropriate ones, determine what is rational or irrational in a relationship, and separate past influences from present ones?

All relationships contain a mixture of reality and fantasy; real relations are influenced by elements of transference, and transferences contain a measure of reality. Thus, for example, in the real relation between parent and child, both parts may project some unrealistic expectations upon the other ('My son has great talent!' 'My father is extraordinarily intelligent!'). On the other hand, patients' feelings about their therapists are frequently based on some real aspects of the therapists' personalities ('You look tired and sad today, I think you work too much!').

However, while it may be difficult to distinguish between real and fictitious aspects of a relationship, it is often possible, on the basis of judging emotional intensity, to determine which of the two aspects is dominant.

In the process of understanding the origins and dynamics of transference relationships, psychoanalysts are in a position in which they have to safeguard both the transference and the working alliance at the same time. The two images which are projected upon them—one from the past and one from the present—demand that analysts take on a double role in which communication is maintained with both poles simultaneously. A suspension of transference would lead to decreased understanding, a breakdown in working alliance to an interruption in treatment. The simultaneous refusal and acceptance of the role/s assigned and the fact that the analyst should play the game and yet not play it create an ambiguous and problematic situation which is discussed at length in the psychoanalytic literature. Greenson (1967) sums it up nicely: 'In a strange way the analyst becomes a silent actor in a play the patient is creating. The analyst does not act in this drama; he tries to remain the shadowy figure the patient needs for his fantasies. Yet the analyst helps in the creation of the character, working out the details by his insight, empathy, and intuition. In a sense, he becomes a kind of stage director in the situation—a vital part of the play, but not an actor' (p.402).

Similarly, Koestler (1969) describes how 'the psychoanalyst induces his patients to relive their conflicts in an illusory drama, where he himself impersonates the central figure—half way between comedian and tragedian. The tragedian creates illusion, the comedian debunks illusion; the therapist does both' (p.188).

According to Moreno, psychodrama offers a better solution to this problem than does psychoanalysis. While transference, in psychoanalysis, arises in the patient as a reaction to the analyst, an auxiliary (sometimes especially trained for this assignment) is introduced in psychodrama and transferences are thus carried over to that person rather than to the person of the therapist. This is preferable because it puts the psychodramatist in a less ambiguous situation in which he or she can focus on directing, rather than on acting as the 'antagonist'.

The process of transference varies in expression during the course of a psychodrama session (Leutz, 1971). During the first phase of warm-up, the protagonist may initially develop some distorted feelings towards the psycho-dramatist. Such transference, however, may be rapidly redirected towards another object, chosen by the protagonist. When the protagonist makes this choice of a significant other person—looking around the group and becoming aware of the various group members—he or she actively transfers feelings and memories upon the group members and, from that point on, the psychodramat-ist is hardly noticed. During the second phase of action, the psychodramatist can direct the session from a more distant position which makes him or her free to engage with the protagonist in a 'real' person-to-person relation. In the third phase of sharing, transferences on the auxiliaries are interrupted and disconti-nued. This may, for example, be done through 'de-roling' ('I am no longer your uncle Sam. Please, view me as myself...') and through 'role-feedback' ('I some-times feel like Sam, but I would have been less violent than he was'). By talking about their own feelings when participating in the psychodrama, the auxiliaries slowly dismantle their acquired roles and return to their original positions in the group.

While it is often true in psychodrama that 'the immediate target of trans-ference switches from the therapist himself to the auxiliary ego' (Moreno & Moreno, 1959, p.96), this is an ideal situation which does not always happen. Schutzenberger (1970) pointed out that transferences onto the psychodramatist certainly occur also in psychodrama, though not so often as in classical psycho-analytic therapies. Similarly, Williams (1989) cautioned us against becoming too idealistic: 'This fortunate situation where the intense preoccupation with the leader is defused by the various functions of the group does not always prevail. For some members, the director is and remains utterly central, and they look only to him or her' (p.193) for satisfaction.

As I have discussed in Chapter 4, certain charismatic leaders who become the object of such infantile expectations are tempted to try to satisfy them and, initially, may feel that their surrogate holding produces immediate and power-ful therapeutic effects. During the course of therapy, however, what started out as a corrective emotional relationship may, in the final analysis, become a destructive and disappointing one, in which a well-meaning therapist is accused of not being a sufficiently 'good' mother. It is therefore suggested that the therapist be aware of the subtle transference and counter-transference responses which tend to arise and, as far as possible, guard the relationship from excessive distortions.

Auxiliary ego

The term used by Moreno to depict the therapeutic assistants in psychodrama was originally 'auxiliary ego'. During the last few years, however, the common usage has, according to Blatner and Blatner (1988), become simply 'auxiliary,' without the added 'ego' (p.160), a change suggested by Zerka Moreno and adopted by Williams (1989). I think it is an appropriate and justified simplification because in actuality the auxiliary is an aid, not only to the 'ego,' but also to inner and outer 'objects,' and to the 'symbolic inner world' at large. As such, the psychodramatic auxiliary fulfills functions which are largely similar to those of the psychoanalyst as transference object. It is therefore not surprising to note that the original term 'auxiliary ego' has entered into psychoanalytic vocabulary with a somewhat different, but in some respects similar, meaning as in psychodrama.

As a consequence of the emergence of psychoanalytic ego psychology and the treatment of the so-called borderline cases, the function of the analyst has changed radically. It has, in fact, become more like the function of the psychodramatic auxiliary ego which was originally described by Moreno (1972, p.54) as the caretaker who helps the infant 'get started' in life.

In psychotherapy with personality disorders, the therapeutic situation is regarded as containing certain elements of the mother-child relationship, and therapists use themselves more or less as instruments to strengthen the patient's developing ego. In recent years, the entire human milieu in such therapies has been described with the term 'holding environment'. Rather than being an object for transferences to these patients, the psychoanalyst takes on a more active role as auxiliary to the patient's own ego-functioning. In addition to being a screen for the patient's projections, the therapist becomes a new empathic object which, if internalized, helps the patient to contain pain, grief and conflicting emotions. In such cases, the therapist takes on a supportive and corrective role which promotes symbolic working through of developmental deprivation.

According to Kernberg (1976) the psychotherapist 'shifts from a consultant's role to an auxiliary ego role, that is, he becomes the "management" of the patient'. What is implied by being 'management,' however, may not be limited to an auxiliary ego role (e.g. helping to focus attention, remember, test reality, synthesize, etc.), but may also develop into an auxiliary superego role (e.g. demanding, setting up tasks, punishing, praising). With almost the same choice of words, Strachey (1934) says that the patient sometimes uses the analyst as an 'auxiliary superego'. The therapist in Dewald's (1964) supportive psychotherapy has the function of a 'substitute ego' or a 'surrogate ego' and, according to Blanck & Blanck (1974), 'it is inherent in the therapeutic situation that the therapist is a potential identification model'. Gitelson (1973) recommended that the analyst present him- or herself as an appropriate object for the patient and as an 'auxiliary ego'. Finally, Anna Freud (1965) described how the child uses the analyst as a new object, as an object of externalization and internalization and as an auxiliary ego. These examples have been selected because they represent the so-called 'orthodoxy' in psychoanalysis. The neofreudian schools have long been in agreement with the Morenian position.

Transparency

In psychoanalysis, the analyst assumes the form of receptive passivity known as 'free floating, or evenly-suspended attention' in order to understand the unconscious meaning of the patient's free associations. In the process of this empathic activity, the analyst assumes a 'blank,' non-transparent and neutral attitude towards the patient and attempts not to 'transfer back' feelings which the patient has transferred upon him or her. This 'mirror' attitude facilitates free association and makes it possible for the patient's distorted and unrealistic reactions to be demonstrated as such. The analyst's neutrality is thus an indirect method of bringing about transference in a non-contagious setting.

However, reality factors, such as the therapist's age, sex, marital status, level of experience and competence, assertiveness, personality traits, personal distance and leadership style, may all significantly influence the patient. Therefore, 'one must conclude that the analyst as a mere screen does not actually exist. He cannot deny his personality, its operation as a significant factor. He will appear as he actually is in manner of speech and general spontaneity' (Gitelson, 1973, p.192). Viderman (1991) recently emphasized the powerful effects of the real person of the analyst—particularly his or her emotional availability—in the process of psychoanalytic cure. The removal of the psychoanalyst, outside the purview of the patient, does not really mitigate this influence. As a result, 'the decisive role of the analyst's total personality in the process and outcome of therapy has become an ever-present consideration, so that the analyst must be careful to distinguish between transference reactions and those reactions to him that are evoked by the person he is' (Witenberg, 1973, p.8).

In contrast to the incognito position of psychoanalysts, psychodramatists frequently assume a highly transparent and self-disclosing attitude towards their patients (compare the relevant papers by Curtis, 1982 and Dies, 1977). The difference is not only a matter of contrasting temperament but also a difference in theoretical orientation. Moreno was discontent with the blank screen posture because of its tendency to stimulate projections and felt that it would be more helpful to encourage a reciprocal tele-relation in which the therapist adopted an authentic posture. In the words of Williams (1989), the psychodramatist 'tends to be active, giving plenty of "personality" and behavior for members to interpret. Psychodramatists tend to adopt a high profile, and put out more cues as to what they are thinking and feeling; the process is more "transparent". They might join in the sharing phase of a psychodrama, for example, and reveal details of their own lives' (p.183).

Conclusion

Psychoanalysts and psychodramatists generally agree that transferences, even though they are universal and inevitable, are undesirable in inter-personal relations. They also agree that transferences evolving within the framework of psychotherapy can be used as valuable clinical material and as 'live' manifestations of interpersonal patterns and thus lead to a better understanding of the patient's interpersonal conflicts.

The aim of interpersonal explorations in psychodrama is to help patients correct their distorted perceptions; to grow out of their transference relations, or to reduce the emotional intensity of these relations to a level which allows for discovering what kind of actual relationship is given to them by therapists and others as real people. In order to achieve this, it is important to distinguish, accept and even encourage the real relation which exists between patient and therapist.

Since it is in practice impossible to conceal oneself totally behind a blank screen, the psychodramatist prefers to maximize the positive elements of the therapist-patient interaction and encourage an open, warm, respecting, empathizing attitude, and confidently accept that conflict and ambivalence in human relations are normal and manageable. Transferences will be present but the real interactions make them easier to acknowledge.

The dilemma of the patient who needs love to become healthy and the therapist who is unable or unwilling to act as a love partner is resolved in psychodrama through the engagement of a third party: an auxiliary ego which is someone other than the therapist him- or herself. This gives the psychodramatist the freedom to develop a real tele relationship toward patients which—if sufficiently warm, authentic and empathic—may be a powerful therapeutic factor in itself.

CHAPTER 9

As-if

'Psychodrama is a way to change the world in the HERE AND NOW using the fundamental rules of imagination without falling into the abyss of illusion, hallucination or delusion' (From J.L. Moreno's 'Magic Charter of Psychodrama', 1969/1972).

'A person is least of all himself when he talks as himself. Give him a mask and he will tell the truth' (Oscar Wilde).

The previous chapters have dealt with the emotional, cognitive and inter-personal aspects of psychodrama which have, by tradition, been regarded as central to the therapeutic process. None of these aspects, however, would have an impact were it not for their location within the framework of imagination and their stimulation by the deliberate activation of 'as-if'. In the present chapter, I will describe the use of imagination in psychodrama and demonstrate the central place of the as-if concept in the methodology and philosophy of psychodrama.

As-if in Psychodrama

The potential for mental imagery, while often underdeveloped, is universal, and intrinsically enjoyable to most people. Whenever possible, we like to picture ourselves in various pleasurable situations and we may resort to daydreaming when external reality becomes too difficult or frightening. Imagination allows for hope and dreams to re-enter our lives, even if only for a moment. When they met, Moreno told Freud: 'I start where you leave off. You analyze their dreams. I try to give them courage to dream again' (Moreno,1972, p.5–6). This brief quote captures the central role of imagination in psychodrama; a belief inherent in psychodrama is that it is a mistake to take away the dreams of people, or merely to use them as psychological 'material' to be interpreted.

In psychodrama, we are encouraged to present our day-dreams in action for the purpose of self-actualization and adaptation to the external world. The entire methodology of psychodrama—its use of role-playing, auxiliaries, the stage, warm-up exercises, props and its deliberate time and place distortion—is based on the principle of 'as-if' (Buchanan & Little, 1983).

Let us consider first the use of role-playing, the 'sine qua non' of psychodrama, which Geller (1978) described as behaviour portrayed *as-if* it were real, although everyone knows it is not. In such role-playing, participants are encouraged to re-enact situations from the past *as-if* these events were happening in the present, relate to inanimate objects *as-if* these objects were alive, and to talk to other group members *as-if* they were old acquaintances or key individuals in their lives. The psychodramatic stage is in itself viewed by both actors and audience *as-if* it were an imaginary arena within which anything, including the impossible, can happen. Thus, within the psychodramatic realm of 'as-if,' inner experiences may be externalized, abstract inter- and intrapersonal relations may be concretized and dreams may be brought to the light of day.

'As-if' is essential to that quality which Moreno (1972) called dramatic spontaneity: 'It is that quality which gives newness and vivacity to feelings, acting, and verbal utterances which are nothing but repetitions of what an individual has experienced a thousand times before...This form of spontaneity has apparently a great practical importance in *energizing* and *unifying* the self. It makes disassociated automaton like acts be felt and look like true self-expression and acts like a 'cosmetic' for the psyche' (p.89).

Most psychodramatic techniques are based on some element of as-if activity. For example, in the technique of role reversal, Arthur acts *as-if* he were Bill and Bill acts *as-if* he were Arthur. In the technique of doubling, Bill acts *as-if* he were Arthur, following Arthur's every move and mood. In the technique of mirroring, Arthur is presented *as-if* he were to appear in a mirror. In the technique of soliloquy, Arthur talks *as-if* no one were listening or *as-if* he were thinking aloud. In the future projection technique and in role-training, Arthur is asked to visualize himself in the future, both as he believes he will become and as he wants to become; Arthur acts *as-if* his later self were a living being. Finally, when Arthur concretizes his feelings, for example through the technique of 'sculpturing,' he presents these feelings *as-if* they existed in physical space.

Psychodramatic warm-up exercises are also frequently founded on the stimulation of as-if. For example, in the 'kingdom of plants,' people are asked to imagine themselves *as-if* they were plants. They are asked first to visualize where they grow, in what kind of earth, in which season, and what conditions they need to fulfill their potentials. Later, they are urged to 'become' the plant and to show the group in detail how they live and develop. In one group, one participant presented himself as 'an old tree without roots,' another as 'a burning bush who was sent from God'. A woman felt like 'a rambler rose without support,' and a man described himself as 'a tree-stump with dogs urinating on his trunk!' The fact that the information is presented in 'as-if' language, which partly hides reality and partly discloses it in an obscured form, makes it easier for some participants to reveal sensitive information about themselves to the group and thereafter to work it through in a psychodrama.

People ordinarily have no difficulty in using their imagination. They can easily make inanimate objects come to life and relate to them as if they were real. For example, a group of people was given an old, disconnected telephone to play with, and immediately started to use it. Someone dialed, calling his wife to let her know that he would be late for dinner. A female group member answered the phone, but she became suspicious and accused him of being unfaithful to her. While the roles taken in this improvisation were made up on the spur of the moment, the interactional content and personal emotions became real, opening up boundless possibilities for further exploration and working-through.

When 'as-if' is blocked, psychodrama does not work. A woman who had vehemently expressed 'I need no one in my life!' was leaning on the wall and I asked her to talk to the wall. She looked at me, puzzled, and I asked, 'Who is it you are leaning on?' But she did not answer my question because to her, the wall was only a wall and nothing else. She was unable, at that point, to 'see'. When she later became the protagonist in psychodrama, we realized that the figure she had been unable to see in the wall was her father on whom she leaned for support and affection. The scene that she had been unable to picture was that of herself as a young girl at her father's grave. In the process of the psychodrama, the symbolism of the wall shifted as in a dream, becoming alternately a tomb-stone, a support to depend on for protection, and a barrier within herself that ultimately had to be torn down.

'As-if' occurs by definition in all imaginative activity, including drama, dreaming and play. The capacity to say, think, and feel 'if...' is manifested in the ability to operate at various levels of hypotheticalness (Sarbin, 1972). In the 'if-statement,' something unreal, untrue, or fictitious is stated but at the same time it is a condition for making any assumptions whatsoever about reality (Vaihinger, 1911). Without the 'if-statement' we would be unable to portray, personify, picture, impersonate or represent the outside reality in symbolic form.

Imagery-Based Therapeutic Methods

'As-if' has been utilized as part of various healing rituals for many years (Sheikh & Jordan, 1983). During the last decade, it has come to be associated with a variety of psychotherapeutic methods. In hypnosis, for example, 'as-if' is associated with trance, suggestion and altered states of consciousness, implying that the more vivid the imagination, the more suggestible the person. In psychoanalysis, the 'as-if' concept is related to unconscious fantasy (Isaacs, 1952), primary process thinking, and free association, serving as a vehicle for the symbolic representation of unconscious conflicts.

Jung attached great importance to the inner world of human beings and to the complex underlying patterns of symbolic representations which are continuously manifested in our dreams. Jung's (1967) utilization of imagery in therapy is best represented by the method he called 'active imagination,' which could grow out of a dream, hypnagogic image, or fantasy. Jung regarded active imagination as a procedure to be employed largely independently by the patient and generally toward the end of analysis or after it. However, several clinicians investigated the potential of imagery for use as a primary method of psychotherapy. The best known of these approaches include Desoille's (1965) 'directed daydream,' Fretigny and Virel's (1968) 'oneirodrama,' and Leuner's (1978) 'guided affective imagery'. Sheikh and Jordan (1983) used the term 'oneirotherapies' to describe these three therapies ('oneiros' meaning 'dream').

Various other imagery techniques, such as the use of daydreaming and imagery in psychotherapy (Singer, 1974; Singer & Pope, 1978), and 'eidetic' psychotherapy (Ahsen, 1968; Ahsen, 1984) actively employ 'as-if' principles in their therapeutic approaches. Imagery is also used as an adjunct in more eclectic techniques such as Psychosynthesis (Assagioli, 1973), modeling (Bandura, 1971), and Neuro-Linguistic Programming (Bandler & Grinder, 1979; Buchanan & Little, 1983).

In a very different fashion, Adlerian Psychotherapy (Mosak, 1979, p.71; Adler, 1963) urges patients to try out new behaviour and to act 'as if'. This more direct, behavioural approach is based on the assumption that while patients can exercise only a limited control over feelings at best, they may be able to channel their thoughts into imaginary pathways and act 'as-if' they had a desired state of mind. In clinical role playing (Kipper, 1986), such an approach is related to the concept of 'simulation' and in Kelly's (1955) fixed role therapy, it is a precondition for behaviour rehearsal.

A rapidly growing body of evidence indicates the value of mental imagery and the effectiveness of 'as-if' techniques in the treatment of a whole spectrum of problems. The proponents of all imagery approaches claim significant successes and cite numerous supporting case histories. Unfortunately, at the present time, very scant experimental work has been devoted to the verification of the assumptions that underlie these procedures.

Numerous mechanisms that presumably underlie the effectiveness of imagery have been suggested. Singer (1974) tends to believe that the efficacy of imagery may essentially depend on the following factors: (1) clear discrimination by the client of his or her own ongoing fantasy processes; (2) clues provided by the therapist concerning alternative ways of approaching various situations; (3) awareness of generally avoided situations; (4) encouragement by the therapist to engage in covert rehearsal of alternatives; and (5) consequent decrease in fear of making overt approaches to the avoided situations.

The Therapeutic Value of 'As-if' in Psychodrama

Psychodrama employs 'as-if' in a variety of directions, including the ones mentioned above. The primary function of 'as-if' in psychodrama, however, is that it helps the protagonist to master stressful life events vicariously within the protected world of make-believe. Participants are encouraged to let go of reality testing and to withdraw temporarily from the external world. They experiment with several new dimensions of reality, building the world according to their own spontaneous ideas. In a paradoxical manner, such a procedure helps a person both to deny and to affirm external reality. For example, when Anna talked to her dead mother in psychodrama, she acted 'as-if' her mother were alive on stage, momentarily denying the fact that her mother was dead. This imaginary encounter, however, helped her to cope better with her mother's death by opening up the natural channels of mourning which had hitherto been blocked.

It is my position that 'as-if' thus employed will strengthen a patient's ego functioning, his or her ability to deal with internal and external pressures. Here I am in agreement with Blatner and Blatner (1988), who described the effectiveness of psychodrama in terms of 'strengthening the patient's ego functioning' (p.95). According to the categories presented by Bellak, Hurvich, & Gediman (1973), such ego functions include reality testing, judgment, sense of reality, regulation and control of drives, affects and impulses, object relations, thought processes, adaptive regression in the service of the ego, defensive functioning, stimulus barriers, autonomous functions, synthetic-integrative functioning, and mastery-competence (reviewed in Blatner and Blatner, 1988, pp.95–99).

The use of 'as-if' in psychodrama may be illustrated by Marianne, a 21 year-old university student, who had been raped at knifepoint while returning home from a party. Consequently, she developed fears of being alone, suffered from frequent nightmares and avoided most contacts with men. She also complained of a sense of guilt and blamed herself for not having resisted sufficiently during the assault. In her psychodrama about a year later, Marianne was urged to confront the rapist again, and to re-live the traumatic experience once more. This second time, however, Marianne was helped to resist the assault, to express her rage towards the rapist and, in an imaginary trial (cf. the 'judgment technique' presented by Sacks, 1965), she prosecuted her attacker and announced his punishment. The vicarious revenge involved in this act helped Marianne to redirect some of the blame which she had directed towards herself onto the aggressor. The psychodrama closed with a guided fantasy trip in which Marianne was asked to imagine that she 'followed a stream to its source'. This imagery journey was chosen here because of its assumed relevance to Marianne, symbolizing her way back to intimacy and warmth through the deliberate use of the healing power inherent in water and cool springs. As a result of this session, Marianne returned to work while remaining mildly anxious for some time. In light of her marriage the following year, it seems probable that psychodrama at least opened the way for further mastery of her feelings and her gradual readjustment to ordinary life.

Surplus Reality

Psychodramatic 'as-if' does not operate in the actuality of life but rather in the semi-real situation of play: this is the so called meta-reality or 'surplus-reality' (Moreno, 1966). 'Surplus' means 'what is left over,' and refers to the part of experience which remains within us when the external world has taken its share of attention. In this sphere, the psychic reality is 'made wider' and the 'intangible, invisible dimensions of the protagonist's life' are given expression (Moreno & Moreno, 1969). In the words of Moreno (1972), 'It is a dream-land in which painful tasks in life are finished by the gesture of a hand or by a smile. Scenes in life which endure for days are here reduced to a minute' (p.214).

According to Blatner (1973), 'the role of surplus reality is misunderstood in our lives. The view of man as *only* existentially being-in-the-world, with one unified "core" of authenticity, denies the phenomenon of-imagination. It is our imagination which accounts for the self-reflective dimensions of our consciousness, the ability to see ourselves at a distance...The imagination represents that dimension of our lives which is our surplus reality. We are kings, we are slaves; we are again children, we exist ten years in the future' (p.124).

The concept of surplus reality was first introduced in psychodrama to facilitate the presentation of personal truth. 'The subject must act out 'his truth,' as he feels and perceives it, in a completely subjective manner (no matter how distorted this appears to the spectator)' (Moreno & Moreno, 1969, p.234). However, not only what 'really' happened in life may be portrayed but also that which never happened yet is nevertheless wished for, feared, or wondered about: the unknown, the unspoken, the unborn, dreams, hopes, deja-vu experiences, fears, disappointments, unfulfilled wishes and expectations (Leutz, 1974; Blatner and Blatner, 1988; Karp, 1988).

> 'What counts is what appears "phenomenologically" true for the protagonist [as it appears in direct experience]. Certainly, consensual validation (as in agreement with the perceptions expressed by others) and checking the protagonist's phenomenal world with the real world (correspondence) figures or may figure later in considering the overall program of therapy for the client. But, during the psychodrama, what appears as true for the protagonist...takes precedence and is given support by the therapist' (Seeman & Weiner, 1985, p.151–152).

This affirmation by the psychodramatist of a protagonist's personal truth and unique experience of reality is called 'existential validation'. The following two examples with psychotic patients—one from psychodrama and the other from psychiatry—may illustrate this central concept in psychodrama.

A successful use of existential validation may be illustrated by one of J.L. Moreno's famous cases, 'A Case of Paranoia' (Moreno & Moreno, 1969). Mary was a psychotic young woman who had escaped into a fantasy world where she persistently searched for 'John,' her imaginary lover. Moreno instructed one of his assistants (an auxiliary) to enact the role of 'John's friend,' who was there to help Mary complete her dramatic search. Acknowledging the adaptive aspects of Mary's fantasy world, Moreno did not challenge her view of reality, but emphasized it and made it a point of departure. Mary's resistance against relating to real persons in the outer world was thus gradually clarified, realized, replaced and, finally, removed. The auxiliary could be de-roled when Mary began to relate to him, not as John's friend, but as himself.

For the sake of clarity, I will here compare this procedure with the contrary methods of 'rational-emotive' and 'cognitive-behavioural' psychotherapies which confront irrational beliefs directly. A failure of such a procedure (cited in Mahoney, 1974) described a schizophrenic patient who went around telling everyone who would listen that he was dead. A psychology intern, in a fit of frustration, was determined to prove to the patient that his belief was erroneous. The intern asked the patient if dead people bleed. The patient responded that everyone knew that dead people did not bleed. The intern then took the patient's finger and pricked it with a pin, bringing forth several drops of blood. Upon examining the evidence (i.e. blood on his finger) the patient replied, 'Son of a bitch, dead people do bleed!' The patient readily accommodated his 'dead people' belief to the new evidence. This anecdote illustrates some of the frustrations that can occur when attempts are made to alter a patient's personal view of the world in a direct manner, without initially entering it with affirmation and existential validation.

It is important to emphasize, however, that there are several ways to deal with external reality in psychodrama, some of which will be briefly described below.

Procedures of Dealing with External Reality

According to Henne (1979) and Pitzele (1991), three different psychodramatic procedures may be employed for the working through of various dimensions of reality: the realistic, the intrapsychic and the imaginary. A fourth, psychoanalytic procedure will also be included.

The 'realistic' (classical) procedure draws material from personal memory and calls upon actual characters, presenting autobiographical experiences and veritable life events. This procedure frequently starts with the presentation of a current complaint, continues with the re-enactment of a traumatic past event and then returns to the present in order to establish a realistic view of the actual life situation. For example, Rebecka presented various scenes from her life before and after her brother's suicide.

The second, 'intrapsychic' procedure (called 'figurative psychodrama' by Gonseth & Zoller, 1982) is a frequently used adjunct to classical psychodrama. It explores the internal world of the self in all its complexity and especially focuses on the various parts of the self and their relation to one another and to the outer world. In the auxiliary chair technique (Lippitt, 1958), aspects of self are projected onto an empty chair. Moving from one chair to another, the protagonist is invited to address aspects of him- or herself in dialogue in order to 're-capture' or re-integrate dissociated aspects in a manner similar to that used in Gestalt therapy.

In such a 'figurative' session, the psyche itself may be presented on stage in a kind of inner drama. Thus we may find the ego, a harassed protagonist who complains that he has no more strength to endure the hardships of life, that he feels helpless and dissatisfied with himself. On the one hand, he has to deal with 'id,' an irresponsible child who demands immediate gratification of every need. On the other hand, the 'super-ego,' a self-righteous tyrant, criticizes every move he makes and demands complete obedience. Moreover, he is reminded of his economic responsibilities and various voices from society let him know, that 'You better get your act together pretty fast because, if you can't cope, you won't survive here long!' The protagonist finally succeeds in making some kind of a compromise between all these conflicting demands and, with the help of some auxiliaries who keep the disorderly fellows in track, he regains some emotional balance.

The third, 'imaginary' procedure is either used as a middle phase in the classical procedure, or as a separate form of psychodrama. It is also called 'metaphoric,' 'surrealistic,' or 'symbolic'. This procedure is very similar to some forms of drama therapy (Jennings, 1986; Landy, 1986) and includes psychodramatic dream reenactment (Nolte, Weistart, and Wyatt, 1977). Its basic characteristic is that the inner reality of protagonists is presented in symbolic form: through imaginary stories, improvisations, theatre exercises, pictures, movements, or sounds. Jane, for example, presented the moods of her life as a colourful rainbow with a hidden treasure on one side and the tax-man on the other. The psychodrama session described in Chapter 1 ('Who Shall Drive My Green Car?'), is another example.

All three psychodramatic procedures include imaginary surplus reality scenes, but they differ regarding the proper timing for the presentation of such scenes. The classical procedure insists on presenting reality before surplus reality. The intra-psychic procedure remains more or less in some kind of surplus reality all through the session. And the 'imaginary' procedure starts in surplus reality and often, but not always, ends in reality.

A fourth, 'psychoanalytic' procedure, represents yet another strategy. Analytic psychodrama, according to Anzieu (1960), rests on the distinction which Lacan called the 'mainspring of psychoanalysis': the imaginary, the symbolic, and the real. 'Insofar as psychodrama expresses fantasies, the theme proposed by the subject places them in the register of imaginary satisfactions. Insofar as it sets forth the roles which the subject wishes to try out, it is part of the symbolic register, intermediary between pure pantomime and pure verbalization, and peculiar to psychodrama. As for the play aspect, it constitutes a test of reality, represented at the same time by the psychodramatist's and the subject's ability to effectively assume the role announced. Thus the efficacy of the as-if element in psychodrama resides in what the ethnologist Levi-Strauss has called "symbolic efficacy"' (p.43–44).

Role-playing and Role-taking

Widely different theories may be used to support cognitively the use of 'as-if' methods in psychodrama. Here I will first briefly mention the importance of play in child development and psychotherapy, and especially the importance of role-playing and role-taking in the crystallization of a unified identity. I will then treat some relevant parallel theories from social psychology, social-learning-theory and psychoanalysis. Finally, I will present some central ideas from role-taking in the theatre.

All playing—especially role-playing—includes elements of 'as-if' and is an activity of central importance throughout life. Moreno disagreed with Freud's (1908) claim that play was abandoned in adulthood. As people grow up, play may become more ritualized, structured, and controlled, but it does not disappear; it coexists with imagination throughout life. Because of the prominent place of play in psychodrama, I sometimes like to think of this method as a kind of 'play therapy,' for children and adults alike.

Play is an active way to master anxiety, to learn socially adaptive behaviour, and to satisfy human needs vicariously. According to Singer (1977), imagination and make-believe activities play an important part in children's acquisition of a varied vocabulary, imagery skill development, ability to tolerate waiting periods, and empathy and social role mastery. He pointed out that 'the dimension of *as if*, the activity of pretending and the world of make-believe has great potentials for enriching the experience of childhood and for preparing the child for the continuing and more formal aspects of education in the years after five and six' (p.141).

Role playing has especially been regarded as effective in helping people to differentiate between fantasy and reality, and between self and others. Role playing thus may contribute to the formation of a unified and consistent sense of self. 'Taking-the-role-of-the-other' is essential for all the internalizing processes: imitation, mirroring, identification, modeling, introjection and assimilation. Piaget (1951) has described the beginnings of symbolism involved in children's play, as it proceeds from imitation in the presence of a model to deferred imitation, and then to internal mental representation. When taking on a role and internalizing it, we initially behave 'as if' we have certain attributes and only later do we feel we can identify with the role and achieve a united sense of self. This process echoes Moreno's (1960a) theory of role-playing and role-taking in child development: 'Roles do not emerge from the self, but the self can emerge from the roles' (p.81).

These views are consistent with the theories of social psychologists such as William James, C.H. Cooley, and G.H. Mead who described personality development in terms of social interaction with generalized others. When looking at the way others see me, I look at myself as in a mirror and thus I build my own image of myself. Through social interaction, role playing and role reversal with others, I learn to 'imitate' their responses and thus I become an 'object' for myself (this is 'Me'). At the same time I exist as a separate entity (this is 'I') who initiates new and spontaneous responses and who represents the subjective, personal part of myself. Playing roles thus becomes a way in which to continually take on new roles, a key skill in personality development, according to Blatner and Blatner (1988).

From a social-learning-theory perspective (Bandura, 1971) the function of roleplaying is slightly different. People acquire new behavioural repertoires and modify their social responses through the observation of models: parents or significant adults who help the individuals to feel good about themselves.

From a psychoanalytic perspective, Jacobson (1964) describes how engaging in as-if and 'make-believe' play helps the young child to develop a sense of self in relation to the outside world and to differentiate between what is inside and what is outside: 'In the beginning the baby's imitations of the mother, of her gestures, her behaviour, her actions, are indeed only formal "as-if" activities without awareness of their meaning, founded merely on the close links of empathy with the mother. Imitating and playing the mother means being or becoming the mother' (p.43).

In a similar manner, Winnicott (1971) suggests that the child uses a kind of intermediate area, a middle sphere of play not unlike the psychodramatic surplus reality, in which the inner subjective world ('I') can meet with the outer reality ('Me'). In this sphere, the infant tries to connect the two worlds and unite them with each other, but still keeps them apart as we do in imagination, fantasy, illusion, and all other as-if activity. Winnicott also described how the child plays with a kind of 'transitional object' —the first 'not-me' possession—to help in the process of differentiation. This object may be a piece of blanket, a pacifier, or a cuddly toy that helps the infant gain an inner representation of an outer object.

Role-taking Within the Theatre
As an outgrowth of classical theatre, psychodramatic role playing may be regarded as an attempt to simulate or represent reality (Kipper, 1986). The goals of theatre, however, are of course different from those of psychodrama. While theatre aims to produce moments of stimulating entertainment for the audience,

psychodrama gives the actors an opportunity to grow. According to Martin (1991), 'In the former, the goal is that of creating a simulated reality for an audience, and the role players adopt whatever techniques, including props, scenery, music, etc., to facilitate the audience's suspension of disbelief. From this point of view, whether or not the role players themselves engage in this suspension is irrelevant, although some argue that such involvement by the actor facilitates the audience reaction (Staninslavski, 1936), while others argue the opposite (Diderot, 1951)' (p.588).

Yet, while goals differ, there is much that is similar. The process of role-taking in psychodrama is similar to the way a professional actor takes on a new part (Sarbin & Allen, 1968; Goldfried & Davidson, 1976; Yablonsky, 1976; Kipper, 1986). Actors do not only strive for technical mastery of their roles. They also attempt to incorporate and emotionally integrate their roles within their own personalities, which is a task requiring an abundance of creativity from the actors. Since they use themselves as instruments of personification, they must establish an inner relationship to the part and be able to maintain this in such a way that the audience sees them as the persons they pretend to be. In order to do this, they have to believe in their own performance to the extent that their behaviour and feelings are experienced as authentic.

This 'authentic' style of acting is usually associated with the school of Stanislavski (1936), who employed what he called a 'magical if' as a kind of 'lever' that lifts the actor from everyday reality to the level of imagination. When using this technique, the actor actively revives an earlier memory and transfers it to the stage. For example, an actor who must personify an angry person will emotionally revive the memory of a situation in which he became angry and use this memory to evoke the same feelings of anger again.

There is of course some controversy regarding the ability of actors to truly take on parts which are set by predetermined manuscripts. According to Moreno (1923), such parts will of necessity be in conflict with the actors as persons because the fact that these parts are prescribed and not evolving spontaneously (sua sponte = by itself from within), demands some amount of deception from the actors. Yardley (1982), however, disagrees with Moreno (1972) on this point, 'for a Stanislavski actor does not merely play a skeletal role but integrates him- or herself with the role and [im-] personates it within an as-if framework, bringing the role to vital embodiment' (p.297). Be that as it may, the tension between the actor as a person and the actor as the role-player reflects a universal human condition: a parallel to the potential conflict between the personal self and the social role which must meet the expectations of the outer world.

Through the use of imagination and 'as-if' techniques, psychodrama actively attempts to solve this apparent conflict and to transform the two polarities into complementary and mutually dependent states. In this process, 'as-if' becomes a powerful therapeutic factor which works as a kind of 'lever' of the self towards actualization. Thus, the 'magic as-if' of Stanislavski becomes with Moreno 'as is' (Ginn, 1974, p.132).

Role-Playing and Authenticity

Because of its reliance on 'as-if,' psychodrama is regarded by some professionals as phony and unauthentic. Janov (1970), for example, described psychodrama as an 'as-if game,' arguing that it is a mistake to instruct patients to act and feel like someone else while they are often incapable of feeling like themselves. This critique is based on the assumption that role playing in itself is pretence and that any use of imagination in psychotherapy of necessity leads to illusions.

Yet the simple fact that Shakespeare's declaration, 'all the world is a stage,' is a popularly accepted and empirically established tenet indicates that all people are role players in one way or another. If this is true, are all people then dissimulators? And why can't a person just be him- or herself, without playing a role? I believe that any psychotherapeutic method which relies on role playing and 'as-if' must solve this apparent contradiction.

Obviously, psychodrama does not employ role playing and 'as-if' to develop a false self. These methods are rather a way to expand the various parts of self through actively trying on new roles in the same way as one tries on a new coat. Such an action does not change the person wearing the coat but sometimes, with a handsome coat and a good fit, one may behave differently and perhaps also feel differently. There is nothing unauthentic or hypocritical about this role-taking process, provided that the new roles played do not disguise the real person. Quite the contrary, the roles may help develop a more flexible and functional identity.

Of course 'as-if' activity is not 'real'. All participants know this. However, it has real results and calls upon real feelings, at least as real as anything we know. The make-believe aspect disappears as soon as participants become emotionally involved in the role-playing (Martin, 1991) and begin to think, feel and act the way they do in real life. The amount of emotional involvement (the level of warm-up) in role playing is the factor which determines the authenticity of 'as-if'.

Such involvement may be aroused through openness to absorbing self-altering experiences ('absorption'), a trait related to hypnotic susceptibility (Tellegen & Atkinson, 1974), or through 'aesthetic distancing' (Scheff, 1979), which in brief means that actors should become emotionally involved in the role playing, but not to the degree that they forget who they are and where they are. Emotional involvement in role playing may, according to Yardley (1982), also be aroused via the following three technical practices which have parallels in theatre stagecraft. (1) *Particularization*, in this context, is the explicit detailing of objects (a chair is a car) and demands some kind of warming up to a situation with a description of the context and the background of the event. (2) *Personalization* is the degree to which particularized material is drawn from the subjects themselves. For example, a protagonist sets the scene in a manner which is personally meaningful for him or her and presents material which is drawn from his own experience. (3) *Presencing*, finally, refers to the presentation in here-and-now of particularized and personalized material, and not a reconstruction of the past. Such involvement enables the protagonist of psychodrama to 'take the game seriously'.

Conclusion

Thus we may conclude that the unrealistic and unauthentic characteristics of 'as-if' disappear as a result of emotional involvement in role playing. The role playing consequently becomes an ingenious circumventing tool for eliciting authentic material. 'Therefore, since it so often produces genuine self-expression behaviour, role playing ought to be regarded as much as an "as it is" behaviour as an "as-if" one' (Kipper, 1986, p.28).

CHAPTER 10

Acting Out

In psychodrama, participants not only talk about their conflicts, they also 'act them out' in overt role playing behaviour within the therapeutic setting. The concept of acting out represents the behavioural dimension of psychodramatic healing because, through its use, earlier events and their emotional residues are repeated in action via a direct motor expression of intrapsychic processes. Inner tensions may thus be transformed into overt behaviour which provides a possibility of gaining 'act-completion,' an experiential satisfaction of act-hunger similar to a complete catharsis. According to Breuer and Freud (1893), 'a complete catharsis depends on whether there has been an energetic reaction to the event that provokes an affect. By "reaction" we here understand the whole class of voluntary and involuntary reflexes—from tears to acts of revenge—in which, as experience shows, the affects are discharged' (p.8).

Acting Out

The tendency to act out increases in a group psychotherapy setting. When otherwise well-integrated neurotic patients are brought together in a group, they sometimes become irrational, impulsive, and chaotic. They may throw objects, drop out from the group, come late, remain silent, form subgroups or behave in other ways that are disturbing to the progress of therapy. The concept of 'acting out' is often used in the analysis of such phenomenon. But acting out is so multifaceted and complex that reviews of the literature show little agreement on its definition (Abt & Weissman, 1965). In addition, two different schools of thought on the question of acting out seem to have developed, one represented by psychoanalysis and the second by psychodrama. While acting out is discouraged in psychoanalysis, Moreno (1972) said that: 'Acting from within, or acting out, is a necessary phase in the progress of therapy' (p. x).

In this chapter I shall try to summarize the various ways in which acting out has been defined by psychoanalytic and psychodramatic authors and to present a comparative discussion. My main object is to show that the concept of acting out should be replaced by several terms from an action-terminology emphasizing doing rather than being, for this allows a finer distinction between the various aspects of actional phenomena in group psychotherapy than is provided by the simple postfix 'out.'

Acting Out in Psychoanalysis

It is beyond the scope of this chapter to present a review of the entire psychoanalytic literature on the concept of acting out. Excellent reviews have been presented by Rexford (1966), A. Freud (1968), and Sandler, Dare & Holder (1973). The most frequently used psychoanalytic definitions of acting out include any or all of the following:

1. Bungled, unconscious, symptomatic, or chance actions;

2. Physical (behavioural) expression of memories and fantasies;

3. Repetition, re-living, re-enactment of a past memory;

4. All motor behaviour occurring within the analytic setting;

5. Actions outside the analytic setting occurring as a reaction to happenings inside the setting;

6. Resistance; process opposed to working through and-attaining insight; replacement of thought by action; substitution for remembering;

7. Motor discharge of feelings, tensions, impulses (abreaction);

8. Attempt at wish fulfilment, satisfaction of infantile needs;

9. Experimental trial actions;

10. Antisocial, impulsive, delinquent, or dangerous behaviour.

I will illustrate these forms of acting out with a few simple examples. When angry with his therapist, Walter simply left the room instead of letting the therapist know how he felt. Tom started a course in assertiveness training when his female therapist was on holiday. In one therapeutic group, group members met between sessions without telling the therapist about this. One young female group member sent the therapist love letters and insisted on seeing him outside the group in a private setting. Such actions may be understood as expressions of any or all of the above-mentioned aspects and have traditionally been considered a hindrance in psychoanalytic therapies. According to Yalom (1975), 'Acting out is, by definition, a resistance to therapy; it is action concealed from the group's analytic eye; patients discharge through action those impulses which should be examined in therapy' (p.427).

But the psychoanalytic understanding of the term, once so narrow, is broadening. Acting out is no longer considered only a hindrance to treatment but has now become a part of the therapeutic process, as a source of information about unconscious mental states and as an indispensable addition to remembering. There is now a whole spectrum of therapists which extends from those who stress the harmful and destructive nature of acting out to those who lay emphasis on its communicative and adaptive nature (A. Freud, 1968).

In a discussion of acting-out incidents in groups, Grotjahn (1976) concludes that in the hands of a skilful and experienced group analyst, acting out can lead to successful analysis, insight, and integration.

Acting Out in Psychodrama

In psychodrama the term acting out means 'enactment'. For example, Moreno (1972) says of acting out: 'Why not let a protagonist act out his or her hidden thoughts and strivings as an alternate to an analysis of resistances? The patient on the couch, for example, may be a woman who suddenly has an urge to get up and dance, or talk to her husband whom she suspects of being disloyal to her, or, ridden by a feeling of guilt, she may want to kneel down and say a prayer' (p.ix).

Psychodramatic definitions of acting out include the following:

1. Living out, enactment through motor means;

2. Abreaction (ventilation of feelings);

3. Re-enactment, re-living of a past happening, or pre-enactment, pre-living of a future happening 'as if' it were occurring in the here-and-now;

4. Expression of an inner reality in the external world;

5. Non-verbal communication, the spontaneous use of 'action-language';

6. All 'doings' (claimed, manifest actions) on the psychodrama stage.

In its widest connotation, acting out in psychodrama refers to all output of an organism, all overt behaviour within the therapeutic setting. A person may move about, stand still, push and pull, make sounds or gestures or pronounce words. It is all acting out—communication through the universal action-language.

When Moreno used the term, he meant acting out that which is within the person, in contrast to reacting to stimulus from the outer world. To him, the 'out' in acting out, meant out of the inner self.

The following is a clinical example: A married woman, Ethel, who lived with her intruding mother, complained that she felt tense and irritable most of the time. She suffered occasional anxiety attacks in which her heart pounded and she broke out in a profuse perspiration. In a psychodrama session, Ethel was asked to present a typical encounter between herself and her mother (played by an auxiliary). In this scene it was clear to the group that Ethel held back many feelings towards her mother and she was asked to tell her mother what she really felt about her. Ethel hesitated, looking at the woman who sat opposite her, and slowly started to talk. She got more and more angry and finally burst out in a furious scream: 'I hate you, I hate you!' It looked as if something was 'breaking through' in her and she started to yell and hit and cry. When she had no more strength left, she fell to the floor exhausted and started to whisper words of forgiveness, expressing intense feelings of guilt for having used such strong words against her mother. The session continued with Ethel playing the roles of her mother, her husband and her children. Ethel 'acted out' her feelings and thoughts, her perceptions and fantasies and, in this process, her anxiety attacks became understandable and thus easier to handle.

In a psychodramatic production, participants are encouraged to continue and complete their actions through dramatization, role-playing, and dramatic self-presentation. Acting out may be a direct motor expression of intrapsychic processes, where inner tensions are transformed into overt behaviour without passing through a symbolic word translation. But the special advantage of psychodramatic acting out is the multifold utilization of both non-verbal and verbal communication (Polansky & Harkins, 1969).

It should be noted that acting out as a valuable ingredient in psychodrama is restricted to acting within the therapeutic setting. Moreno (1972) clearly differentiated 'irrational, incalculable acting out in life itself, harmful to the patient and others,' from 'therapeutic, controlled acting out taking place within the treatment setting' (p.x). However, while making this distinction, Moreno did not differentiate between aspects of acting out within the setting.

The Postfix 'Out'

There is a tendency on the part of some psychotherapists to refer to any social misbehaviour on the part of the patient during treatment as acting out. According to Menninger & Holzman (1973), it would be better if 'some of this were differentiated as "acting up" or "acting in" or just "acting!" For certainly not all behaviour that the analyst doesn't approve of can be put in the category of "acting out"' (p.11). Sandler, et al. (1973) have suggested substitution of the term 'enactment' for acting out on the ground that some of the confusion about acting out arises from a mistranslation of the German "agieren"': '...and in particular the inclusion of the preposition "out"' has contributed to some of the changes in meaning of the concept' (p.95).

Many other authors have also attempted to clarify the concept by changing its postfix. Eidelberg (1968) restricts it to acting *outside* the analytic setting. For example: 'A patient suddenly refuses to make his alimony payable to his ex-wife, displacing his resistance against paying his analyst's fees' (p.11). Eidelberg suggests the term 'acting-in' for actions inside the consultation room, for example, a patient getting up from the couch and removing a book from the shelf during a session. Zeligs (1957) and Rosen (1965) discuss 'acting-in,' as distinct from 'acting out inside analysis'. Another change in postfix was proposed by Robertiello (1965) who coined the expression 'acting-through' to describe the meaningful repetition of the past which leads to mastery and change. In a panel discussion of acting out in group psychotherapy (Hulse, 1958) and in a paper by Bromberg (1958), attempts were made to differentiate non-realistic acting out from realistic, everyday acting.

Within the psychodramatic frame of reference, Blatner (1973) suggests that the term 'acting-in' be used to describe the application of action methods 'which turn impulses into insights' (p.2). This change in postfix further confuses the issue as it is unclear whether 'in' refers to the internalization *into* the personality, to the growth of *in*sight, or to the acting with*in* the setting.

The postfix 'out' is no less ambiguous for it, too, has at least three meanings:

(1) Resistance: out of the therapeutic setting, that is, out of the influence and purview of the therapist;

(2) Abreaction: outflow of energy, discharge of tension, letting out of feelings;

(3) Communication: out into the external world (from the internal).

These three meanings of 'out' reflect some of the most widely held conceptions about what acting out includes. Together with repetitive action (actualization in the transference), they comprise the main components of the phenomenon called acting out.

It is my thesis that the postfix 'out' is inadequate to describe all these components and that we need another terminology to replace the term. Mani-festations of actions are indicative of much more than mere acting out. They include all the *doings* of a person. Instead of calling some actions 'acting out' and others 'acting-in' or 'acting-through,' all actions should be described and analysed in terms of their meaning in the therapeutic process.

The distinction between actions which occur within and outside the thera-peutic setting is trivial and blurs the more relevant distinction of intrapsychic versus overt action (Boesky, 1982). 'In' and 'out,' as traditionally used, merely locate the patient's action without describing the nature of that action. To describe actions which occur outside the setting as a reaction to experiences inside the setting, a more general term should be used, such as displacement. To call them acting out is misleading for such actions are not only 'acting out' but also 'feeling out' and 'thinking out,' a displacement of feelings and thoughts. As Rangell (1968) points out: 'All relevant psychic content kept defensively outside the analysis is to be brought into it' (p.200).

Action-Terminology

The use of an action-terminology can replace the term acting out in a beneficial way. For the purpose of psychological description, I suggest translating the above-mentioned components of acting out into the following new action-ter-minology: (1) counter-action (resistance); (2) abreaction (ventilation); (3) com-municative action (expression), and (4) repetitive action (re-living in the transference) and that we refrain from using the multifaceted concept 'acting out' when describing specific phenomena in psychodrama and psychotherapy in general.

Furthermore, we may find it clinically useful to distinguish between rational, controlled, social, and other appropriate actions and their opposites. Depending on our theory of psychotherapeutic technique and on our value-system, we may thereafter suggest that some actions are therapeutically useful and normal, and that others are destructive and abnormal.

This does have its complications. Behaviour which is viewed by some practitioners as impulsive and uncontrolled may be viewed by others as spontaneous and expressive. Some of these different values may be illustrated by the responses to an earlier version of this paper which were published in *Group Analysis* in 1985. Jean-Claude Rouchy, a group analyst from Paris, found the paper 'humorous' (p.63), while Marcia Karp, a psychodramatist from England, 'missed the humour' (p.65).

All this emphasizes the need for basic action theory (Parsons and Shils, 1951; Moreno, 1953; Hartmann, 1964) in which regressive-progressive action, passive-active action, spontaneous-inhibited action, conscious-unconscious action, external-internal action, manifest-latent action, and determined-free action are properly defined.

Examples

The following examples from group sessions illustrate my argument:

Let us consider the situation in which a patient gives the therapist a kiss. Is this acting out? If so, when is the kiss constructive and when is it destructive to the progress of therapy? It would be meaningless merely to say that this is acting out, for the word acting out is a blank that may be filled in with any meaning the speaker or listener desires. The meaning of the kiss may be better analyzed in terms of the four basic aspects described above. The kiss may be understood as any or all of the following: (1) As a counter-action it may be an attempt to seduce the therapist, with the patient refusing to examine or allow the group to examine the meaning of the action. As such, it is destructive to the progress of therapy and if possible, should be minimized. (2) As an abreaction it may be an affective discharge of pent-up erotic feelings towards the therapist. Abreaction and catharsis are important to the group therapeutic process. However, as I have pointed out in Chapter 6, they are only partial processes and must be complemented by other factors in order to become truly therapeutic. (3) As a communication, the kiss may convey affection. With the inclusion of verbal as well as non-verbal expressions, communications are of course vital to the to the progress of therapy. (4) As a repetition, the kiss may represent a false connection between the therapist and a person the patient had wanted to kiss years before, a re-enactment of a kiss given in the past, or an experimental recollection, a primitive mode of reconstruction (Ekstein & Friedman, 1957). Repetitive actions, or actualizations in the transference, are generally considered to be indispensable ingredients in dynamic psychotherapy and in psychodrama.

A second example illustrates a case in which something happening outside the psychodrama setting was a reaction to a situation existing within the setting.

After two unsuccessful individual psychotherapies, Iris, a 32-year-old woman, started psychodrama because of a failure to finish her academic degree and because of an inability to establish a long-lasting heterosexual relationship. After a few months in the group, Iris revealed that the previous weekend she had participated in a two-day marathon EST workshop. This came as a surprise to the group who had known nothing of Iris's intentions. Iris explained that she had withheld her plans because she was afraid that the group members, and especially the leader, would disapprove.

While most group therapists would probably interpret Iris's behaviour as a simple form of 'acting out,' a more productive approach would be to analyze the various actual meanings of this situation. The first and most obvious aspect is of course the resistive one: Iris's escape from the group. When asked about this, Iris admitted feeling bored by the group and pessimistic about its ability to help her change. Further exploration revealed fantasies of being helped by some magic force without any involvement or responsibility on her part. This in turn led to a discussion of the second, repetitive, aspect: Iris's inability to remain involved in the group was a re-enactment of her inability to remain involved in any long-lasting and intimate relationship, which was precisely her reason for coming to therapy in the first place. The third, communicative aspect, was verbally translated and expressed in terms of distrust and disbelief in the group. Finally, during the group discussion Iris admitted that she had felt pleasantly unfaithful to the therapist during her participation in the week-end workshop. This led to the fourth aspect, Iris's abreaction of rebellious feelings towards authority figures, a reconstruction of an ambivalent relationship with her seductive father. Giving consideration to these four action meanings turned out to provide helpful guidelines for the therapist and was beneficial to Iris's therapy.

Various actions such as throwing objects, coming late, sub-grouping, sexual relations, silence, and withdrawal occurring during the progress of therapy should be understood in terms of their actional meanings and not merely tossed into the general category of acting out.

Conclusion

There is an often-neglected consensus between psychoanalysis and psychodrama on the therapeutic usefulness of counter-action, abreaction, communicative action and repetitive action (Montagna, 1982).

While it is true that motor behaviour is generally interpreted as a resistance in psychoanalysis and that refraining from motility would be resistance in psychodrama, both approaches emphasize the importance of analysing and resolving counter-actions. Counter-action in psychodrama is a non-invocation of spontaneity operating counter to the therapeutic progress; a definition which is congruent with Schafer's (1976) proposal that 'resisting is engaging in actions contrary to analysis while also engaging in analysis itself...it is analytic counter-action' (p.244). Irrational actions performed outside the therapeutic setting are potentially destructive and, as a matter of course, both psychodrama and psychoanalysis discourage and try to minimize harmful behaviour where participants endanger their own or others' safety.

Some authors criticize psychodrama because it gratifies the patients' affectional needs in opposition to the psychoanalytic rule of abstinence, encourages defensive regression on a very primitive level and strengthens resistance vis-à-vis verbal activity. Lebovici (1974), himself a psychoanalyst, counters this argument, saying that psychodrama does nothing of the sort. It is my view that the psychodramatic principle of 'act-completion,' where past actions are re-enacted and integrated in the present, is congruent with psychoanalytic practice, and that psychodramatic enactment is not defensive regression opposed to working through but rather regression in the service of the ego, a therapeutic process of reorganization.

No adequate therapy is possible unless all actions—whether emotional, cognitive, or behavioural—are allowed to emerge within the therapeutic setting. Impulse-ridden patients will characteristically react to therapy without restraint while inhibited patients will control and delay their actions. Psycho-analysis and psychodrama provide opportunities for both kinds of patient to communicate and express themselves verbally and non-verbally without encountering disapproval or retaliation. In psychoanalysis, patients are encouraged to say what comes into their mind in order to uncover unconscious material. In psychodrama, patients are encouraged to do what comes to their body-mind in order to enhance spontaneous action. In spite of this difference in technique, what emerges through words or behaviour is regarded by both approaches as important information about the inner self of the patient.

Repetitive action and re-enactment of repressed experiences are necessary in order to secure recall and translate some of the most unacceptable, unconscious fantasies into conscious thoughts. Both psychodrama and psychoanalysis agree on the importance of transforming non-spontaneous, 'there-and-then' actions (whether impulse-ridden or inhibited) into more spontaneous 'here-and-now' actions. By the same token, both agree on the aim of narrowing the gap between conscious experience (of motor and affective discharge) and the unconscious meanings of these same actions.

The original controversy between psychoanalysis and psychodrama regarding acting out has thus lost much of its relevance.

CHAPTER 11

Magic

To this point, the discussion of healing in psychodrama has been limited to aspects specific to this method, such as catharsis, action-insight, tele, as-if and acting out. It seems, however, that there are other, more general but not less powerful aspects of healing at work in psychodrama which influence the outcome as well. These general, or '*non-specific*,' aspects are common to diverse and universal forms of healing and occur in most psychotherapies (Frank, 1961). In their relationship to such general aspects of healing, psychodramatists may be viewed as modern versions of the shamen: witch doctors and magic healers who have learned or who possess inherent powers to bring about remedies which are difficult, if not impossible, to explain.

I first noticed the effects of such non-specific factors in a psychodrama which I directed many years ago. At the beginning of the session, I felt tense about my own performance. I wanted to do something in order to make some progress but I was stuck and obviously failing. While searching for clues to continue the drama, I gently touched the protagonist's neck. This seemed to release her and she started to open up. As her words resonated against the palm of my hand, a warm surge of energy rose up from within and I could feel my head clearing up. At the same time I began to empathize with her, becoming her psychodramatic double. I no longer felt her as a separate person but as a part of myself. I think that she felt that and it may have made her able to open up. From that point onwards the session progressed by itself from scene to scene to a satisfactory therapeutic completion, which appeared to arise from within the protagonist without a deliberate effort of mine. When I had finished, I think even old Moreno himself might have given me the nod. The protagonist and the group looked positively entranced. As it was, I was unsure of what had happened and felt exhausted. Whatever it had taken to direct like that also drained me of energy, physically and mentally. 'There's magic in psychodrama,' I thought to myself, 'and it's working on all of us'.

This experience gave me an uncomfortable feeling of practicing some primitive form of magic healing. Ever since, I have occasionally participated in similar sessions in which some extraordinary but invisible powers seemed to be at work. When talking to other practitioners and participants about such experiences, I was surprised to learn that many of them had also experienced mysterious healing processes in psychodrama: hidden parallel processes which led to conflict resolution, physical touch which provided a sense of healing, suggestions which produced relaxation, symbolic rituals which facilitated reconciliation with death, self-fulfilling prophecies, and sudden moments of creativity which aroused powerful emotions, disbelief, or utter confusion. The more I heard, the more I started to feel that there was more to psychodrama than met the eye. The nature and function of such mysterious elements, however, have been largely neglected in the psychodramatic literature. At most, they have been described as manifestations of the 'epic qualities' of psychodrama and of the spiritual and creative dimensions of the 'cosmic man' (Moreno, 1966).

> 'Psychodrama is most loved for its epic qualities, its richness, for showing people the value and intentionality of their lives, for validating a viewpoint, or making sense of a crazy experience, for expression of pent-up emotion, for providing a spark, a moment of epiphany, intensity, or poetry' (Williams, 1989, p.79).

It seems clear that the value of the unexplained in psychodrama has not yet been fully appreciated. It will therefore be the purpose of this chapter to present some preliminary ideas about this subject—to give a glimpse, as it were, of the 'magic' or non-specific aspects of psychodrama.

Magic

The role of magic in healing has been recognized by many theorists, including Coriat (1923), Frazer (1951), Malinowsky (1954), Kiev (1964), LeShan (1966), Middleton, (1967), Ehrenwald (1967), Dossey (1982), and Versluis (1986). Bandler & Grinder (1975) used the metaphor of the magician when describing the skills of effective psychotherapists in Neuro-Linguistic Programming (NLP). Buchanan and Little (1983) used the same metaphor to describe psychodramatists who have difficulties translating their directorial styles into 'exact measurable components of behavior which can be taught to others' (p.114) and Karp (1988) recommended that the psychodrama director 'should be unafraid to be a magician' (p.49).

However, despite the fact that the structure of a psychodrama session may have certain similarities with that of a spiritual session (Bonilla, 1969) or a primitive ritual (Collomb & dePreneuf, 1979), psychodramatists are not 'real' magicians who deal directly with supernatural phenomena such as spiritism, parapsychology or ESP, and they are not stage magicians who pull rabbits out of a hat. Psychodramatists should rather be regarded as 'magicians of make-believe,' who perform illusions that actualize the inner self of the participants. Such a role is excellently captured in the following declaration by Tom Wingfield in Tennesse Williams' *Glass Menagerie* (Gassner, 1947): 'Yes, I have tricks in my pockets. I have things up my sleeve. But I am the opposite of a stage magician.

He gives you illusion that has the appearance of truth. I give you truth in the pleasant disguise of illusion.'

The magic practices of psychodrama are based on the notion that illness results from a disharmony among the various energies that are present in the individual, in society and in nature. Psychodramatists employ different names to describe such energies: spontaneity-creativity-conserve (Moreno, 1953), Yin and Yang, ego-superego-id (Freud), social-class conflict, person-by-situation interaction (Magnusson & Endler, 1977), cybernetic epistemology (Bateson, 1972), or field theory (Lewin, 1951). In order for a person to become healthy, he or she must find a suitable equilibrium, or integration, among these various forces.

Non-Specific Healing Aids

Mysterious or 'magic' healing which lead to a 'spontaneous remission' have been observed in psychotherapy for many years; psychiatry, according to Fenichel (1946), 'is tainted with magic' (p.3). Initially, such healing was referred to in terms of placebo effects (Shapiro, 1971)—remedies which in themselves were ineffective but which, through their suggestive influence, could effect a cure. As such, placebos were viewed as detrimental to any sound therapy and researchers on psychotherapy tried to minimize their effects. Later, the mysterious healing aspects were described as 'common denominators' (Frank, 1969): factors of healing which were active in various methods of psychotherapy, regardless of therapeutic philosophy. Finally, the term 'non-specific factors' (Strupp, 1972, 1973; Kazdin, 1979) came into use because, while being causally responsible for the amelioration of a patient's distress, these healing agents were not specific to a particular treatment technique or theoretical orientation.

Despite the universality of their presence, non-specific healing aids are defined differently in various therapeutic approaches. In psychoanalysis, for example, 'non-interpretive' (Stone, 1981) elements are considered non-specific, while in behaviour therapy it is the therapist-patient relationship that is considered non-specific. An illuminating illustration of the transition from yesterday's (non-specific) placebo to today's behaviour therapy was the consideration of desensitization as a placebo control for the effects of psychoanalytic psychotherapy (Goldstein, 1960).

Catharsis, action-insight, tele, as-if, and acting out have long been regarded as having a direct and specific influence on patient change in psychodrama. These aspects are believed to substantially increase the likelihood that psychodrama will be effective and are considered the conventional agents of change. Yet without a consideration of non-specific healing aids, the picture is incomplete.

The following may serve as a simple example. When I asked a woman who had participated in psychodrama groups for many years what she had found most helpful in her psychodramatic experience she said: 'My own psychodrama sessions were of course important and I worked through many important issues which troubled me. But in the long run, the most important thing for me was that I established a close relationship with Zerka, a kind of friendship which extended beyond the ordinary patient-therapist relation. She took me to restaurants and on trips and treated me like my own mother had never done. That friendship had such a great impact on me that I can feel its effects to this very day!'

Participants, however, are usually relatively unaware of the existence of non-specific healing aspects. Such factors are therefore difficult to operationalize and almost impossible to research. As a result, in my research on participants' perception of therapeutic aspects in psychodrama (Kellermann, 1985a; 1986; 1987c), it came as no surprise that the non-specific aspects were considered less helpful than other aspects of healing.

Nonspecific healing aids may be described as falling into the following four categories (Frank, 1971; Hobbs, 1962; Strupp, 1973). First, there is the emotionally charged, 'real' therapist-patient relationship which optimally includes caring, confidence and the absence of ulterior motives (described in this book as the 'tele-relationship'). Second, the patient is persuaded to perceive the therapist as possessing special healing powers (described in Chapter 4). Third, there is a healing context which provides a sense of hope and safety through suggestion. Finally, therapeutic rituals and healing ceremonies with symbolic relevance are performed to help people make important transitions in their lives.

As far as I understand them, non-specific healing aids may be actualized in psychodrama through the deliberate activation of these four processes. Here I will discuss the latter processes—suggestion and ritualization—in some detail. In a psychodrama session, participants are first emotionally stimulated and warmed up through suggestion. They are then invited to participate in a healing ritual, a kind of ceremony which helps them to adjust to a new situation.

The Healing Context of Suggestion

The element of suggestion is a powerful therapeutic factor in most psychotherapies, including psychoanalysis (Bibring, 1954; Wolberg, 1977; Appelbaum, 1988). In psychodrama, participants are constantly being influenced by various authoritative formulations and directives.

At the beginning of a psychodrama session, participants are stimulated by the use of 'warm-up' techniques, such as relaxation, emotionally arousing music, exercises for the imagination, and improvisational role playing. Such techniques are suggestive in themselves, invoking an altered state of consciousness which makes people more susceptible to outside influence and more open to change. Powerful words are spoken to open doors to hidden layers of the soul, and physical touch conveys subtle and powerful subliminal messages.

Many of these techniques are wrapped in clouds of secrecy. This, according to Luhrman (1989), in itself has a magic effect on people. 'Secrecy is about control. It is about the individual possession of knowledge that others do not have, and from the psychological consequences of this privileged possession follow its effects in magical practice. Secrecy elevates the value of the thing concealed. That which is hidden grows desirable and seems powerful, and magicians exploit this tendency to give their magic significance' (p.161).

Participants are persuaded to 'feel more and think less;' the explicit focus of exploration being on emotional experiences rather than on cognition, reason, and rationality. As a result, expectations are raised that something extraordinary is going to happen. A sense of hope is fostered that the method will work, and participants are persuaded to believe that they will get what they need 'if they only reach out their hands to take it'. A tacit message is that 'without faith, psychodrama will not work,' and that 'the director must trust the psychodrama method as the final arbiter and guide in the therapeutic process' (Zerka Moreno, 1965). The psychodramatist, through words and action, conveys a belief in the healing procedure and in the creative potential of every individual.

Suggestion in psychodrama is based on the deliberate arousal of 'magical thinking,' a kind of thinking especially prevalent in small children (Fraiberg, 1958). Magical thinking remains in a hidden part of each person throughout his or her life and can be brought back to life throughout adulthood by various methods. People are easily persuaded to resort to magical thinking because it offers a system of answers to difficult questions and provides an orderly picture of a sometimes chaotic universe. 'The principle governing magic,' according to Freud (1913–14),' is the principle of the 'omnipotence of thought,' (p.85) a belief that one can alter the external world merely by thinking. Such total power over the environment is brought about by a belief that wishes can bring about real events. In the words of Appelbaum (1988):

> 'In summary, a helpful context of healing implicates a primitive level of reality and experience, with heightened suggestibility, more feeling and less cognition, needfulness, and the expectation of external help with that need, all of which dispose one toward the feeling that anything is possible; in short, a particular kind of controlled regression in the service of the therapeutic ego. If these characteristics sound familiar it is because they are the ways in which psychoanalytic textbooks describe orality—a phase that is characteristic of a primitive stage of life, that encompasses a need for nurturance and expectation of healing in the form of lowering bodily tensions, a belief in magic and omnipotence, and mass discharge of feeling. We thus arrive at a characterization of the healing relationship as being derived from the earliest form of what obtains between mother and child' (p.203).

Magic Shop

A suitable illustration of magical thinking in psychodrama is the use of the adjunctive technique 'Magic Shop' (Weiner, 1959; Schutzenberger, 1970; Petzold, 1978). In this technique, personality characteristics and their actualizations are translated into economic transactions between a buyer and a seller.

A shop-keeper is chosen to manage the shop and participants come in, one by one, to buy real or imaginary things from the past, present or future that they feel they need. In such a Magic Shop, people can buy a pound of courage, some fantasy, the ability to say 'No,' or any other unfulfilled wish or need. One person wanted to buy a part of himself that he had lost, another wanted to become famous, and still another person wanted to buy the ability to laugh at himself.

The price, which does not include money, is determined by the shopkeeper after some bargaining. 'How much is a bottle of self-confidence?' One shop-keeper suggested that the price be some of the buyer's sensitivity, which was unacceptable for the customer. The prices asked for an item should represent something which is relevant to the item required and be a part of the qualities of the buyer, and the buyer has to give up something which is valuable to him. A man who wanted to buy the ability to be loved by his wife was asked to give up hours from work, be less selfish and hand in a large amount of social prestige.

The Magic Shop is loaded with symbolic and projective content as well as with elements of external reality, making this technique an excellent diagnostic tool. According to Petzold (1978), however, the Magic Shop does more than simply serve as a stimulus for projective material. If it includes some working through of intra-personal conflicts, it can also be a therapeutic agent in itself, leading to symbolic wish-fulfilment, insight into the hidden contents of personal needs and an exploration of pathways to more creative adaptation to outer reality.

Rituals

The entire procedure of psychodrama may be regarded as a kind of ritual, a healing ceremony with symbolic relevance for the protagonist. Such cere-monies, however, are also employed as adjunctive technique or as closure scenes within the psychodramatic process. In both larger and smaller contexts, these rituals have mystical therapeutic effects.

Traditionally, rituals are employed to help people making transitions from one phase of life to another. Rituals are performed at birth, confirmation, and marriage for the purposes of initiation, and at funeral ceremonies to help the living separate from the deceased. Rituals have a strongly formalized structure with a distinct framework of action. The very dramatization of important life-events helps people to adjust to their new circumstances and, according to Hart & Ebbers (1981), rituals are 'powerful instruments for the stimulation and stabilization of change' (p.189).

Rituals may be used in psychodrama as 'initiation rites,' for example with adolescents who need to come to terms with their inner selves (Pitzele, 1991), or as 'reconciliation rites' for couples who consider divorce (Williams, 1989). Aguilar & Wood (1976) described the use of drama rituals for even more highly symbolic purposes, for example, burying someone's past.

The most frequent use of rituals in psychodrama, however, is to help people complete unfinished business from the past, and particularly to help them take leave from persons who have died. In psychodramatic 'leave-taking rituals,' protagonists are helped to solve unresolved grief in a symbolic manner, and to give new meanings to traumatic happenings. Psychodrama sessions frequently involve actual ceremonies of 'saying goodbye' (Blatner and Blatner, 1988, p.166), death scenes (Siroka & Schloss, 1968) in which the protagonist speaks to an important person (played by an auxiliary) who is dying or has died, or various mourning ceremonies which help the protagonist to accept his or her loss and to adjust to a new reality.

In a recent psychodrama, a woman who had miscarried reenacted the process of becoming pregnant and then losing her baby. She mourned her dead child, expressed anger at her physicians, and received ambivalent support from her husband (played by an auxiliary) who had fainted in the delivery room. In the actual scene of the spontaneous abortion, her child had been taken away from her and she was urged, in the psychodrama, to take it in her arms, to say goodbye to it, and to bury it symbolically. In the closure scene, the unborn child (played first by the protagonist and later by an auxiliary) asked her to remember him with the happiness she had felt when she got the message that she was pregnant.

According to Hart (1983), re-enactments of funeral rituals are particularly helpful to people who have unresolved feelings about the death of someone close, often because they were not present at the real funeral and thus could not participate in the original mourning process. In such cases it may be important to perform separation rituals using actual objects which serve as symbols for the relationship with the deceased person. For example, clothing of deceased children may be burned, buried or given away (Selvini-Palazzoli et al., 1977), letters may be written to doctors, and real objects of symbolic significance may be destroyed (such as wedding rings, photographs and love letters).

Conclusion

While our goal is to understand as much as possible about psychodrama, many things remain incomprehensible and mysterious in the cold light of reason. Regarding the processes described in this chapter, I have little more to say than that this part of psychodrama will always remain a mystery. And perhaps it is best that way. Because once the hidden forces of magic have been aroused in the psychodramatic process, one does well to follow with the naivete of a child, not saying more about it than can be understood in simple terms. In the words of Wittgenstein (1922), 'whereof one cannot speak, one must be silent.'

CHAPTER 12

Resistance

In the previous chapters, I have described the various aspects of psychodrama which facilitate its therapeutic progress and have shown the ways psychodrama *works*. Frequently, however, obstacles arise which interfere with the effective employment of psychodrama's therapeutic aspects. Such obstacles, or *resistances*, are activated by participants when they feel a need to defend themselves against some real or fantasized threat.

Psychodrama currently has only partial theories regarding resistance. This chapter will propose a more consistent theory of resistance and suggest some techniques which may be useful to resolve them in a proper manner, through analysis and/or neutralization.

Resistance.

'Resistance is a function of spontaneity; it is due to a decrease or loss of it' (Moreno, 1953, p.liv). In psychodrama, resistance is defined as the protagonist's security tactic against becoming involved, warmed up and spontaneous. In other words, it is a force which restrains or inhibits spontaneous action, a non-invocation of spontaneity operating counter to the therapeutic process.

Resistance is also one of the ways in which protagonists respond inappropriately to new situations, thereby preventing their use of spontaneity as an adaptive, coping and mastering agent. Resistance becomes a form of compulsive role-playing supplanting the spontaneous flexibility of the self, playing to the tune of role-conserves (frozen, habituated behaviour). When protagonists resist, they reduce their involvement with a present situation to a minimum by substituting a simple, repetitive response for the new response that the situation demands. This allows them to continue living with a low amount of spontaneity, and prevents them from dealing creatively and flexibly with their problems.

Since many theories hold that resistances appear when a therapeutic investigation touches upon crucial anxiety-provoking conflicts, there are as many theories of resistance as there are theories about the origins of anxiety. Resistance can be understood from both psychodynamic and behavioural points of view (Wachtel, 1982), to name just two. For the purposes of the present discussion, I will adopt the view of Moreno (1953) who postulated that anxiety results from a 'loss of spontaneity' (p.42), an inability to live in the here-and-now. According to this theory, protagonists become anxious and resist when they cannot find adequate responses to internal and external pressures.

In an operational sense, 'resistance means merely that the protagonist does not wish to participate in the production' (Moreno, 1972, p.viii). Resistance here refers to the nonexistence of a treatment-alliance and to behaviour in opposition to the psychodramatic process. This definition has its pitfalls, however; some opposition to shortcomings in the method and/or in the therapist may be justified and realistic, and should therefore not be confused with resistance.

The principles of resistance may be illustrated by John, who participated in a psychodrama group because he had interpersonal problems. As a warm-up exercise, the psychodramatist asked the group members to present a short but important situation from their past. All presented their scenes except John, who sat silent and uncooperative. When asked for the reason for his refusal to present a scene, he said: 'I can't do this. This is stupid! I came here to make friends, not to play childish games!'

Another participant, Mary, resisted in a more subtle manner. She volunteered to present a situation in action but chose to leave out all conflicting feelings and problematic issues. Overtly she seemed eager to embark on the therapeutic journey but covertly she remained in full control of the situation and continued to conceal her inner chaotic world. She obviously enjoyed getting attention from the group and it took a long time before the group realized that she was playing a resistance game with them.

If we regard psychodrama as a gradual progress of integration, then resistance can be described variously as a counter-force (Greenson, 1967), a counter-pressure (Menninger & Holzman, 1973), a counter-will (Rank, 1957), or a counter-attack (Perls, Hefferline, & Goodman, 1950) against this progress. However, to emphasize the active participation of protagonists, I prefer to describe resistance as a *counter-action*. Taken as active manifestations of defence, resistances become the protagonists' own creations, not things imposed or inflicted by the outside world. Protagonists who refuse to get involved in the therapeutic process, even when this refusal is manifested in extreme passivity, are in fact *acting* to block their spontaneous energy.

Accepting the fact that protagonists do resist, we should make distinctions regarding the ways in which they resist, when and where they resist, what they are attempting avoid, and why they do so. The ways in which protagonists resist will be described as 'manifestations of resistance,' and what they resist as 'functions of resistance'.

Manifestations of Resistance

How do protagonists resist? There are many ways to remain uninvolved in the psychodramatic process. All aspects of mental life can serve a defensive function and may manifest themselves as resistances. The expression of one feeling, such as laughter, can be a defence against the expression of another feeling, such as sadness. An attitude of indifference may be a kind of complacent avoidance of ego-involvement. We all have our own ways of avoiding involvement. Among the numerous escape routes which allow people to refrain from feeling, the most common ones will be mentioned here.

Psychoanalytic authors have described in detail how patients resist by being late, missing hours, dropping out of therapy or forgetting to pay, or by becoming silent, withdrawn, passive, stubborn, bored or shy. While a patient who resists in psychoanalysis often does not 'feel like talking,' a protagonist who resists in psychodrama does not 'feel like acting'. The message behind both these statements is, of course, that they do not want to feel or express their feelings, either through talking or acting.

People may resist, either in a passive or in an active manner, manifesting their avoidance in a subtle and disguised way ('I have nothing to say...') or in a more direct protest ('This method doesn't work on me!'). Some express an initial enthusiasm, only to add their inevitable 'but' when they themselves are required to reveal themselves. One participant said: 'Personally, I do not mind becoming a protagonist. I simply find, for various reasons, that it would be better if someone else used the time of the group.' But a moment later, when he had gained more confidence, he added with abandon: 'You see, there is something about this play-acting which upsets me physically!'

People who participate in a psychodrama group for the first time usually present an initial resistance to the role-playing itself. This resistance may be due to embarrassment at being the centre of attention, a fear of public exposure expressed in stage fright, or a lack of sufficient emotional preparation (warm-up). Bentley (1967) believes that most adults initially react with some hesitation: 'I could never do that. I'd sink through the floor!' Leveton (1977) describes the initial questions and fears of a person entering psychodrama: 'Do you have to be able to act? I'm not an actor, I can't be phony, pretend to be someone else. Do you have to perform? In front of an audience? They'll just make a fool of me, make me act out my problems and then ridicule me...I'm just going to sit quietly and hope that the leader doesn't look at me' (p.16).

But even when protagonists are properly warmed-up to action and motivated to work, resistances may develop during the course of any session, making them avoid certain scenes or specific roles. When sensitive areas are prematurely uncovered, protagonists will become stuck and uncooperative, causing a stalemate in the therapy.

According to Korn (1975), one way of avoiding getting emotionally involved in psychodrama is 'to prevent an interhuman situation from "mattering". The group member defends himself from "getting involved"—and his lack of involvement prevents the group situation from becoming urgently and demandingly relevant to his basic personal concerns. The other group members are merely "other patients". The group situation is merely "treatment". The dramaturgical transformation of therapy into real life does not occur' (p.187).

Seabourne (1966) describes various kinds of 'difficult' protagonists, for example, the protagonist who narrates and intellectualizes; the one who is able to tolerate very little participation in a session; the one who will not get up on stage or who tends to leave before the scene is closed; the one who 'has no problem'; the one who cannot limit or focus the material presented; the one who dominates the group; and the disruptive patients (psychotic, hysteric, or suicidal/homicidal) who act in a way that will not permit the rest of the group to proceed in its activities. These participants are not only resisting emotional involvement in the psychodramatic process, they are also disturbing the development of a constructive working group climate. In a similar manner, Sacks (1976b) describes some subtle forms of resistances among psychodrama participants who may become confused, forgetting the purpose of the session, express themselves only in short sentences, laugh inappropriately, inhibit body expression or block their voices.

Mental health professionals who participate in psychodrama for their own personal growth may, according to Quin (1991), be especially likely to find subtle ways to resist: 'My experience of working with mental health professionals as protagonists is that they can be creative, exciting and courageous in the risks that they will take but that when they become stuck, they do so with great thoroughness. Skilled and sensitive people will suddenly start crying "crocodile tears" and avoiding the real distress, or sidetracking the director maybe using talking to avoid action, or allowing themselves to be led down well-known pathways rather than face the unknown areas' (p.241).

Barriers between members of the group and between the members and the psychodramatist can also be regarded as manifestations of resistance. Moreno (1972) called these resistances 'interpersonal' (p.215), indicating the tendency of people to avoid spontaneous involvement with each other, not taking each other for what and whom they are. The past has a distorting influence on such relationships, which would, in psychoanalytic terminology, be regarded as transference resistances. This aspect of resistance is emphasized by Kruger (1980), who defined resistance in psychodrama as 'interpersonal concretization of the intrapsychic defense in the transference relationship between members and group or members and therapist' (p.243).

An interpersonal resistance may be illustrated by the case of Ralph, who had 'unfinished business' with his mother. Ralph consciously refrained from choosing an older woman in the group to play his mother because he was afraid that that woman's resemblance to his mother might cause him to be overwhelmed by 'real' aggression. Instead, Ralph chose a good friend in the group who actually represented his ideal mother; a choice which prevented him from dealing with his aggressive feelings and from making progress in therapy.

Not only protagonists but also auxiliaries and entire groups may resist in psychodrama. The most common resistance among auxiliaries is that they refuse to play certain antagonist roles. According to Moreno (1972, p.xvi), the reasons for such refusals may be either 'therapeutic' (the protagonist 'uses' the role playing situation without any willingness to reverse roles with the auxiliary), or 'private' (indicating personal difficulties with certain roles).

The group norms, the group climate, and the sociometric structure of the group may also cause resistances in individual members. One group member, Sam, sat frozen and silent through a number of sessions, refusing to take part in the work because he perceived himself as an 'isolate,' a sociometric solitary outcast. Sam had to be integrated into the group through getting the entire group to attend to his problem in psychodrama before he felt safe enough to participate in a more active manner.

Group resistances may be further described either in terms of Bion's (1961) 'basic assumption groups' (dependency, fight-flight, and pairing), or in terms of Whitaker and Lieberman's (1964) related concept of 'group focal conflict' (the solution of a shared group-conflict).

A situation that appeared in a psychodrama group that I led, may illustrate such group resistances. It was a group for adolescents, within an educational setting. From the very beginning, I was met with suspicious silence and antagonism, as if the entire group had joined forces against me in passive opposition. The group resistance was so intense and the silence so compact that I initially was tempted to leave the group and would probably have done so if I had not contracted the work with the institution long in advance. What surprised me, however, was that the participants continued to attend the sessions regularly and, despite their long silences, seemed to enjoy coming to the group. It took a long time for me to realize that the group had developed a kind of group norm which seemed to paralyze them. The tacit message of the group was that 'if we only keep quiet, perhaps nobody will get hurt...' and any interference with this norm was met with fierce opposition. Little by little, I learned that there was a lot of old, pent-up aggression between members of the group: aggression which could not be expressed because of fear of retaliation, abandonment and guilt, with the possible result of suicide. Thus, the group norm 'Let's be quiet...' represented a solution of a group focal conflict which it seemed impossible to resolve. Although some of the interpersonal issues had to be left unattended, some were taken up and worked through in the group with a positive effect on the entire group process.

Functions of Resistance

What do protagonists try to ward off? Resisting protagonists are mainly avoiding discomfort and unpleasant feelings such as anxiety, guilt, or shame. A young man refused to show the group how he interacted with women because it

brought back painful memories of failure and rejection in him. Another protagonist got stuck when he suddenly became burdened with guilt for having told
mother that he hated her. Still another person became blocked when talking
about his shame about wetting his bed. Resistances should be viewed as the
overt manifestations of defence mechanisms or security operations which
people use to cope with inner and/or outer threat. Upon perceiving danger,
people may either guard themselves offensively through, for example, sarcasm,
criticism, and assault, or escape defensively through repression, withdrawal,
and indifference. Henry Kellerman (1979) describes resistances in terms of their
ability to effectively deal with 'it'—the assumed threat. A person may start with
'denial' and then follow a kind of circular defence logic until finding the escape
route which works best for him or her: 'Denial is *don't see it*. If that doesn't work
then insulate yourself and *don't feel it*. If that doesn't work then repress it and
therefore *don't remember it*. If that doesn't work then *do something else about it like
act-out*; or you could regress and *cry for it*, or you could compensate and *try to
get it back*. If none of these methods work then you might fantasize or daydream
about it. If even this doesn't work then you might as well criticize or project and
blame it; or, even better, you might displace it and *attack something that represents
it*. When these attempts are also inadequate you might as well *join it*. How?;
well, you might identify with it or *be like it*. A good way to be like it is to introject
or *take it in*. Once you've finally taken it in, you'd better not show it—rather you
could *recategorize it* by intellectualizing it. How is that possible?; well, you might
rationalize or *make an excuse for it*, or...' (p.101–102).

Protagonists who insist that they feel 'nothing,' that they are 'empty,' or
'blocked,' have chosen a more primitive way of escaping feelings, sometimes
called 'isolation'. For whatever reasons, such persons prefer to be spectators in
the theatre of life and present strong resistances to becoming participant actors.
If their feelings continue to be thus 'isolated' over a long period of time, the
blocked energies may develop into a permanent 'muscular armour,' a biophysi-
cal block in motility according to a concept coined by Reich (1929/50). Such a
muscular armour, or 'character resistance' as it is also called, may require more
active handling of the physical aspects of the person by the psychodramatist,
for example using bioenergetics, rolfing, breathing exercises, or expressive
movements.

In his paper on psychodramatic shock therapy, Moreno (1939) describes how
a patient who has recuperated from a psychotic episode shows a violent
resistance to throw himself back into the earlier hallucinatory experience. 'His
natural bent is to forget—not to talk about it. He is full of fears that his new
freedom may be shattered. The mere suggestion, and still more the actual
process, frightens him' (p.3). For the same reason, people who have been
through a crisis—the loss of a family member, an automobile accident, or a
failure in pregnancy—which evoked overwhelming feelings of grief and
anxiety accompanied by spells of reality diffusion and inner turmoil, will do

everything to avoid re-living the traumatic event. Having worked hard to reach some emotional equilibrium after the trauma (no matter how adaptive the new sense of balance may be), they will not readily give it up, even for a moment.

Thus we come to the conclusion that resistances, in the final analysis, function to maintain the psychic equilibrium of the individual, and that resistances are best understood within the framework of psychoanalytic ego-psychology. According to this theory, protagonists have more or less strong egoes and they need more or less rigid defences. People who are 'ego-strong,' use resistances to defend the status quo in their neuroses. The aim of psychodrama in these cases is to help them regress, abreact, progress and reach a new integration. Ego-weak protagonists, however, such as borderline and other personality disorders, use resistances to maintain a fragile emotional homeostasis which protects them from excessive anxiety or ego fragmentation. With such protagonists, the aim of psychodrama is to strengthen their ego functions and to build up an independent ego-structure, rather than to stimulate regression and loss of control. According to Blanck and Blanck (1979), resistance in such personalities represents unsuccessful attempts at separation-individuation, rather than opposition to treatment. If the threat to ego-weak protagonists is great enough they may (adaptively) defend themselves by resisting or by terminating treatment: 'The technical decisions to be made when dealing with manifestations of oppositionalism, negativism, stubbornness, withholding, defiance, and the like, are more complex than was heretofore thought. When withholding or refusal, for example, is partly in the service of growth...we have to support it to acknowledge the developmental and adaptive aspects' (p.149).

Techniques of Resolving Resistances

Since the manifestations and functions of resistance differ with each protagonist, technical interventions must be applied differently to each individual in each situation.

A main question when handling resistances is whether to probe for resistances analytically in order to understand them better and/or to circumvent them with the help of manipulative techniques. Let's take the case of the protagonist who suddenly gets an urge to leave the stage. One possible intervention is to ask: 'What do you fear will happen on stage? What do you avoid?' Another intervention, not unusual among psychodramatists, is simply to take the protagonist's hand and suggest: 'Let's do it together. I will help you!'

Exploring the motives for resistant behaviour—the first strategy listed above—represents a re-constructive strategy which aims to give the protagonist a better understanding of his or her defence processes, including their historical roots. The second, somewhat manipulative, strategy of reassurance aims to help the protagonist to 'get over' or to neutralize the obstacles in therapy in order to reach his or her feelings directly. The first strategy may be likened to the gradual peeling of an onion while the second strategy is more similar to the immediate chopping, pressing and squeezing of the onion; while both strategies lead to some evacuation of tears, one is more gentle than the other.

It is my position that both analysis and neutralization may be employed effectively in psychodramatic resistance resolution, with different protagonists and at different stages in the treatment process. While it is grossly inappropriate to offer precise recommendations regarding the 'when' and 'for whom' aspects of resistance resolution, the general guideline should, in my experience, be *analysis before neutralization*. The techniques involved in these two strategies will therefore be described below in that order.

Analysis

One of the major challenges facing psychodramatists is assisting protagonists to examine those feelings that threaten the protagonists' sense of mastery. Psychodramatists try to reach beyond the noninvolved 'I don't feel like,' to the protagonists' unconscious cries for help, and, in the process, attempt a look behind the facade of resistances, searching for expressions of genuine spontaneity.

The analysis of resistances in psychodrama may be roughly described as progressing through the following three stages.

(1) First, the protagonist must become aware that he or she is resisting. Then the resistances must be identified as such and verbalized. ('It seems to me that you do not want to become emotionally involved in this...') Because resistance appears in the context of time and space, the psychodramatist must try to find out when—whether in the beginning, middle, or ending phase—and where—in which situations and scenes—the protagonist is resisting. ('At the end of every session, you withdraw and leave the room a few minutes early, without saying goodbye...') The manifestations of resistance are then explored in greater detail with no efforts to neutralize them. In the words of Z.T. Moreno (1965), 'First we must accept this inability, and assist him to accept himself; gradually we try to release him from his own bonds by various methods...' (p.236). According to Hart, Corriere, and Binder (1975), 'the first step toward completing a feeling is to feel the defenses which make particular feelings incomplete. For example, a patient might have to feel and express, "I don't care about people" for a long time before "I don't care" can give.way to "I do care, it hurts not to care"' (p.40).

(2) Protagonists are then invited to explore what they are warding off, what they prefer not to feel, think or do. Rather than being focused on finding intellectual answers to the question 'Why,' this process is directed towards an experiential understanding of the functions of resistance in the

here-and-now. ("I am afraid you would leave me if I told you I care about you").

(3) Finally, protagonists are encouraged to give up their resistances, by first identifying their act-hunger, their drive toward fulfilment of desires and their need for act-completion. ('It would be nice to-be able to embrace someone and really feel close, without any strings attached to this closeness...') The psychodramatist then tries to convince them that they might achieve what they want by doing what is suggested.

Neutralization

The most important issue in neutralizing resistances in psychodrama is to establish a context which fosters spontaneity. According to Blatner (1973), 'the necessary conditions for spontaneous behaviour include (1) a sense of trust and safety; (2) norms which allow for the inclusion of nonrational and intuitive dimensions; (3) some feeling of tentative distance, which is one element of "playfulness;" and (4) a movement toward risk-taking and exploration into novelty' (p.36). Some sort of warm-up activity is therefore usually required at the beginning of a psychodrama session. The resistance displayed during this period should not be regarded as resistance per se, but as a necessary phase in the process of getting started. Verbal and nonverbal exercises, games and other playful activities increase spontaneity, decrease anxiety, and loosen resistant positions. Members of a group may, for example, walk around the room, look one another in the eyes, touch and talk to one another to set up an easy-going atmosphere. A more structured warm up is to ask each group member to complete a sentence, for example: 'The next step I am going to take in my life is...'

Moreno (1972) recommends that resistant protagonists begin their psychodrama with a symbolic production to eliminate fear of personal involvement. Protagonists are inspired to perceive the role playing 'as if it were reality' which, in itself, can neutralize resistances. Hand puppets and masks may be especially effective when working with children and adolescents. The distance provided by these props gives the participants a secure feeling of being able to hide behind a mask while presenting a painful inner reality. For example, a sexually abused girl was able to talk about her feelings of guilt with the help of a hand puppet she called 'Bertha'. 'Bertha was a bad girl. Not only had she done dirty things with her father. She had also revealed their secret and, as a consequence of this betrayal, her father had been sent to prison. Bertha was to be severely punished!'

When a protagonist presents a situation from the past, the psychodramatist helps to recreate the feelings which were prevalent in that time and place. In scene-setting, the protagonist is helped to regain the sense of 'there-and-then' by rebuilding the physical surroundings, describing colours, textures, furniture arrangements, etc. This helps to revive memory and increase involvement and makes the enactment more authentic. Initial resistances are often eliminated when the authentic feelings connected to that section of time and space have been recreated in the here-and-now.

I will illustrate this process with a resistant, depressed woman, Mrs. A., who had mentioned that she was unsatisfied with her marriage. When she was asked to show how she interacted with her husband, she moved slowly, seemingly without interest and initiative and complained about having lost all pleasure in life. The director asked Mrs A. to set the scene, to show the room where she used to be together with her husband. But Mrs A. refused: 'There is no point in doing this anyway. Let's stop here!' Despite her resistance, the director continued to ask questions about the room: 'What colours are the walls? What can you see from this window? Who gave you this souvenir?' And gave his reaction: 'That's nice!' Pointing out every object, the director succeeded in staging the room carefully. During this scene-setting, Mrs. A. remembered a picture of her husband taken before they were married. The picture, which showed her husband as a soldier, was personified on stage by a young man from the group. When seeing the picture thus recreated, Mrs. A. suddenly came to life. Her eyes shone when she talked about her husband the way she knew him then. The picture became a kind of 'resistance remover' which enabled Mrs. A. to become emotionally involved and to present her feelings of despair when losing her newborn baby more than thirty years earlier.

Most of the major psychodramatic techniques can be used in analyzing and/or neutralizing resistances. Here, only the most common ones (soliloquy, double, mirror, role reversal, maximizing and concretizing) are explained in relation to resistance resolution.

Soliloquy

The soliloquy technique is useful in revealing hidden thoughts and feelings and in discovering the motives and functions of resistance manifestations. Tom was an ambivalent group member who, having applied for membership in the group with great enthusiasm, remained negative during many sessions. When asked to soliloquize, Tom associated freely for a while and then, in a few words, expressed his fear of a certain group member. He had the feeling that she would make fun of him if he presented himself. After this interpersonal resistance was brought out into the open, the threatening group member turned out to be very helpful as an auxiliary for Tom, playing the role of his dominating and ridiculing mother.

Double

The double technique, which is used to express verbally the hidden contents of a protagonist's communication, may be the most effective instrument in understanding resistances. Jane, a shy woman, came to a psychodrama group for over a year without ever volunteering to become a protagonist. When the director made this an issue for exploration and asked Jane to talk about her feelings in the group, she said that she was afraid to present herself because she felt less secure than the others. When the group suggested that she become a protagonist to explore this issue, Jane responded with a repetitive 'Yes, but...' which was identified as a resistance game. A group member who was chosen to be Jane's double focused on her contradictory feelings: 'I need therapy, but I can manage without it. I want to participate, but something stops me from revealing my real feelings. I do not know what I want...' With the help of the double, the main issue of Jane's psychodrama became her general ambivalence, both in the group and in her daily life. After the psychodrama, Jane was proud of herself and pleased with her session, volunteering immediately for continued work at the next session.

Mirroring

Mirroring is useful in portraying nonverbal resistance communication. William was asked to leave the stage and to watch a mirror production of himself played by an auxiliary. The auxiliary took his place, his body posture, and imitated him both verbally and nonverbally. When William looked at himself from a distance, seeing how his body expressed the message 'Don't touch me!' he exclaimed: 'No, that is not true! I want people to touch me, I need touching!' Moreno & Moreno (1969) hold that 'with resisting protagonists, the mirror may be exaggerated, employing techniques of deliberate distortion in order to arouse the patient to come forth and change from a passive spectator into an active participant, to correct what he feels is not the right enactment and interpretation of himself' (p.241).

Role Reversal

Protagonists who resist when playing themselves may resist less if allowed to play the role of someone else. Paul, for example, resisted playing himself as a child, preferring to play the role of his own father. Once he realized that his father had also once been a child, however, Paul could more easily deal with his fear of being in the 'child ego-state'. A nonassertive, female protagonist who felt she was a victim of male aggression seemed to present herself without emotional involvement. Only when reversing roles with her aggressor was she able to express her anger.

A radical and uncommon technique, employed with very resistant neurotic protagonists who do not respond to other devices, is to reverse roles with the psychodramatist who directs the session. Protagonists are thus confronted with the basic therapeutic contract: whether or not they want to continue the session. If they choose to continue, they then become active as their own therapists, which may provide important clues for the observing psychodramatist about possible ways to reach out to the protagonist. In such a session, the psychodramatist can either play the role of the protagonist or step out of the scene and designate an empty chair or an auxiliary to represent the protagonist. A situation in which direction is thus turned over to the protagonist is called 'auto-' or 'mono-drama'.

Maximizing

Resisting protagonists are often instructed to maximize their counter-actions, to exaggerate their blocks and to intensify their noninvolvement. In such instances, the psychodramatist controls the relationship by 'prescribing the symptom' in a paradoxical manner. For example, an intellectualizing protagonist may be instructed to use only intellectual talk for a specific period, or an overdramatic protagonist may be directed to maximize dramatic performance and exaggerate unauthentic behaviour. In maximizing the manner in which they act out their resistances, protagonists learn to claim responsibility for their actions, which subsequently enhances their ability to change. The idea behind this strategy is that those who can produce resistances at will are also able to remove them at will and the cure is thereby elicited in a manner that allows protagonist-initiated change.

Concretizing

Concretizing is used to make abstract resistances more tangible. Resistances which are manifested as tensions in the body, for example, by trembling in the hands, blocks in the chest or difficulty in breathing, may be physically concretized. Marilyn said that she could not participate because she did not like the leader. She felt that there was a wall between them. The wall, which symbolized Marilyn's resistances, was first concretized by group members who stood in a line between Marilyn and the leader and then by Marilyn herself. By being the wall and imagining herself in the role of her resistance, Marilyn could more easily understand what she was up against. As a wall she announced her functions: 'I am a barrier to Marilyn—she cannot cross me! But I am also protecting her against threat!' After this scene, Marilyn was able to talk about her simultaneous wish to be close to the leader and her fear of rejection by him, which she immediately connected to her feelings towards her father. Thus she was helped to deal with her feelings of resentment in a therapeutically useful manner.

Additional Techniques

When the interaction between protagonist and director becomes negative, Z.T. Moreno (1965) suggests that the psychodramatist ask the protagonist to designate another director or to choose another scene; the psychodramatist can also explain the rationale for the direction given, or leave the enactment, to return to it at a later time. Seabourne (1966) suggests a variety of approaches in dealing with her previously mentioned 'difficult' protagonists: constructing pleasant scenes, encouraging the protagonist to participate in many different stage experiences, letting the protagonist play all the roles in a particular situation, using fantasy material or confrontation scenes, allowing for group reactions or providing talking sessions with the psychodramatist before the session.

One may hold that the entire psychodramatic undertaking becomes a paradox in that its goal is spontaneity, which it is impossible to elicit by the power of will. Telling someone to be spontaneous is like telling a person in front of a camera to smile. It inhibits rather than releases authenticity. The photographer must say or do something that makes the person smile, if the smile is to be genuine. And the psychodramatist must likewise influence the protagonist indirectly, utilizing what Watzlawik, Weakland, and Fish (1974) called 'change of the second degree'. A protagonist who does not want to go up on stage may, for example, be told: 'When you go up on stage soon, you may either walk up slowly, so that you become aware of every step, or you may jump up, spring up, crawl up, or walk on your hands. Which way do you choose?' In this way, the going up itself is hidden among the given alternatives.

Therapeutic Strategy

The handling of resistances is the most difficult task in all therapeutic endeavours, testing the art of the therapist more than any other. Not only is it difficult to know what to do with a resisting protagonist, therapists often respond with negative feelings of their own when dealing with avoidance behaviour and hostility. Patients who are stuck or who progress slowly may evoke 'counter-resistance' in their therapists. In such situations, the interaction between patients and therapists may develop into a kind of battle—'a battle of wits' (Moreno & Enneis, 1950, p.2)—which includes manoeuvers initiated for the purpose of *winning*.

While some strategic psychotherapists still view therapeutic interactions in such terms, I believe that most practitioners of psychodrama hold that resistances are best resolved when the therapist does not oppose them.

I have found that if the psychodramatist forms an ad hoc alliance with the resistant force, he or she may succeed in redirecting it, giving it a progressive and growth-stimulating potential. Like a skier, you try to keep your knees loose, you bend, you go along with the turns and twists of the protagonist and, although stumbling on blocks, you just ride it out, going wherever the skis lead you, seeking the path of least resistance. 'By taking advantage of the aggressive feelings to which the patient is warmed up at the moment, a negative and resisting patient may be turned into a productive and clarifying agent' (Moreno & Moreno, 1959, p.97). Family therapists use the expression 'coupling' to describe this process in which the therapist joins the family system in order to change it from within. When entering the system and meeting the protagonists from within their own frame of reference, the psychodramatist estimates which resistances the protagonists can deal with and which should be avoided for the moment. In this empathic assessment of the personalities of protagonists, the psychodramatist tries to evaluate ego strength, anxiety tolerance, adaptive defensive capacity and general level of spontaneity, and to choose techniques accordingly.

Conclusion

In psychodrama, the therapist works along with resistance, so as to keep from being put in a counterposition and thereby endangering the working alliance and tele-relation. Pressuring protagonists to give up their resistances prematurely would lead to increased anxiety, diminished self-esteem and further repression of the protagonists' inner worlds. Instead, the psychodramatist must let 'the warming-up process proceed from the periphery to the center' (Z.T. Moreno, 1965) which is compatible with the recommendation of Blanck and Blanck (1979), that the therapist 'navigate with the wind and tide, making the best use of these to carry the patient a small distance beyond where he is' (p.224). Blatner (1973) conveys the same message: 'I find that if the director works *with* the resistances, there can often be a way found to gradually explore the deeper conflicts. Dr. Moreno puts it this way: "We don't tear down the protagonist's walls; rather, we simply try some of the handles on the many doors, and see which one opens"' (p.63).

CHAPTER 13

Closure

The earlier chapters of this book explored the therapeutic process of psychodrama from various points of view. What remains to be done in order to complete to picture is to add a study of 'closure,' the significant termination stage of psychodrama. Such a study summarizes, in a way, many of the therapeutic principles which have been previously discussed and translates them into action through the use of effective termination strategies.

Finis Corona Opus; the end crowns the production. The end of a successful psychodrama production often includes a suitable scene that terminates the drama in a fulfilling manner. This scene is the high point of the session, completing the action by providing a sense of closure for the protagonist and for the group.

Such a scene is generally described as a *closure scene* and is of special importance when conceptualizing the therapeutic process of psychodrama. But closure has been largely neglected in major textbooks and the termination of psychodrama is often an inadequately handled process. Although various other aspects, such as the warm-up process, have been discussed at length, comparatively little has been written about closure. As a result, our understanding of the closure aspect and of the termination phase of psychodrama remains rather limited.

The significance of closure was emphasized by Yalom (1975), who stated that 'termination is more than an act signifying the end of therapy; it is an integral part of the process of therapy and, if properly understood and managed, may be an important factor in the instigation of change' (p.365).

The purpose of this chapter is to define the closure concept in psychodrama and to discuss its therapeutic purposes. In addition, and in consideration of the technical challenge that closure presents to all psychodrama practitioners, some common closure scenes will be described briefly.

The Concept of Closure

The word closure is not an original psychodramatic concept and, as far as I know, it does not appear in any of Moreno's writings. 'Closure' may have entered the vocabulary of psychodrama from gestalt psychology or gestalt therapy. Within these fields it is used to describe the process in perception and personality organization wherein an integrated and whole gestalt is completed.

Currently, the word closure is used in psychodrama from two different points of view.

From the point of view of drama, closure puts a time-perspective on experience and is used simply to describe the final scene in a psychodrama. It is the stopping place of the action on stage, before the postaction sharing phase (Barbour, 1977). As such, closure is regarded as the grand finale, the culmination of a drama. It becomes a 'staging problem for the director, who attempts to end the drama in an aesthetically pleasing way' (Warner, 1975, p.9).

From the point of view of psychotherapy, closure is a kind of intrapsychic conclusion for the protagonist. As such, it represents the maturation of a healing process, the final station of a therapeutic journey, and the goal of a session, ideally giving a feeling of emotional relief and a sense of therapeutic progress. It is in this termination phase of psychodrama therapy that the definite work of resolution is anchored.

Such resolution is important not only for the protagonist, but also for the auxiliaries, the group, and the director. The auxiliaries may find closure in role feedback and de-roling. The group may find closure in identification and ventilation aspects of the sharing phase. And the director may also achieve closure after the session, during the processing phase of psychodrama.

Intrapsychic closure may occur not only during the action part of the session, but at any time after the session. Such closure implies that there is no absolute end to the therapeutic process as such. As one session leads to the other, it is misleading to speak of any definite intrapsychic conclusions. On the contrary, the protagonist will experience continued change after a successful psychodrama session and, it is hoped, continue to reintegrate new growth experiences all through life.

The principles of closure may be illustrated by the psychodrama of Paula. Paula was going to get married but felt uncomfortable with certain aspects of her relationship with her boyfriend. She had adopted a self-sufficient attitude toward him that led to an inability to ask him to take care of her in times of need. Tracing her feelings back to childhood revealed a number of similar situations in which Paula had become her own 'parent' during her mother's depressions. Remembering those situations from the past brought out a flood of pent-up feelings and revealed largely unsatisfied dependency needs from childhood. Having reached some emotional release (and with the awareness that she was reenacting an old script from the past), she was prepared to confront her boyfriend again, this time in a more mature and satisfying manner.

Here, Paula's psychodrama could have ended. But the director felt that there was a need to enact one last scene that would close the session in a more therapeutic fashion. The director suggested a closure scene in which each group member was instructed to 'be' Paula and to empathize with her original problem. Paula was then asked to be her own therapist and tell each of those doubles what to do to change the old role of being a strong and undemanding 'parent' in the future. In a role reversal after this enactment, Paula then listened as each group member repeated her earlier words to them. This scene closed the drama and the director invited the group to share with Paula.

Adding this closure scene to the others in Paula's psychodrama was important for several reasons. First, the closure scene initiated a therapeutic process that went beyond mere catharsis and insight as these were translated into behavioural action. Further, by exploring the possibilities for such actions in the future, the closure scene provoked a real-life confrontation for the protagonist to enact after the psychodrama and outside of the therapeutic setting. And, in taking on the role of her own therapist, Paula was faced with the final responsibility of deciding what to do in the future. Finally, by actively involving the other group members in Paula's problem, the scene facilitated sharing and helped Paula to return to the group.

Very little has been written about closure in the literature of psychodrama and role playing. Perhaps the best-known text is the paper on 'sum-up' by Weiner & Sacks (1969). Sum-up is a form of closure that recapitulates, in a succinct form, high points of a session. Barbour (1977) emphasizes the closure aspect involved in psychodramatic sharing. Another conceptualization of closure is presented by Levy (1969), who describes how people warm up to emotional and subjective involvement in role playing and how they later 'warm down' to a level of objectivity and noninvolvement. This kind of thinking is based on the simplified view of people who 'warm up' or 'open up' in the beginning of the session and who later 'cool down' or 'close down' at the end. This 'switch-on-switch-off' attitude towards feelings is, of course, erroneous and misleading and does not adequately describe human opening-and-closure patterns.

It is more productive to describe closure as the end of a therapeutic journey. Typically, classical psychodrama progresses through the various stages of warm-up, action, closure, and sharing as illustrated by, for example, a 'normal' curve (Hollander, 1969), a spiral (Goldman & Morrison, 1984), or a feeling cycle (Hart, Corriere, & Binder, 1975). Closure constitutes the termination phase of this process, rather than a sudden cessation of activity. 'Once the emotional peak has been achieved, the director should assist the protagonist in 'closing down' the drama. Rather than further exploration and disclosure, the protagonist is urged to concentrate upon closing the session and building integration into the psychodrama' (Hollander, 1969, p.5).

Another conceptualization of closure as a specific phase in the therapeutic process of psychodrama is given by Schramski (1979), who mentions the portion of role training that seems to be a kind of closure because it occurs after action but before sharing. Similarly, Petzold (1978) describes a behaviour modification closure phase that he calls 'new-orientation'; it is introduced after the diagnostic-anamnestic and the psycho-cathartic phases but occurs before the final feedback phase of psychodramatic sharing. A framework for structuring a psychodramatic production—the 'central concern model'—is presented by Buchanan (1980).

If we regard psychodrama in such process terms as a journey of mind through life, closure may be thought of either as a final destination, like arriving at the top of a mountain where the view is finally clear, or as returning to the starting point, completing a full circle. An example of the latter closure strategy is the re-enactment of the first scene at the end of the session. Such psychodramas often begin with one or more scenes from the here and now, proceed to scenes from the there and then, and finally return to a closure scene in the here and now. This strategy is in agreement with the recommendation of Z. T. Moreno (1965) that sessions should proceed 'from the periphery to the center,' and that a session should come 'full circle back to the present' (Goldman & Morrison, 1984, p.27).

When closure is absent or insufficient, the protagonist is left with an uncomfortable feeling of unrest. This feeling can be likened to the sense of suddenly waking up from the middle of some dramatic dream before its natural ending. In drama therapy, the lack of closure is manifested by the director who neglects to close the primal cathartic force of the drama; he or she walks away 'leaving potential Hamlets at the edge of their graves' (Landy, 1986, p.115). With regard to psychodrama, such a lack of closure calls for a continuation in a new session in which the protagonist is given sufficient time to finish the process and to reach action-completion.

At what point has closure been achieved? According to Warner (1975), 'closure has been achieved when there are not too many loose ends, and when both protagonist and group sense a completion, even though the final statement may specify unresolved tensions and future directions' (p.9).

Therapeutic Purposes of Closure Scenes

Closure scenes are used by directors for specific purposes. According to Goldman & Morrison (1984), one purpose of a closure scene is to conclude the psychodrama 'on a high note or some other positive possibility' (p.31). For Warner (1975), closure scenes prevent protagonists from being left 'high and dry' (p.9), helping them to regain emotional balance and control before leaving the psychodrama stage. According to Kipper (1986), the closing stage is expected to accomplish (1) deroling for the protagonist of the roles he or she has portrayed in the session; (2) restoration of the protagonist's emotional stability; (3) comfort from the recognition that problems are shared by others; (4) optimism and hope that problems can be solved; (5) enhancement of the protagonists' understanding of themselves; and (6) help for the protagonist in formulating future plans. Some of the other general purposes of closure scenes and termination strategies may be to (1) provide symbolic or real satisfaction; (2) neutralize regression and transference; (3) make separation a maturational event; (4) transform surplus reality into 'common' reality; (5) bring about a cognitive reorganization or re-evaluation of emotional experiences from the session; (6) provide behavioural learning for the future; (7) facilitate the return to the outer world of day-to-day responsibilities (from the regressive inner world); and (8) maximize the transfer of learning to situations outside therapy.

Happy Endings

A major controversy regarding closure is the use of so-called 'happy endings,' which are sometimes introduced in order to provide wish fulfilment at the end of the session. For example, Hollander (1969) pointed out that the final stages of psychodrama enactment require the inclusion of two principles, surplus reality and a purposeful positive ending: 'As the protagonist draws his session to a close, the director must aid the protagonist by introducing rehearsal for life situations, corrective alternatives, self-confrontation, or psychodramatic ego-re-pair endings. By doing this he encourages the protagonist to spontaneously evolve new creativity for his life without fear of reprisal or embarrassment. Psychodrama enactment is provided for creative and productive objectives. One ethic inherent in the methodology is the suppression of destructive behaviour. Therefore, no session may conclude with a destructive act such as suicide or murder, nor may it terminate in an artificial manner' (p.6). Other advocates of positive endings claim that they are helpful in evoking a sense of optimism and hope, giving protagonists a good feeling as they leave the stage, providing some light at the end of a dark tunnel. Critics, however, dispute these benefits or deny them completely. They claim that fantasized ideal closure scenes tend to distort reality by emphasizing only its positive aspects; they argue that without any fundamental growth process experienced by the protagonist, progress must be regarded as only superficial. Advocates of happy endings, while acknow-ledging the imaginary aspects of some closure scenes, assert that people need dreams to help them to cope with life, just as children (and some adults) find consolation in the classical happy endings of literature. Critics feel that such endings deceive the protagonist into accepting illusions rather than coping with reality.

It is my feeling that a 'happy' closure scene may have its therapeutic value as well as its aesthetic charm, especially by demonstrating how conflicts may be successfully resolved and thus arousing hope for the future. However, I do not think that all sessions must be terminated on an optimistic tone. Some psychodramas that end like fairy tales, with the protagonist hero riding off into the sunset after a 'perfect victory,' giving the illusion of living happily ever after, are deceptive if there has been no significant working through of conflicts. It may be more productive in such cases to introduce a closure scene in which the

protagonist recognizes unresolved conflicts, faces difficult situations, or antici-
pates an uncertain future. Such closure scenes are open-ended, signifying that
life itself is open to unforeseen occurrences and that there are no guarantees of
future happiness. This thinking assumes that there are no perfect psychodrama
sessions, only more or less honest and human ones.

Thus, while we may be susceptible at times to the fantasy quest for a
'complete cure,' we must agree with Freud (1937), that psychotherapy is 'interminable;' that it can never resolve all problems, remove all symptoms, or result
in full self-actualization. At best it is preparatory; a place where we switch trains
in order to continue on our journey.

Examples of Closure Scenes in Psychodrama

Closure scenes that are productive for one protagonist may be useless for
another; each protagonist needs to conclude in a most personal manner according to the specific therapeutic journey he or she has embarked upon. Closure
should be consistent with the nature of the therapeutic focus and goals of the
session. Sarah ended her psychodrama with a joyful, spontaneous dance. Jill's
closure was explosive; she put an end to her alcoholism by smashing bottles and
throwing them away. Paul ended his psychodrama sitting in the lap of an
auxiliary who was enacting the role of his ideal father. Li gave a speech to the
group, asserting her own right to chose what to do with her life. Tom went
around the group asking how people felt about him after he had revealed his
secret.

Achieving suitable personal closure scenes demands an understanding not
only of the psychological apparatus of the individual protagonist, but also of
the specific healing experiences that each person requires in order to make
progress. Some protagonists require symbolic need fulfillment, others forgiveness from guilt, concrete suggestions for the future, or new experiences that
plant seeds of trust and hope. Finding such appropriate closure scenes is a major
challenge for every director of psychodrama.

Ideally, closure scenes evolve naturally from the drama and are initiated by
the protagonists themselves. If this does not happen, the director may suggest
a closure scene based on earlier experience and clues from the current drama.
Common closure scenes found in the literature (Z.T. Moreno, 1965; Weiner &
Sacks, 1969; Blatner, 1973; Warner, 1975; Treadwell, Stein & Kumar, 1990) and in
my own experience lend themselves to the following categorizations:

> Action Completion. The protagonist is encouraged to complete his or her
> fantasies; to do what was left undone and to undo what was done wrong.

> Audience Analyst. A group member sums up reactions from the audience
> about a psychodrama.

Award Experience. The protagonist is given an award and is asked to give a 'thank-you' speech to the group.

Concretization. A closure scene is constructed in which 'all threads of a session come together' (Goldman & Morrison, 1984) p.31) thereby making a situation concrete and tangible.

Conflict Solving. A scene is enacted in which a balance is found between at least two inner tendencies that are in conflict with one another.

Correction. A corrective scene is enacted in which, for example, crime or injustice is admitted and forgiven.

Epilogue. Retrospective analysis of the past in light of how things actually turned out.

Final Dialogue. The protagonist has a final talk with a significant person from his or her life.

Future Work. The protagonist plans for future sessions, for example, with the help of empty chairs, each signifying an unresolved problem. Another variety of this closure is to plan and give homework assignments to be done by the protagonist after the session.

Future Projection. A continuation of life is anticipated. One example would be the enactment of an imagined situation 10 years from now.

Goal Setting. The protagonist is urged to be specific about at least some plans for the future and to generalize learning from the session to outside life, for example by making a contract to use some skills after the psycho-drama session.

Grand Finale. The protagonist finally renounces, forgives, or gives a clear statement 'on stage' to a large group of significant others.

Group Choice. Various endings suggested by the group.

Happy Endings. A scene is enacted that presents a situation of wish fulfil-ment, love, or triumphant victory.

Leave-Taking Ritual. The protagonist is instructed to separate from an important person with the help of a ritual. One example of such a ritual, described by Hart (1983), is writing farewell letters and then burning them.

Open Endings. The drama is deliberately left uncompleted in order to provoke future action and continued working through after the session. Like a book with chapters to fill, open-ended psychodramas emphasize how life proceeds through continuous experiences and cycles that go beyond any single phase and therefore never reach a final end point.

Recovery Room. Having undergone 'deep surgery of an emotional nature' (Z.T. Moreno, 1990, p.43), the protagonist is put in a recovery room where he or she gets tender, loving, and individualized care until regaining balance.

Reenactment. The protagonist reenacts the first or any other important scene from the psychodrama in a new or different way.

Relaxation. Protagonist and group members are given a moment of physical relaxation with suitable music at the end of the session.

Re-parenting. The protagonist is exposed to group members who enact the roles of good parents who hold and take care of him or her in a new way, thus providing a corrective emotional experience.

Role Training. The protagonist learns how to enact various roles and how to behave in difficult situations.

Rituals. The group performs a ritual, for example standing together in a circle and holding hands to join in spiritual union with the protagonist.

Separation. The protagonist separates from a person or from a group as a whole for the purpose of individuation. 'The closure of separation,' according to Kempler (1973) 'acknowledges the pain of separation as it simultaneously tastes the glory of separateness' (p.95).

Sum Up. Director and protagonist recapitulate the process and the scenes from the psychodrama or give a summary of what has taken place.

Support. Each person in the group tells the protagonist something he or she likes about the protagonist.

Surplus Reality. A fantasy scene is enacted to express symbolic material, for example, the voice of God declaring that everything will be all right.

Symphony. The group produces an orchestration of the social atom; a musical improvisation of the relations between people.

Take a Picture. An actual or imagined picture is taken of the final scene.

Thanksgiving Gift. The protagonist gives a symbolic or real parting gift to the group members or receives a gift from them.

While the scenes mentioned above may help describe common termination strategies and universal patterns of closure, they cannot substitute for the creative use of specific endings for each individual psychodrama. The success of a psychodramatic endeavour depends in large part on the artistic flexibility of the director. Any mechanization of technique leading to predictable closures, therefore, is entirely out of place.

Conclusion: Beyond Closure

Consummatum est. La commedia e finita.

The psychodrama is done, finished, and over; actions are completed; tears are shed; wounds are healed; and the past is a part of forever. Another cycle of life is closed. However, while closure terminates the therapeutic journey on stage, it should not be regarded as an absolute end. In the words of Merlyn Pitzele (personal communication, 1987), 'Strictly speaking there is no such thing as closure save death. What we want is transition in which we hold on to what we have been through but get on with our lives.' In the final analysis, the ultimate purpose of closure in psychodrama is to extend the drama beyond its natural end and induce a transition to a new beginning. At the cross-road of closure, the protagonist reflects upon what happened in the past, recognizes what exists in the present and looks toward the uncertain future that awaits. If properly understood and managed, psychodramatic closure conveys the truism that even as something ends, it begins again and again and again. That's about the only thing we can be sure of.

CHAPTER 14

Processing

Psychodrama training sessions are usually followed by didactic conferences in which the performance of the psychodrama director is evaluated and the therapeutic process of the session is analyzed. Such a didactic conference is called process-analysis, or simply 'processing,' connoting the systematic investigation of the developing process in psychodrama. The main purpose of processing is to improve the professional skills of students in training.

The procedure of processing in psychodrama is unique among psychotherapy training and supervision methods for several reasons. First, it is based on direct, in vivo observation by the trainer of the trainee and not on second-hand reports or audio/video recordings. Second, clients are invited to participate in the supervision session and listen to the feedback given to the student director. Third, new skills may be taught and practiced with experiential action-methods in addition to verbal descriptions.

In spite of these original features of training, psychodramatic processing has not received sufficient attention in literature. The purpose of the present chapter is to describe the basic procedure of processing in psychodrama and to discuss some of its problematic components. In addition, a processing checklist is included as a systematic aid in evaluating the professional skills of psychodrama directors.

The Procedure of Processing

The processing phase should be clearly separated from the sharing phase. Although both phases constitute a kind of 'echo' from the group members of what they experienced during the session, each has different objectives and focuses on different participants. Sharing, with its focus on universality and existential validation, encourages identification with the protagonist in a personal, emotionally involved manner. Processing, on the other hand, focuses on learning and understanding, encouraging analysis and evaluation of the student director in a more detached and intellectual manner. While sharing continues the personal growth process of the session, processing introduces a normative dimension which is often in striking contrast to the earlier accepting climate.

For this reason, processing should not be conducted immediately after the sharing phase, but rather following at least a short intermission. The duration of this pause varies according to the time it takes for the participants to detach themselves emotionally from the session. Moreover, enough time must have elapsed after the session for the trainee to have reconstructed the psychodrama and prepared a comprehensive self-evaluation. If too much time has elapsed between the session and the processing, however, significant material may have been forgotten and the subsequent discussion will lack energy.

Processing typically includes the person who was the protagonist in the session, the trainee (or student director) who directed the psychodrama, the auxiliaries, the group members (or fellow students), and the trainer (or teaching director) who was a participant observer in the session. All take turns in giving their comments during the processing phase.

First, the protagonist—the leading person in the drama—gives his or her view of the session and of the director. The protagonist is not expected to evaluate the psychodrama from the point of view of its therapeutic effect. Rather, he or she is encouraged to comment on the central issues presented, on crucial scenes and encounters with significant people, and on the kind of interpersonal relationships which evolved during the action. This is an excellent opportunity for the protagonist to integrate material from the session and to achieve further closure.

Second, the student director—the 'second protagonist'—evaluates his or her own work. This can be done through an exploration of the basic theme, the sequence of scenes, the techniques employed, the choice points and perceived clues, and/or the rationale for the direction. At this time, suggestions as to what could have been done differently may be verbalized. Goldman & Morrison (1984) found that the degree to which students are able to evaluate their own skills reflects their ability to understand the psychodramatic process; 'when the neophyte director is aware of the missed cue or mistake before being told, he/she is less likely to repeat that error' (p.95).

Third, participants who were auxiliaries in the session give their feedback, not only from the point of view of the roles they played (role-feedback), but also as assistant therapists who were actively involved in the work and who may contribute valuable 'inside information' about the session.

Fourth, group members in training are invited to evaluate the session. They may mention what they liked and disliked or what they would have done differently had they been directing, or ask specific questions about the direction. In an attempt to improve the efficiency of processing, Goldman & Morrison (1984) suggested that no one repeat a comment already made, that comments be specific to a scene and/or a particular dynamic aspect, and that students ask and attempt to answer their questions themselves in a Socratic fashion.

Finally, the trainer gives a general appraisal of the session in a straightforward yet sensitive manner, offering additional general comments on the points of view already mentioned. Basing these comments on careful observation and recording of director performance, the trainer attempts to exemplify each general point with specific material from the session.

I have preferred not to call psychodrama trainers 'supervisors' because, as far as I can see, they do not oversee or inspect the work of students. Neither are they watching the action 'from above' with 'super-vision.' Trainers should rather be viewed as facilitators, educators and participating colleagues who share an experience with the group. Their main task is to help students in training to develop a professional identity by teaching empathic/analytic, therapeutic, staging and group leadership skills (as explained in Chapter 3).

Some trainers feel that their task is accomplished when they have given a verbal summary of their findings and identified problematic points and issues. Others attempt to translate their findings into training recommendations and to use some of the processing time for systematic teaching. Such teaching may include specially adapted training exercises and training tips (Warner, 1975), instruction in co-directing methods (Goldman, Morrison, & Schramski, 1982), or experiential re-enactments and role-playing demonstrations suitable for the students in this phase of their professional development (Emunah, 1989; Shalit, 1990). In addition, trainers may encourage students to conceptualize the psychodramatic process in terms of various theoretical models, such as those presented by Goldman & Morrison (1984), Hale (1974), Hollander (1969), and/or Schramski (1979). According to Kempler (1973), 'The art of processing is not some clever invention of men's minds, but rather a re-minding, a realization, a bringing into consciousness of the mind's own inherent mechanism for orienting Man in his earthbound existence' (p.61).

Psychodramatic processing is similar to the Open Live Supervision used for training family therapists (Olson & Pegg, 1979). In this kind of supervision, supervisor and trainees are present together with the therapist and the family creating a complex system of relations which influences the entire process.

Problematic Issues in Processing
Psychodramatic processing creates a complex situation which may at times be difficult to manage. Four specific problematic issues are common.

1. Focus
One basic problem is caused by the variety of contradictory goals and feelings which participants seem to experience when processing. For example, protagonists want to be unconditionally accepted and are often curious of what people think about them after their psychodrama. They are also sensitive to criticism of their director and tend to defend his or her work.

According to Zerka Moreno (personal communication), 'I've known protagonists to throw their arm around a director whom they feel has helped them and say: 'But he/she did such a fine job with me!' That's good, but of course I've had to explain that this is a teaching process as well as what has been a therapeutic process.' Correspondingly, student directors frequently feel protective of their protagonists and somewhat defensive about their own work. Auxiliaries search for recognition and appreciation. Some group members are impatient with the group for being engaged in such 'head trips' for too long. Others identify with the student director and emphasize only positive aspects of the direction. And trainers frequently feel frustrated for not being able to teach. These contradictory goals and feelings make it difficult for the training group to decide upon a common focus. Some would prefer to focus on the student director, others on the protagonist or on the group-as-a-whole. This leaves us with three variations of processing which may function separately or in combination with one another: (1) director-centred processing which focuses on the student director; (2) protagonist-centred processing which focuses on the protagonist; and (3) group-centred processing which focuses on the group-as-a-whole.

If the purpose of processing is to teach psychodrama and not to do psychotherapy or group dynamics, it is my position that processing should focus on the student director. This includes the director's analysis of protagonist and group, but excludes working through for the protagonist and for the group of what is verbalized. While every protagonist may benefit from additional re-examination and re-integration of the issues raised in a previous psychodrama, this should not be done during processing, but rather during later sessions. By the same token, the conflicts which tend to inhibit a group's development may be worked on during specially scheduled group exploration sessions, but not during processing.

2. Professional skills or personality

A second difficulty in processing concerns the amount of personal versus technical feedback to be given to the trainee.

It is my experience that processing becomes a more constructive learning experience when feedback is generally restricted to professional skills and methodological issues, which tend to be easier to assimilate nondefensively and may be shared by the whole group. Individual difficulties of a personal nature, such as character traits, blind spots, unresolved counter-transference issues, etc., which surely affect the work of any director, can be mentioned in processing, but should be worked through later in a psychodrama session or in individual psychotherapy/supervision.

3. Protagonist presence

A third difficulty is the presence of the protagonist in processing. When student directors explain a rationale for their direction, they cannot refrain from analyzing the personality of the protagonist (normally an inappropriate activity in psychodrama groups). When listening to this analysis, the protagonist either agrees or disagrees with the director. If he or she agrees, it may be a valuable opportunity for integrative insight; if the protagonist disagrees, it may evoke defensive processes and erase some of the therapeutic gain made in the psychodrama. Analysis is especially inapt in such sessions, since to talk about the protagonist in the third person, as if he or she were not present, would be highly inappropriate within a Morenean framework of open encounter.

Extensive discussion of protagonist personality serves the single purpose of teaching personality theory. It may have nothing to do with the protagonist and should therefore be kept to a minimum if the protagonist is present. Various contributions from other group members to such a discussion should also be discouraged in order not to transform the processing session into an analysis by the group of one individual, or, if matters get more personal, into a sociometric exploration of interpersonal relations.

If there is a didactic need to discuss the personality characteristics of the protagonist, this should be done in the absence of the protagonist and with the pronounced aim of improving the analytical knowledge of the students.

4. Trainer Type

A fourth general difficulty with processing concerns the educating style of the trainer. There are two extreme types of trainers: the supportive and the critical.

Supportive trainers give mostly positive feedback, emphasizing the strong sides of each student's work, providing a climate of unconditional acceptance. They formulate their comments carefully, for example communicating criticism in terms of possible other ways of directing, so as not to hurt the ego of the student and create a need for defensiveness. Such trainers develop a sense of confidence and safety among their students, but because their requirements seem relatively easy to satisfy, their views become less important with time.

Critical trainers are more difficult to satisfy. They give mostly negative feedback, confronting students with mistakes and weaknesses in an inconsiderate manner. These trainers argue that external evaluation is essential for any learning process and believe that straightforward and honest criticism is the best way to learn the skills required for psychodrama. Depending on the response of students, these trainers tend to become authority figures arousing either admiration or rebellion.

In order to make processing a truly educational event, trainers are advised either to take on a double role or work together with someone who can take on the complementary role. Students need both the protection and 'mothering' of the supportive trainer and the confrontation and 'fathering' of the critical one. Alone, neither is complete. Students will benefit from exposure to both support and confrontation, praise and criticism. Both these elements are necessary to push or pull them a step further in their professional development.

Systematic methods of processing

Various methods of observation and recording of psychodrama sessions have been employed as the basis for processing. Typically, teachers observe sessions in an unsystematic fashion, taking notes of what they feel is important and raising questions and comments as they arise during the process. However, some training programs have introduced more systematic methods of observation and recording, such as evaluation sheets which focus on specific elements, role diagrams of the psychodramatist (Frick, 1985), dramaturgical analysis (Hare, 1976) or processing checklists which describe observed phenomena in terms of specific categories.

As psychodrama develops into a more structured method of psychotherapy, the need for such systematic evaluation tools is increasing. Provided that such tools are not used as mechanical devices and that they do not impair the creativity of the director, it is my experience that they are valuable as didactic aids in psychodrama training programs. Moreover, they may help us develop the common framework needed to build standardized criteria for certification.

A simple tool for evaluating the professional performance of psychodrama directors may be found in the 'Psychodrama Director Processing Checklist,' which is presented in Appendix 1. This 100-item checklist can be used as a questionnaire for appropriate psychodramatist performance, as a guideline for observation for group members, as a self-evaluation instrument for the director, as a list of topics to be discussed in processing, or as standardized criteria for examination of candidates.

Most of the questions originated in actual processing sessions with my own teachers, Zerka Moreno and Merlyn Pitzele. The rest arose from the teaching of other psychodramatists, from the literature (Blatner, 1968; Kelly, 1977;) from various training and standard manuals (American Board of Examiners, 1989; Australian and New Zealand Psychodrama Association, 1989), and from my own students-in-training.

When tried out in a number of training groups and in the examination of psychodramatists in Scandinavia and in Israel, the processing checklist was a useful and stimulating aid in the evaluation process. Systematic methods of processesing, such as the checklist presented here, may help us clarify what we want to know but forgot to ask. Although long and time-consuming and in spite of the lack of experimental data on validity, it was largely appreciated by students and teachers and helped improve the didactic effectiveness of processing.

Conclusion

Psychodramatic processing is based on an alternative educational concept which reflects a considerable extension of the educational concept used in classical psychotherapy supervision. The fact that feedback is given in a setting which includes all participants—client, student, trainer and group—creates both potential benefits and potential hazards. If the difficulties in management are resolved, processing may provide an opportunity for a profound learning experience, helping to make sense of the complex processes activated in psychodrama.

Psychodrama Director Processing Checklist

For each item, circle one of the following:
(Y) = Yes (correct performance)
(N) = No (incorrect performance), or
(?) = Don't know (inadequate information or questionable performance).

A. WARM-UP

1. Was the director able to stimulate individual group members sufficiently and warm them up to action? Y N ?
2. Was the director able to build sufficient cohesion and a constructive working climate in the group? Y N ?
3. Was the type of warm-up exercise/s appropriately chosen? Y N ?
4. Were the instructions to warm-up exercise/s sufficiently clear? Y N ?
5. Was there adequate follow up to warm-up exercise/s? Y N ?
6. Was the director able to help the group develop a specific theme upon which to focus? Y N ?
7. Did the director consider group dynamic aspects and sociometry sufficiently at the beginning of the session? Y N ?
8. Was the director sufficiently warmed up to directing? Y N ?

B. SELECTING THE PROTAGONIST

9. Was the protagonist selected in a suitable manner? Y N ?
10. Were other potential protagonists considered and taken care of? Y N ?

C. TREATMENT CONTRACT (action-preparation)

11. Were overall time-boundaries of the session taken into consideration sufficiently before the session? Y N ?
12. Was the stage, or action-space, prepared sufficiently? Y N ?
13. Was a therapeutic alliance (tele) established? Y N ?
14. Was a treatment contract sufficiently negotiated? Y N ?

15. Was the protagonist assisted in the transition from
audience to drama in a manner which developed the
warm-up process?   Y N ?

D. INTERVIEWING (focusing)

16. Was the protagonist interviewed adequately with respect
to time—not too long or too short?   Y N ?
17. Was a basic theme or focal issue identified correctly?   Y N ?
18. Was the protagonist given sufficient freedom to select the
focus of exploration?   Y N ?
19. Were other concerns adequately identified?   Y N ?
20. Were non-verbal messages of the protagonist identified?   Y N ?
21. Were anamnestic, symptomatic, and/or other essential
clinical information sufficiently gathered?   Y N ?

Action Phase :

E. SCENE-SETTING

22. Was the first scene chosen properly in terms of protagonist
warm-up and relevance to the focal issue?   Y N ?
23. Were subsequent scenes chosen properly?   Y N ?
24. Were the scenes sufficiently 'anchored' in time (when)?   Y N ?
25. Were the scenes sufficiently 'anchored' in place (where)?   Y N ?
26. Were symbolic scenes, representing the imaginary world of
symbols and dreams, properly staged?   Y N ?
27. Was the director able to capture the overall atmosphere of
location properly, so as to arouse the group's imagination?   Y N ?
28. Were light and sound used properly to enhance atmosphere?   Y N ?
29. Were relevant (and/or significant) objects used correctly?   Y N ?
30. Were transitions between scenes correctly handled?   Y N ?
31. Could the group hear and see the action sufficiently?   Y N ?
32. Was the stage properly 'set' for action (taking into
consideration the positioning of walls and furniture,
for example)?   Y N ?
33. Was the stage adequately 'cleared' between scenes?   Y N ?
34. Were relevant clues adequately picked up?   Y N ?

F. PUTTING AUXILIARIES INTO ROLE

35. Were the auxiliaries chosen properly?   Y N ?
36. Were the auxiliaries put into role properly, receiving
sufficient instructions on their role performance?   Y N ?
37. Were the auxiliaries optimally mobilized to function as
extensions of the director and protagonist?   Y N ?
38. Were dysfunctional auxiliaries tactfully dismissed?   Y N ?

39. Were auxiliaries sufficiently protected against physical
harm?   Y N ?

G. ENACTMENT

Beginning.

40. Was the director able to perceive important clues, identify
the central issues, and translate them into action?   Y N ?
41. Was the protagonist instructed to act in the here-and-now?   Y N ?
42. Was the protagonist instructed to 'show' the group what
happened rather than talk about it?   Y N ?
43.Were resistances properly identified, concretized and worked
through before and during the action?   Y N ?
44.Was reality enacted before surplus reality (affirmation before
correction)?   Y N ?
45. Were the various time dimensions; past, present, and
future, properly differentiated?   Y N ?
46. Were the various reality dimensions; subjective, objective
and surplus reality, properly differentiated?   Y N ?
47. Was the protagonist helped to make a transition from the
world of experience to the world of representation?   Y N ?

Middle.

48. Did the sequence of events and scenes move logically?   Y N ?
49. Was the technique of role reversal used correctly?   Y N ?
50. Was the technique of doubling used correctly?   Y N ?
51. Was the technique of mirroring used correctly?   Y N ?
52. Was the technique of soliloquy used correctly?   Y N ?
53. Were other techniques and adjunctive methods, such as
dream work, axiodrama, bibliodrama, playback theatre,
living newspaper, magic shop, hypnodrama and role
training used correctly?   Y N ?
54. Did the session move from the periphery to the center?   Y N ?
55. Was the physical contact between director and protagonist
adequate?   Y N ?
56. Was the tempo of the director the same as, or in tune with,
that of the protagonist?   Y N ?
57. Were abstractions concretized correctly?   Y N ?
58. Were expressions maximized correctly in accordance with
the need of the protagonist?   Y N ?
59. Was catharsis allowed to emerge spontaneously in its own
time   Y N ?
60. Was catharsis allowed to be fully expressed?   Y N ?

61. Was the protagonist encouraged to complete his or her
    actions and given the opportunity to 'un-do' and to 'do
    again'?   Y N ?
62. Were insights correctly induced?   Y N ?
63. Were new behaviours suggested and trained correctly?   Y N ?
64. Was the involvement of the group taken into consideration,
    and did the director maintain contact with the group,
    during the session?   Y N ?
65. Was the protagonist sufficiently protected against physical
    harm?   Y N ?

End.
66. Was the psychodrama allowed to evolve 'by itself' without
    a pre-fixed strategy or a 'script'?   Y N ?
67. Did action end in reality?   Y N ?
68. Did action end in here-and-now?   Y N ?
69. Was the protagonist in his/her own role at the end of action? Y N ?
70. Were adequate suggestions from the group encouraged?   Y N ?

H. CLOSURE
71. Was sufficient closure provided at the end of the session? Y N ?
72. Did the director assist the protagonist in integrating
    material from the session?   Y N ?
73. Were hints for further exploration proposed?   Y N ?
74. Did the director encourage constructive feedback and/or
    alternative solutions from the group?   Y N ?
75. Was the protagonist sufficiently helped to re-enter the group
    after the session?   Y N ?

I. SHARING
76. Was the protagonist's need for 'recovery time' satisfied? Y N ?
77. Was the audience allowed its catharsis of integration in the
    sharing portion of the drama?   Y N ?
78. Was de-roling of the auxiliaries encouraged?   Y N ?
79. Was role-feedback encouraged?   Y N ?
80. Was the group allowed to respond honestly?   Y N ?
81. Was the director able to protect the protagonist from well-
    meaning advice and interpretations?   Y N ?
82. Did the director share with the group?   Y N ?

J. PROCESSING
83. Was the director willing to ask for help when stuck or in
    need of assistance?   Y N ?

84. Was there a clear rationale, a theoretical assumption, or a working hypothesis behind the direction?   Y N ?
85. Was the director able to provide a sound evaluation of his or her own work?   Y N ?

K. GENERAL

86. Were instructions and interventions verbalized clearly?·   Y N ?
87. Were transference issues properly handled?   Y N ?
88. Were countertransference issues properly handled?   Y N ?
89. Did the director practice according to the code of ethics; (responsibility, moral standards, confidentiality, client welfare, public statements, client relationships, etc.)?   Y N ?
90. Did the director seem to 'understand' the protagonist (empathic ability)?   Y N ?
91. Was the director able to hear correctly what was said?   Y N ?
92. Was the director able to identify emotionally with the protagonist?   Y N ?
93. Was the director able to comprehend the underlying messages which were communicated by the protagonist?   Y N ?
94. Was the director able to report back to the protagonist, at the right moment, what was understood? (timing)   Y N ?
95. Was the director able to verify his or her understanding and correct it if mistaken?   Y N ?
96. Did the director find the proper balance between support and confrontation?   Y N ?
97. Did the director function well in the role of group leader? (establish group norms, build cohesion, encourage active participation by all members, and facilitate interaction)?   Y N ?
98. Did the director find the proper balance between leading and following (working together)?   Y N ?
99. Did the director function well in the role of therapist (influencing, healing, changing)?   Y N ?
100. Did the director seem to trust the potential power of the psychodramatic method?   Y N ?

References

Abt, L., & Weissman, S. (Eds.) (1965). *Acting Out: Theoretical and Clinical Aspects*. New York: Grune & Stratton.

Adler, A. (1930). Individual Psychology. In C. Murchison (Ed.), *Psychologies of 1930*. Worcester, Mass.: Clark University Press.

Adler, A. (1963). *The Practice and Theory of Individual Psychology*. Paterson, N.J.: Littlefield Adams.

Adorno, T.W., Frenkel-Brunswik, E., Levinson, D.J., & Sanford, R.N. (1950). *The Authoritarian Personality*. New York: Norton.

Aguilar, J., & Wood, V.N. (1976). Therapy Through Death Ritual. *Social Work*, 21, 49–54.

Ahsen, A. (1968). *Basic Concepts in Eidetic Psychotherapy*. New York: Brandon House.

Ahsen, A. (1984). Imagery, Drama and Transformation. *Journal of Mental Imagery*, 8, 53–78.

Alexander, F., & French, T. (1946). *Psychoanalytic Therapy*. New York: Ronald Press.

American Board of Examiners in Psychodrama, Sociometry and Group Psychotherapy, (1989). *Practitioner Evaluation Form*.

Anzieu, D. (1960). Aspects of Analytical Psychodrama applied to Children. *International Journal of Sociometry*, 2, 42–47.

Appelbaum, S.A. (1988). Psychoanalytic Therapy: A Subset of Healing. *Psychotherapy*, 25, 201–208.

Aristotle (1941). *The Basic Works of Aristotle*. New York: Random House.

Assagioli, R. (1973). *The Act of Will*. London: Wildwood House.

Aulicino, J. (1954). Critique of Moreno's Spontaneity Theory. *Group Psychotherapy*, 7, 148–158.

Australian and New Zealand Psychodrama Association, Inc. (1989). Board of Examiners; *Training and Standards Manual*.

Bales, R.F., & Cohen, E. (1979). *SYMLOG: a System for Multiple Level Observation of Groups*. New York: McMillan, Free Press.

Bandler, R., & Grinder, J. (1975). *The Structure of Magic: 1.* Palo Alto: Science & Behavior Books.

Bandler, R., & Grinder, J. (1979). Frogs into Princes. *Neurolinguistic Programming*. Moab, Utah: Real People Press.

Bandura, A. (1971). *Social Learning Theory*. Englewood Cliffs, N.J.: Prentice-Hall.

Bandura, A. (1977). Self-efficacy: Toward a Unified Theory of Behavioral Change. *Psychological Review*, 84, 191–215.

Bandura, A., & Walters, R.H. (1965). *Social Learning and Personality Development*. New York: Holt, Rinehart & Winston.

Barbour, A. (1977). Variations on Psychodramatic Sharing. *Group Psychotherapy, Psychodrama & Sociometry*, 30, 122–126.

Bateson, G. (1972). *Steps in the Ecology of Mind*. New York: Ballantine.

Bellak, L., Hurvich, H., & Gediman, H.K. (1973). *Ego Functions in Schizophrenics, Neurotics, and Normals*. New York: Wiley.

Bentley, E. (1967). Theatre and Therapy. In W. Anderson (Ed.), *Therapy and the Arts: Tools of Consciousness*. New York: Harper & Row.

Bergson, H. (1928). *L'evolution Creatrice*. Paris.

Berkowitz, L., Green, J.A., & Macanlay, J.R. (1962). Hostility Catharsis as the Reduction of Emotional Tension. *Psychiatry*, 25, 23–31.

Berman, E. (1982). Authority and Authoritarianism in Group Psychotherapy. *International Journal of Group Psychotherapy*, 32, 189–200.

Berzon, B., Pious, C., & Parson, R. (1963). The Therapeutic Event in Group Psychotherapy: A Study of Subjective Reports by Group Members. *Journal of Individual Psychology*, 19, 204–212.

Bibring, E. (1954). Psychoanalysis and the Dynamic Psychotherapies. *Journal of the American Psychoanalytic Association*. 2, 745–770.

Binstock, W.A. (1973). Purgation Through Pity and Terror. *International Journal of Psychoanalysis*, 54, 499–504.

Bion, W.R. (1961). *Experiences in Groups*. London: Tavistock Publications.

Bischof, L.J. (1964). *Interpreting Personality Theories*. New York: Harper & Row. (2nd edition 1970)

Blanck, G., & Blanck, R. (1974). *Ego Psychology (Vol 1)*. New York: Columbia University Press.

Blanck, G., & Blanck, R. (1979). *Ego Psychology (Vol 2)*. New York: Columbia University Press.

Blatner, H.A. (Ed.) (1966). *Psychodrama, Role Playing and Action Methods; A syllabus*. Thetford, England: Author. (2nd edition 1968).

Blatner, H.A. (1968). Pitfalls In Directing. In: H.A. Blatner, (Ed.), *Psychodrama, Role-playing and Action Methods; A syllabus*. Thetford, England: Author, (pp.71–74).

Blatner, H.A. (Ed.) (1970). *Practical Aspects of Psychodrama*. Belmont, California: Author,

Blatner, H.A. (1973). *Acting-In: Practical Applications of Psychodramatic Methods*. New York: Springer.

Blatner, H.A.(1985). The Dynamics of Catharsis. *Journal of Group Psychotherapy, Psychodrama & Sociometry*, 37, 157–166.

Blatner, A., & Blatner, A. (1988). *Foundations of Psychodrama: History, Theory & Practice*. New York: Springer. (3rd edition)

Bloch, S., & Crouch, E. (1985). *Therapeutic Factors in Group Psychotherapy*. Oxford: Oxford University Press.

Boesky, D. (1982). Acting Out: A Reconsideration on the Concept. *International Journal of Psychoanalysis*, 63, 39–55.

Bohart, A.C. (1980). Toward a Cognitive Theory of Catharsis. *Psychotherapy: Theory, Research & Practice*, 17, 192–201.

Bohart A.C., & Wugalter, S. (1991). Change in Experiental Knowing as a Common Dimension in Psychotherapy. *Journal of Integrative and Eclectic Psychotherapy*, 10, 14–37.

Bonilla, E.S. (1969). Spiritualism and Psychodrama. *Group Psychotherapy*, 22, 65–71.

Boria, G. (1989). Conceptual Clarity in Psychodrama Training. *Journal of Group Psychotherapy, Psychodrama & Sociometry*, 42, 166–172.

Bowers, W., Gaurone, E. & Mines, R. (1984). Training of Group Psychotherapists: An Evaluation Procedure. *Small Group Behavior*, 15, 125–137.

Breuer, J., & Freud, S. (1893). *Studies on Hysteria*. Standard Edition, Vol. 2, London: Hogarth Press.

Bromberg, W. (1958). Acting and Acting Out. *American Journal of Psychotherapy*, 12, 264–268.

Buber, M. (1923). *Ich und Du*. (English translation: *I and Thou*. New York: Scribner, 1937).

Buchanan, D.R. (1980). The Central Concern Model. A Framework for Structuring Psychodramatic Production. *Journal of Group Psychotherapy, Psychodrama & Sociometry*, 33, 47–62.

Buchanan, D.R., & Little, D. (1983). Neuro-Linguistic Programming and Psychodrama: Theoretical and Clinical Similarities. *Journal of Group Psychotherapy, Psychodrama & Sociometry*, 36, 114–122.

Buchanan, D.R., & Taylor, J.A. (1986). Jungian Typology of Professional Psychodramatists: Myers-Briggs Type Indicator Analysis of Certified Psychodramatists. *Psychological Reports*, 58, 391–400.

Buer, F. (Ed.) (1989). *Morenos Therapeutische Philosophie*. Opladen: Leske & Budrich.

Buhler, C. (1979). Humanistic Psychology. *Journal of Humanistic Psychology*, 19, 5–22.

Butcher, J., & Koss, M. (1978). Research on Brief and Crises-oriented Therapies. In. S. Garfield & A. Bergin (Eds.), *Handbook of Psychotherapy and Behavior Change (2nd ed.)*. New York: Wiley.

Butler, T., & Fuhriman, A. (1980). Patient Perspective on the Curative Process: A comparison of day treatment and outpatient psychotherapy groups. *Small Group Behavior*, 11, 371–388.

Butler, T., & Fuhriman, A. (1983). Curative Factors in Group Therapy: A Review of the Recent Literature. *Small Group Behavior*, 14, 131–142.

Buxbaum, H. (1972). The Psychodramatic Phenomenon of 'Illumination.' *Group Psychotherapy and Psychodrama*, 25, 160–162.

Collomb, H., & de Preneuf, C. (1979). N'Doep und Psychodrama. *Integrative Therapie*, 5, 303–312.

Coriat, I.H. (1923). Suggestion as a Form of Medical Magic. *Journal of Abnormal Psychology*, 18.

Cornyetz, P. (1947). Action Catharsis and Intensive Psychotherapy. *Sociatry*, 1, 59–63.

Corsini, R.J. (1967). *Role Playing in Psychotherapy: A Manual*. Chicago: Aldine Publications.

Corsini, R.J., & Rosenberg, B. (1955). Mechanisms of Group Psychotherapy: Processes and Dynamics. *Journal of Abnormal and Social Psychology*, 51, 406–410.

Curtis, J.M. (1982). The Effect of Therapist Self-disclosure. *Psychotherapy: Theory, Research & Practice*, 19, 54–62.

D'Amato, R.C., & Dean, R.S. (1988). Psychodrama Research: Therapy and Theory: A Critical Analysis of an Arrested Modality. *Psychology in the Schools*, 25, 305–313.

Davies, M.H. (1976). The Origins and Practice of Psychodrama. *The British Journal of Psychiatry*, 129, 201–205.

Deutsch, A. (1980). Tenacity of Attachment to a Cult Leader: A Psychiatric Perspective. *American Journal of Psychiatry*, 137, 1569–1573.

Desoille, R. (1965). *The Directed Daydream*. New York: Psychosynthesis Research Foundation.

Dewald, P.A. (1964). *Psychotherapy: A Dynamic Approach*. New York: Basic Books.

Dickoff, H., & Lakin, M. (1963). Patients' View of Group Psychotherapy: Retrospections and Interpretations. *International Journal of Group Psychotherapy*, 13, 61–73.

Diderot, D. (1951). *Le Paradoxe du Comedien, De la Poesie Dramatique*. Paris: Oevres. (Original work published 1830).

Dies, R.R. (1977). Group Therapist Transparency: A Critique of Theory and Research. *International Journal of Group Psychotherapy*, 27, 177–197.

Dilthey, W. (1944). Selected Passages from Dilthey. In H. Hodges (Ed.), *Wilhelm Dilthey: An introduction*. London: Routledge.

Dollard, J., Doeb, L.W. Miller, N.E. Mowerer, O.H., & Sears, R.R. (1939). *Frustration and Aggression*. New Haven: Yale University Press.

Dossey, L. (1982). *Space, Time & Medicine*. London: Shambhala.

Ehrenwald, J. (1967). The Therapeutic Process and the Rival Schools. *American Journal of Psychotherapy*, 21, 44–53.

Eidelberg, L. (1968). *Encyclopedia of Psychoanalysis*. New York: Free Press.

Ekstein, R., & Friedman, S.W. (1957). Acting Out, Play Action, and Acting. *Journal of the American Psychoanalytic Association*, 5, 581–629.

Emunah, R.(1989). The Use of Dramatic Enactment in the Training of Drama Therapists. *The Arts in Psychotherapy*, 16, 29–36.

Farson, R. (1978). The Technology of Humanism. *Journal of Humanistic Psychology*, 18, 5–36.

Fenichel, O. (1946). *The Psychoanalytic Theory of Neurosis*. London: Routledge & Kegan Paul.

Ferenczi, S., & Rank, O. (1925). *The Development of Psychoanalysis*. Washington: Nervous & Mental Disease Publishing.

Feshbach, S. (1956). The Catharsis Hypothesis and Some Consequences of Interaction with Aggressive and Neutral Play Objects. *Journal of Personality*, 24, 449–462.

Fine, L.J. (1979). Psychodrama. In R.J. Corsini (Ed.) *Current Psychotherapies*. Itasca, Illinois: Peacock. (pp.428–459)

Fine, L.J. (1959). Nonverbal Aspects of Psychodrama. In J. Masserman and J.L. Moreno (Eds.) *Progress in Psychotherapy, Vol 4*. New York: Grune & Stratton.

Fiske, D.W., Luborsky, L., Parloff, M.B., Hunt, H.F. Orne, M.T., Reiser, M.F., & Tuma, A.H. (1970). Planning of Research on Effectiveness of Psychotherapy. *American Psychologist*, 25, 727–737.

Fox, L.J. (1972). *Psychology as Philosophy, Science, and Art*. Pacific Palisades, Cal.: Goodyear Publishing Company.

Fox, J. (Ed.) (1987). *The Essential Moreno: Writings on Psychodrama, Group Method, and Spontaneity by J.L. Moreno*. New York: Springer.

Fraiberg, S.H. (1958). *The Magic Years*. New York: Charles Scribner's Sons.

Frank, J.D. (1961). *Persuasion and Healing: A Comparative Study of Psychotherapy*. Baltimore: John Hopkins University Press. (Revised edition 1973).

Frank, J.D. (1969). Common Features Account for Effectiveness. *International Journal of Psychiatry*, 7, 122–127.

Frank, J.D. (1971). Therapeutic Factors in Psychotherapy. *American Journal of Psychotherapy*, 25, 350–361.

Frazer, J.G. (1951). *The Magic Art and the Evolution of Kings*. New York: The MacMillan Company.

Fretigny, R., & Virel, A. (1968). *L'imagerie Mentale*. Geneva: Mont-Blanc.

Freud, A. (1965). *Normality and Pathology in Childhood*. New York: International Universities Press.

Freud, A. (1968). Symposium: Acting Out and its Role in the Psychoanalytic Process. *International Journal of Psychoanalysis*, 49, 165–170.

Freud, S. (1894). *The Neuro-psychoses of Defence*. Standard Edition, Vol. 3, London: Hogarth Press.

Freud, S. (1908). *Creative Writers and Day-Dreaming*. Standard Edition, Vol. 9, London: Hogart Press.

Freud, S. (1910). *Five Lectures on Psycho-Analysis*. Standard Edition, Vol. 11, London: Hogarth Press.

Freud, S. (1913–14). *Totem and Taboo*. Standard Edition, Vol. 13, London: Hogarth Press, 1953.

Freud, S. (1914). *Remembering Repeating and Working Through*. Standard Edition, Vol. 12, London: Hogarth Press.

Freud, S. (1921). *Group Psychology and the Analysis of the Ego*. Standard Edition, Vol. 18, London: Hogarth Press, 1955.

Freud, S. (1931). *Libidinal Types*. Standard Edition, Vol. 21, London: Hogarth Press, 1961.

Freud, S. (1937). *Analysis Terminable and Interminable*. Standard Edition, Vol. 23, London: Hogarth Press.

Frick,L.C. (1985). Role Diagram of the Psychodrama Director. In A.Hale (Ed.), *Conducting Clinical Sociometric Explorations*, Roannoke, Va: Royal, (pp.140–146).

Fromm, E. (1965). *Escape from Freedom*. New York: Avon. (Original work published 1941)

Fromm-Reichmann, F. (1950). *Principles of Intensive Psychotherapy*. Chicago: University of Chicago Press.

Gassner, J. (1947). *Tennesse Williams: The Glass Menagerie*. Best Plays of the Modern American Theatre, Second series. New York: Crown Publishers.

Geller, D.M. (1978). Involvement in Role-playing Simulations: A Demonstration with Studies on Obedience. *Journal of Personality and Social Psychology*, 36, 219–235.

Gendlin, E.T. (1961). Experiencing: a Variable in the Process of Psychotherapeutic Change. *American Journal of Psychology*, 15, 233–245.

Gendlin, E.T. (1964). A Theory of Personality Change. In: P. Worchel and D. Byrne (Eds.), *Personality Change*. New York: Wiley.

Ginn, I.B. (1973). Catharsis: Its Occurrence in Aristotle, Psychodrama, and Psychoanalysis. *Group Psychotherapy and Psychodrama*, 26, 7–22.

Ginn, R. (1974). Psychodrama, a Theatre for Our Time. *Group Psychotherapy and Psychodrama*, 27, 123–146.

Giorgi, A. (1970). *Psychology as a Human Science*, New York: Harper & Row,

Gitelson, M. (1973). *Psychoanalysis: Science and Profession*. New York: International Universities Press.

Goldfried, M.R., & Davidson, G.C. (1976). *Clinical Behavior Therapy*. New York: Holt, Rinehart & Winston.

Goldman, E.E., Morrison, D.S., & Schramski, R.G. (1982). Co-Directing: A Method for Psychodramatist Training. *Journal of Group Psychotherapy, Psychodrama & Sociometry*, 35, 65–69.

Goldman, E.E., & Morrison, D.S. (1984). *Psychodrama: Experience and Process*. Dubuque, Iowa: Kendall/Hunt.

Goldstein, A.P. (1960). Patient's Expectancies and Non-specific Therapy as a Basis for (Un)spontaneous Remission. *Journal of Clinical Psychology*, 16, 399–403.

Gonen, J.Y. (1971). The Use of Psychodrama Combined with Videotape Playback on an Inpatient Floor. *Psychiatry*, 34, 198–213.

Gonseth, J.P., & Zoller, W.W. (1982). Das Figurative Psychodrama; eine Einfuhrung. *Integrative Therapie*, 8, 24–37.

Goodman, G. & Dooley, D. (1976). A Framework for Help-Intended Communication. *Psychotherapy: Theory, Research & Practice*, 12, 106–117.

Gould, R. (1972). *Child Studies Through Fantasy*. New York: Quadrangle.

Greben, S.E. (1983). Bad Theater in Psychotherapy: The Case for Therapists' Liberation. *American Journal of Psychotherapy*, 37, 69–76.

Greenberg,I.A. (Ed.)(1974). *Psychodrama: Theory and Therapy*. New York: Behavioral Publications.

Greenson, R.R. (1967). *The Technique and Practice of Psychoanalysis*. New York: International Universities Press.

Grotjahn, M. (1976). A Discussion of Acting Out Incidents in Groups. In L.R. Wolberg and M.L. Aronson (Eds.), *Group Therapy, 1976*. New York: Intercontinental Medical Books.

Hale, A.E. (1974). Warm-up to a Sociometric Exploration. *Group Psychotherapy and Psychodrama*, 27, 157–172.

Hale, A. (1985). *Conducting Clinical Sociometric Explorations (rev.ed.)*, Roanoke, Virginia: Royal Publishing Co.

Hall, I. (1977). *The Effects of an Intensive Weekend Psychodrama vs. Spaced Psychodrama Sessions on Anxiety, Distress and Attitude Toward Group Interaction in Nursing Students*. Unpublished doctoral dissertation, University of New Mexico.

Hare, A.P. (1976). *Handbook of Small Group Research (2nd ed.)*. New York: Free Press.

Hare, A.P. (1976). A Category System for Dramaturgical Analysis. *Group Psychotherapy, Psychodrama & Sociometry*, 29, 1–22.

Hare, A.P. (1987).The Complete Bibliography of Moreno's writing. *Group Psychotherapy, Psychodrama & Sociometry*, 39, 95–128.

Hart, J., Corriere, R., & Binder, J. (1975). *Going Sane: An Introduction to Feeling Therapy*. New York: Dell.

Hart van der, O. (1983). *Rituals in Psychotherapy: Transition and Continuity*. New York: Irvington.

Hart van der O., & Ebbers,J. (1981). Rites of Separation in Strategic Psychotherapy. *Psychotherapy: Theory, Research & Practice*, 18, 188–194.

Hartmann, H. (1964). *On Rational and Irrational Action. Essays on Ego Psychology*. New York: International Universities Press.

Haskell, M.R. (1975). *Socioanalysis: Self Direction via Sociometry and Psychodrama*. Long Beach, Cal.: Role Training Associates.

Heider, J. (1974). Catharsis in Human Potential Encounter. *Journal of Humanistic Psychology*, 14, 27–47.

Heimann, P. (1950). On Countertransference. *International Journal of Psycho-Analysis*, 31, 81–84.

Henne, A. (1979). Psychodrama im Rahmen der Analytischen Psychologie von C.G. Jung. *Integrative Therapie*, 5, 79–98.

Hempel, C.G. (1965). *Aspects of Scientific Explanation and Other Essays in the Philosophy of Science*. New York: The Free Press.

Hobbs, N. (1962). Sources of Gain in Psychotherapy. *American Psychologist*, 17, 741–747.

Hokanson, J.E. (1970). Psychophysiological Evaluation of the Catharsis Hypothesis. In E.I. Medgargee and J.E. Hokanson (Eds.), *The Dynamics of Aggression*. New York: Harper & Row.

Hollander, C. (1969). *A Process for Psychodrama Training: The Hollander Psychodrama Curve*. Denver, Colorado: Evergreen Institute Press. [monograph]

Hollander, E.P. (1967). Leadership Innovation and Influence: An Overview. In E.P. Hollander & R.G. Hunt (Eds.), *Current Perspectives in Social Psychology*. New York: Oxford University Press.

Holmes, P., & Karp, M. (1991). *Psychodrama: Inspiration and Technique*. London: Tavistock/Routledge.

Horney, K. (1950). *Neurosis and Human Growth*. New York: Norton.

Horsley, J.S. (1943). *Narco-Analysis*. London: Oxford University Press.

Hulse, W.C. (1958). (Chairman of panel discussion) Acting Out in Group Psychotherapy. *American Journal of Psychotherapy*, 12, 87–105.

Isaacs, S. (1952). The Nature and Function of Phantasy. In J. Riviere (Ed.) *Developments of Psycho-Analysis*. London: Hogarth Press.

Jacobson, E. (1964). *The Self and the Object World*. New York: International Universities Press.

James, W. (1909). *A Pluralistic Universe*. New York: Longmans, Green & Co.

Janov, A. (1970). *The Primal Scream*. New York: Putnam's Sons.

Janzen, W.B., & Myers D.V. (1981). Assertion for Therapists. *Psychotherapy: Theory, Research & Practice*, 18, 291–198.

Jennings, H.H. (1950). *Leadership in Isolation*. New York: Longmans.

Jennings, S. (1986). *Creative Drama in Groupwork*. New York: Winslow Press.

Jung, C.G. (1967). The Symbolic Life. (R.F. Hull, transl.), *Collected Works of C.G. Jung*, Vol 18. Princeton: Princeton University Press. (Original work published 1935)

Kahn, M. (1966). The Physiology of Catharsis. *Journal of Personality and Social Psychology*, 3, 278–286.

Kahn, S. (1964). *Psychodrama Explained*. New York: Phil. Library.

Karle, W., Corriere, R., & Hart, J. (1973). Psychophysiological Changes in Abreactive Therapy: Study 1, Primal Therapy. *Psychotherapy: Theory, Research & Practice*, 10, 117–122.

Karp, M. (1988). Psychodrama in Britain: Prophecy and Legacy. *Group Psychotherapy, Psychodrama & Sociometry*, 41, 45–50.

Kazdin, A.E. (1979). Nonspecific Treatment of Factors in Psycho therapy Outcome Reserach. *Journal of Consulting & Clinical Psychology*, 47, 846–857.

Kellerman, H. (1979). *Group Psychotherapy and Personality: Intersecting Structures*. New York: Grune & Stratton.

Kellermann, P.F. (1979). Transference, Countertransference, and Tele. *Group Psychotherapy, Psychodrama & Sociometry*, 32, 38–55.

Kellermann, P.F. (1982). Psychodrama—Eine 'Als-Ob'-Erfahrung. *Integrative Therapie*, 8, 13–23.

Kellermann, P.F. (1983). Resistance in Psychodrama. *Journal of Group Psychotherapy, Psychodrama & Sociometry*, 36, 30–43.

Kellermann, P.F. (1984a). Acting Out in Psychodrama and in Psychoanalytic Group Psychotherapy. *Group Analysis*, 17, 195–203.

Kellermann, P.F. (1984b). The Place of Catharsis in Psychodrama. *Group Psychotherapy, Psychodrama & Sociometry*, 37, 1–13.

Kellermann, P.F.(1985a). Charismatic Leadership in Psychodrama. *Group Psychotherapy, Psychodrama & Sociometry*, 38, 84–95.

Kellermann, P.F. (1985b). Participants' Perception of Therapeutic Factors in Psychodrama. *Group Psychotherapy, Psychodrama & Sociometry*, 38, 123–132.

Kellermann, P.F. (1986). *Therapeutic Aspects of Psychodrama*. Ph.D. Thesis. University of Stockholm, Sweden.

Kellermann, P.F. (1987a). Outcome Research in Classical Psychodrama. *Small Group Behavior*, 18, 459–469.

Kellermann, P.F. (1987b). A Proposed Definition of Psychodrama. *Group Psychotherapy, Psychodrama & Sociometry*, 40, 76–80.

Kellermann, P.F. (1987c). Psychodrama Participants' Perception of Therapeutic Factors. *Small Group Behavior*, 18, 408–419.

Kellermann, P.F. (1988). Closure in Psychodrama. *Group Psychotherapy, Psychodrama & Sociometry*, 41, 21–29.

Kellermann, P.F. (1991). An Essay on the Metascience of Psychodrama. *Group Psychotherapy, Psychodrama & Sociometry*, 44, 19–32.

Kelly, G.A. (1955). *The Psychology of Personal Constructs*. New York: Norton.

Kelly, G.R. (1977). Training Mental Health Professionals Through Psychodramatic Techniques. *Group Psychotherapy, Psychodrama & Sociometry*, 30, 60–69.

Kempler, W. (1973). *Principles of Gestalt Family Therapy*. Oslo: Nordahl.

Kernberg, O.F., Burstein, E.D., Coyne, L., Appelbaum, A., Horwitz, L., & Voth, H. (1972). *Psychotherapy and psychoanalysis: Final report of the Menninger Foundation's psychotherapy research project*. Topeka: Menninger Foundation.

Kernberg, O. (1976). *Object Relation Theory and Clinical Psycho-Analysis*. New York: Jason Aronson.

Kiev, A. (1964). *Magic, Faith and Healing: Studies in Primitive Psychiatry Today*. New York: Free Press.

Kipper, D.A. (1967). Spontaneity and the Warming-up Process in a New Light. *Group Psychotherapy & Psychodrama*, 20, 62–73.

Kipper, D.A.(1978). Trends in the Research on the Effectiveness of Psychodrama: Retrospect and Prospect. *Group Psychotherapy, Psychodrama & Sociometry*, 31, 5–18.

Kipper, D.A. (1983). Book Review. *Group Psychotherapy, Psychodrama & Sociometry*, 36, 123–125.

Kipper, D.A. (1986). *Psychotherapy Through Clinical Role Playing*. New York: Brunner / Mazel.

Kipper, D.A. (1988). On the Definition of Psychodrama: Another View. *Group Psychotherapy, Psychodrama & Sociometry*, 41, 164–168.

Kipper, D.A. (1989). Psychodrama Research and the Study of Small Groups. *International Journal of Small Group Research*, 5, 4–27.

Knight, M. (1950). *William James*. Middlesex: Penguin Books.

Kobler, J. (1974). The Theater that Heals Men's Minds. In I.A. Greenberg (Ed.), *Psychodrama: Theory and Therapy*. New York: Behavioral Publications. (Original work published 1962)

Koestler, A. (1969). *The Act of Creation*. London: Hutchinson.

Kohut, H. (1978). *The Search for the Self*. New York: International Universities Press.

Kohut, H. (1984). *How Does Analysis Cure?* Chicago: University of Chicago Press.

Korn, R. (1975). The Self as Agent and the Self as Object. *Group Psychotherapy and Psychodrama*, 28, 184–210.

Kris, E. (1952). *Psychoanalytic Explorations in Art*. New York: International Universities Press.

Kruger, R.T. (1980). Gruppendynamik und Widerstandsbearbeitung im Psychodrama. *Gruppenpsychotherapie und Gruppendynamik*, 15, 243–270.

Kuhn, T. (1970). *The Structure of Scientific Revolutions (2nd ed.)* Chicago: University of Chicago Press.

Kutter, P. (1985). 'Insight' and 'Corrective Emotional Experience'—Two Important Curative Factors in Psychoanalytic Group Therapy. *Group Analysis*, 18, 18–24.

Lacoursiere, R.B. (1980). *The Life of Groups: Group Developmental Stage Theory*. New York: Human Sciences Press.

Landy, R. (1986). *Dramatherapy: Concept and Practice*. New York: Charles Springer.

Lazarus, A.A. (1973). Multimodal behavior therapy: Treating the 'Basic Id.' *Journal of Nervous and Mental Disease*, 156, 404– 411.

Lebovici, S. (1958). Psychoanalytic Applications of Psychodrama. *Journal of Social Therapy*, 2, 280–291.

Lebovici, S. (1960). Uses of Psychodrama in Psychiatric Diagnosis. *International Journal of Sociometry and Sociatry*, 3, 175–181.

Lebovici, S. (1974). A Combination of Psychodrama and Group Psychotherapy. In S.De Schill (Ed.), *The Challenge for Group Psychotherapy*. New York: International Universities Press.

Lesche, C. (1962). *A Metascientific Study of Psychosomatic Theories and their Application in Medicine*. New York: Humanities Press.

LeShan, L. (1966). *The Medium, the Mystic, and the Physicist*. New York: Ballantine.

Leuner, H. (1978). Basic Principles and Therapeutic Efficacy of Guided Affective Imagery (GAI). In J.L. Singer and K.S. Pope (Eds.), *The Power of Human Imagination: New Methods in Psychotherapy*. New York and London: Plenum.

Leutz, G.A. (1971). Transference, Empathy and Tele: the Role of the Psychodramatist as Compared with the Role of the Psychoanalyst. *Group Psychotherapy and Psychodrama*, 24, 111–116.

Leutz, G.A. (1974). *Psychodrama, Theorie und Praxis*. Berlin: Springer.

Leutz, G.A. (1976). Jacob Morenos Therapeutische Trieade. In A. Uchtenhagen (Ed.) *Gruppentherapie und Soziale Umwelt*. Bern: Huber.

Leutz, G.A. (1977). The Integrative Force of Psychodrama in Present-day Psychotherapy. *Group Psychotherapy, Psychodrama & Sociometry*, 30, 163–172.

Leutz, G.A. (1985a). Psychodrama in Psychiatry: its Imaginary Reality and Auxiliary World. In P. Pichot, P. Berner, R. Wolf and K. Thau (Eds.,). *Psychiatry, Vol 4*. New York: Plenum, (pp.245–250).

Leutz, G.A. (1985b). What is Effective in Psychodrama? In. G.A. Leutz, Mettre Sa Vie En Scene. Paris: Epi. Leveton, E. (1977). *Psychodrama for the Timid Clinician*. New York: Springer Publishing Company.

Leveton, E. (1977) Psychodrama for the Timid Clinician. New York: Springer.

Levi-Strauss, C. (1949). L'efficiacite Symbolique. Revue d'Histoire des Religions, 135, 5–27.

Levy, R.B. (1969). Human Relations: A Conceptual Approach. New York: International Textbook.

Lewin, K. (1951) Field Theory and Social Science: Selected Theoretical Papers. New York: Harper & Row.

Lieberman, M.A., Yalom, I.D., & Miles, M.B. (1973). Encounter Groups: First Facts. New York: Basic Books.

Liff, Z.A. (1975). The Charismatic Leader. In Z.A. Liff (Ed.), The Leader in the Group. New York: Aronson.

Lippit, R. (1959). The Auxiliary Chair Technique. Group Psychotherapy, 11, 8–23.

Lippit, R., & White, R.K. (1958). An Experimental Study of Leadership and Group Life. In E.E. Maccoby, T.M. Newcomb, & E.L. Hartley (Eds.), Readings in Social Psychology. New York: Holt.

Little, M. (1951). Countertransference and the Patients Response to it. International Journal of Psycho-Analysis, 32, 32–40.

Lowen, A. (1975). Bioenergetics. New York: Coward, McCann & Geoghegan.

Luborsky, L., Crits-Christoph P., Alexander, L., Margolis, M. & Cohen, M. (1983). Two Helping Alliance Methods of Predicting Outcomes of Psychotherapy. Journal of Nervous and Mental Disease, 171, 480–491.

Luhrman, T.M. (1989). The Magic of Secrecy. Ethos, 17, 131–165.

Magnusson D., & Endler, N.S. (Eds.)(1977). Personality at the Crossroads: Current Issues in Interactional Psychology. Hillsdale, N.J.: Wiley.

Mahler, M.S. (1968). On Human Symbiosis and the Vicissitudes of Individuation. New York: International Universities Press.

Mahoney, M.J. (1974). Cognition and Behavior Modification. Cambridge, Mass.: Ballinger.

Malan, D.H. (1976a). The Frontier of Brief Psychotherapy. New York: Plenum Press.

Malan, D.H. (1976b). Toward the Validation of Dynamic Psychotherapy. New York: Plenum Press.

Malinowsky, B. (1954). Magic, Science and Reigion, and Other Essays. London: Doubleday.

Mallick, S.K., & McCandless, B.R. (1966). A Study of Catharsis of Aggression. Journal of Personality and Social Psychology, 4, 591–596.

Marineau, R.F. (1989). Jacob Levy Moreno 1889–1974. International Library of Group Psychotherapy and Group Process. London & New York: Tavistock/Routledge.

Marker, L., & Marker, F.J. (1982). Ingmar Bergman: Four Decades in the Theater. Cambridge: Cambridge University Press.

Marmor, J. (1962). Psychoanalytic Therapy as an Educational Process. In. J.H. Masserman (Ed.). Science and Psychoanalysis, Vol 5. New York: Grune & Stratton, (pp.286–299).

Martin, R.B. (1991). The Assessment of Involvement in Role Playing. Journal of Clinical Psychology, 47, 587–596.

Maslow, A.H. (1968). Toward a Psychology of Being. New York: Van Nostrand.

Maslow, A.H. (1971). The Farther Reaches of Human Nature. New York: Penguin Books.

Mead, G.H. (1934). Mind, Self & Society. Chicago: University of Chicago Press.

Menninger, K.A. & Holzman, P.S. (1973). Theory of Psychoanalytic Technique. New York: Basic Books.

Middleton, J. (1967). Magic, Witchcraft, and Curing. New York: Natural History Press.

Montagna, P.L. (1982). 'Acting out' und Psychodrama. Integrative Therapie, 8, 113–121.

Moreno, J.D. (1974). Psychodrama and the future of social sciences. Group Psychotherapy & Psychodrama, 27, 59–70.

Moreno, J.L. (1914). Einladung zu einer Begegnung. Wien: Anzengruber Verlag.

Moreno, J.L. (1920). Das Testaments des Vaters. Berlin: Gustav Kiepenheuer. (English translation: The Words of the Father, New York: Beacon House, 1941; 1971).

Moreno, J.L. (1923). Das Stegreiftheater. Potsdam: Kiepenheuer. (English translation: The Spontaneity Theatre, New York: Beacon House, 1947; 1970).

Moreno, J.L. (1937). Interpersonal Therapy and the Psychopathology of Interpersonal Relations. Sociometry. (Reprinted in Psychodrama, Volume 1, 1972).

Moreno, J.L. (1939). Psychodramatic Shock Therapy. Sociometry, 2.

Moreno, J.L. (1940). Mental Catharsis and the Psychodrama. *Sociometry*, 3, 209–244.

Moreno, J.L. & Enneis, J.M. (1950). Hypnodrama and psychodrama. *Group Psychotherapy*, 3, 1–10.

Moreno, J.L, (1951). *Sociometry, Experimental Method and the Science of Society*. New York: Beacon House.

Moreno, J.L. (1953). *Who Shall Survive? A New Approach to the Problem of Human Interrelations*. Washington: Nervous and Mental Disease Publishing Co. (Original work published 1934)

Moreno, J.L. (1954). Transference, Countertransference and Tele: Their Relation to Group Research and Group Psychotherapy. *Group Psychotherapy* (October, 1954), 7 (2).

Moreno, J.L. (1959). Psychodrama. In S. Arieti (Ed.), *American Handbook of Psychiatry, Vol. 2*. New York: Basic Books.

Moreno, J.L., & Moreno, Z.T.(1959). *Psychodrama, Volume 2: Foundations of Psychotherapy*. New York: Beacon House.

Moreno,J.L. (Ed.) (1960a). *The Sociometry Reader*. Glencoe, Ill.: The Free Press of Glencoe.

Moreno, J.L. (1960b). Concept of the Encounter. *Journal of Existential Psychiatry*, 1, 144–154.

Moreno, J.L. (1961). The Role Concept, a Bridge between Psychiatry and Sociology. *American Journal of Psychiatry*, 188, 518–523.

Moreno, J.L. (1963). Behavior Therapy. *American Journal of Psychiatry*, 120, 194–196.

Moreno, J.L. (1966). Psychiatry of the Twentieth Century: Function of the Universalia: Time, Space, Reality and Cosmos. *Group Psychotherapy*, 19. (Reprinted in *Psychodrama, Vol. 3*).

Moreno, J.L. (1968). The Validity of Psychodrama. *Group Psychotherapy*, 21, 3.

Moreno, J.L., & Moreno, Z.T. (1969). *Psychodrama, Volume 3: Action Therapy & Principles of Practice*. New York: Beacon House.

Moreno, J.L. (1971). Psychodrama. In H.I. Kaplan & B. Sadock (Eds.), *Comprehensive Group Psychotherapy*. Baltimore: Williams & Wilkins.

Moreno, J.L. (1972). *Psychodrama, Volume 1*. New York: Beacon House. (Original work published 1946)

Moreno, J.L. (1969/1972). The Magic Charter of Psychodrama. *Group Psychotherapy & Psychodrama*, 1972, 25, 131.

Moreno, Z.T. (1959). A Survey of Psychodramatic Techniques. *Group Psychotherapy*, 12, 5–14.

Moreno, Z.T. (1965). Psychodramatic rules, techniques, and adjunctive methods. *Group Psychotherapy*, 18, 73–86.

Moreno, Z.T. (1971). Beyond Aristotle, Breuer and Freud: Moreno's contribution to the concept of catharsis. *Group Psychotherapy & Psychodrama*, 24, 34–43.

Moreno, Z.T. (1976). In Memoriam: Jacob Levy Moreno. *Group Psychotherapy, Psychodrama & Sociometry*, 29, 130–135.

Moreno, Z.T. (1990). Note on Some Forms of Resistance to Psychodrama. *Group Psychotherapy, Psychodrama & Sociometry*, 43, 43–44.

Mosak, H.H. (1979). Adlerian Psychotherapy. In R.J. Corsini (Ed.), *Current Psychotherapies*. Itasca, Illinois: Peacock.

Newman, R.G. (1983). Thoughts on Superstars of Charisma: Pipers in Our Midst. *American Journal of Orthopsychiatry*, 53, 201–208.

Nichols, M.P. (1974). Outcome of brief cathartic psychotherapy. *Journal of Consulting and Clinical Psychology*, 42, 403–410.

Nichols, M.P., & Zax, M.(1977). *Catharsis in Psychotherapy*. New York: Gardner.

Nichols, M.P., & Efran, J.S. (1985). Catharsis in Psychotherapy: A New Perspective. *Psychotherapy: Theory, Research, and Practice*, 22, 46–58.

Nolte, J., Weistart, J. & Wyatt, J. (1977). Psychodramatic Production of Dreams: 'the end of the road'. *Group Psychotherapy & Psychodrama*, 30, 37–48.

Olson, U.J., & Pegg P.(1979). Direct Open Supervision: A Team Approach. *Family Process*, 18, 463–469.

Orcutt, T.L. (1977). Roles and Rules: the Kinship and Territoriality of Psychodrama and Gestalt Therapy. *Group Psychotherapy, Psychodrama and Sociometry*, 30, 97–107.

Orlinsky, D.E., & Howard, K.I.(1978). The Relationship of Process to Outcome in Psychotherapy. In S. Garfield and A. Bergin (Eds.), *Handbook of Psychotherapy and Behavior Change (2nd ed.)*. New York: Wiley.

Ossorio, A.G., & Fine, L.J. (1959). Psychodrama as a Catalyst for Social Change in a Mental Hospital. In J.L. Moreno (Ed.), *Progress in Psychotherapy: Vol. V.* New York: Grune & Stratton, pp.212–218.

Palmer, R.E. (1969). *Hermeneutics.* Evanston: Northwestern University Press.

Parsons, T. (1967). *Social Theory and Modern Society.* New York: Free Press.

Parsons, T., & Shils, E.A. (1951). *Toward a General Theory of Action.* Mass.: Cambridge University Press.

Peirce, C.S. (1931). *Principles of Philosophy.* Cambridge: Harvard University Press.

Perls, F.S. (1969). *Gestalt Therapy Verbatim.* Moab, Utah: Real People Press.

Perls, F.S., Hefferline, R., & Goodman, P. (1950). *Gestalt Therapy: Excitement and Growth in the Human Personality.* New York: Brunner/Mazel.

Petzold, H.(Ed.) (1978). *Angewandtes Psychodrama.* Paderborn: Junfermann-Verlag.

Petzold, H. (1978). Die therapeutischen Moglichkeiten der psychodramatischen 'Magic-Shop-Technik'. In. H. Petzold, (Ed.), *Angewandtes Psychodrama.* Paderborn: Junfermann-Verlag, pp.159–177.

Petzold, H. (1979). *Psychodrama-Therapie: Theorie, Methoden, Anwendung in der Arbeit mit Alten Menschen.* Paderborn: Junfermann-Verlag.

Petzold, H, (1980). Modelle und Konzepte zu Integrativen Ansatzen der Therapie. *Integrative Therapie,* 6, 323–350.

Polansky, N.A. (1982). Ego Functions in Psychodrama. In N. Polansky (Ed.), *Integrated Ego Psychology* (Chapter 11). New York: Aldine.

Polansky,N.A., & Harkins, E.B. (1969). Psychodrama as an Element in Hospital Treatment. *Psychiatry,* 32, 74–87.

Polanyi, M. (1962). *Personal Knowledge.* London: Routledge & Kegan Paul.

Piaget, J. (1951). *Play, Dreams and Imitation in Childood.* London: Routledge & Kegan Paul.

Pitzele, P. (1991). Adolescents inside out: Intrapsychic Psychodrama. In: P. Holmes and M. Karp (Eds.), *Psychodrama: Inspiration and Technique.* London: Tavistock/Routledge, (pp.15–32).

Quin, B.J. (1991). Healing the Healers: Psychodrama with therapists. In P. Holmes & M. Karp (Eds.), *Psychodrama: Inspiration and Technique.* London: Tavistock/Routledge, (pp.227–244).

Racker, H. (1968). *Transference and Countertransference.* London: Hogarth Press.

Radnitzky, G. (1970). *Contemporary Schools of Metascience.* Goteborg: Akademiforlaget.

Rangell, L. (1968). Symposium: Acting Out. *International Journal of Psychoanalysis,* 49, 195–201.

Rank, O. (1957). *Will Therapy and Truth and Reality.* New York: Alfred A. Knopf.

Rapoport, L. (1970). Crisis Intervention as a Mode of Brief Treatment. In Roberts & Nee (Eds.), *Theories of Social Case Work.* Chicago: University of Chicago Press.

Rapaport, D. (1960). *The Structure of Psychoanalytic Theory. Psychological Issues.* New York: International Universities Press.

Reich, W. (1929). *Character Analysis.* London: Vision Press, 1950.

Rexford, E.N. (Ed.)(1966). *A Developmental Approach to Problems of Acting Out.* New York: International Universities Press.

Riebel, L. (1990). Doctor, Teacher, Indian Chief: Metaphor and the Search for Inherent Identity. *Journal of Integrative and Eclectic Psychotherapy,* 9, 119–135.

Rioch, M.J. (1970). The Work of Wilfred Bion on Groups. *Psychiatry,* 33, 56–66.

Rioch, M.J. (1971). 'All we like sheep—' (Isaiah 53:6): Followers and Leaders. *Psychiatry,* 34, 258–268.

Robertiello, R.C. (1965). Acting Out or Acting Through. In: L. Abt and S. Weissman (Eds.), *Acting Out.* New York: Grune & Stratton.

Rogers, C.R. (1957). The Necessary and Sufficient Conditions of Therapeutic Personality Change. *Journal of Consulting Psychology,* 21, 95–103.

Rogers, C.R. (1969). *Freedom to Learn,* Columbus, Ohio: Bell & Howell.

Rose, S. (1976). Intense Feeling Therapy. In: P. Olsen (Ed.), *Emotional Flooding.* New York: Human Sciences Press.

Rosen, J. (1965). The Concept of Acting In. In: L. Abt and S. Weissman (Eds.), *Acting Out.* New York: Grune & Stratton.

Rouchy, J-C., & Karp, M. (1985). Commentary. *Group Analysis,* 18, 63–65.

Rutan, J.S., & Rice, C.A. (1981). The Charismatic Leader: Asset or Liability? *Psychotherapy: Theory, Research & Practice*, 18, 487–492.

Rycroft, C. (1968). *A Critical Dictionary of Psychoanalyis.* New York: Penguin Books.

Sacks, J.M. (1965).The Judgment Technique in Psychodrama. *Group Psychotherapy*, 18, 69–72.

Sacks, J. (1976a). The Psychodrama Group: Formation and Beginning. *Group Process*, 7, 59–78.

Sacks, J.M. (1976b). Shut Up! A Psychodramatic Technique for Releasing Anger. In P.Olsen (Ed.), *Emotional Flooding.* New York: Human Sciences Press.

Sandler, J., Dare, C., & Holder, A. (1973). *The Patient and the Analyst.* New York: International Universities Press.

Sandler, J., & Rosenblatt, B. (1962). The Concept of the Representational World. *Psychoanalytic Study of the Child*, 17, 128–145.

Sarbin, R.R. (1972). Imagining as Muted Role-Taking. In Sheehan (Ed.), *The Function and Nature of Imagery.* New York: Academic Press.

Sarbin, T., & Allen, V. (1968). Role Theory. In G. Lindzey & E. Aronson (Eds.), *The Handbook of Social Psychology, Vol. 1.* Reading, MA: Addison-Wesley.

Scheidlinger, S. (1982). *Focus on Group Psychotherapy.* New York: International Universities Press.

Schafer, R. (1976). *A New Language for Psychoanalysis.* New Haven: Yale University Press.

Schaffer, N.D. (1983). The Utility of Measuring the Skillfulness of Therapeutic Techniques. *Psychotherapy: Theory, Research & Practice*, 20, 330–336.

Schecter, D.W. (1973). On the Emergence of Human Relatedness. In: E.G. Witenberg (Ed.), *Interpersonal Explorations in Psychoanalysis.* New York: Basic Books.

Scheff, T.J. (1979). *Catharsis in Healing, Ritual, and Drama.* Los Angeles: University of California Press.

Scheidlinger, S. (1982). *Focus on Group Psychotherapy.* New York: International Universities Press.

Schiffer, I. (1973). *Charisma: A Psychoanalytic Look at Mass Society.* Toronto: University of Toronto Press.

Schneider-Duker, M. (1991). Psychodrama als Forschungsmethode und Forschungsgegenstand. In M. Vorwerg and T. Alberg (Eds.), *Psychodrama Psychotherapie und Grenzgebiete, Band 12.* Heidelberg: Johann Ambrosius Barth.

Schramski, T.G. (1979). A Systematic Model of Psychodrama. *Group Psychotherapy, Psychodrama & Sociometry*, 32, 20–30.

Schramski, T.G., & Feldman, C.A. (1984). *Selected Abstracts of Outcome Research and Evaluation in the Action Methods.* Unpublished Manuscript, Tucson Center for Psychodrama.

Schutz, W.C. (1966). *FIRO: The Interpersonal Underworld.* Palo Alto: Science & Behavior Books.(Original work published 1960).

Schutz, W.C. (1971). *Here Comes Everybody.* New York: Harper & Row.

Schutzenberger, A.A. (1970). *Precis de Psychodrame (Rev. ed.).* Paris: Editions Universitaires. (Original work published 1966)

Seabourne, B. (1953). The Action Sociogram. *Group Psychotherapy and Psychodrama*, 16, 145–155.

Seabourne, B. (1966). Some Hints on Dealing with Various Kinds of Protagonists. In A. Blatner (Ed.), *Psychodrama, Role-playing and Action Methods: Theory and Practice: A syllabus.* (2nd edition 1970).

Seeman, H., & Weiner, D. (1985). Comparing and Using Psychodrama with Family Therapy: Some Cautions. *Group Psychotherapy, Psychodrama & Sociometry*, 37, 143–156.

Selvini-Palazzoli, M., Boscolo, L., Cecchin, G.F. & Prata, G. (1977). Family Rituals: a Powerful Tool in Family Therapy. *Family Process*, 16, 445–454.

Shalit, E. (1990). Experiential Supervision as an Adjunct to Regular Supervision of Psychotherapy. *The Clinical Supervisor*, 8, 109–130.

Shapiro, A.K. (1971). Placebo Effects in Medicine, Psychotherapy and Psychoanalysis. In A. E. Bergin and S. L. Garfield (Eds.), *Handbook of Psychotherapy and Behavior Change.* New York: Wiley.

Sheikh, A.A., & Jordan, C.S. (1983). Clinical Uses of Mental Imagery. In A.A. Sheikh (Ed.), *Imagery: Current Theory, Research, and Application.* New York: Wiley.

Singer, E. (1970). *Key Concepts in Psychotherapy (2nd ed.).* New York: Random House.

Singer, J.L. (1974). *Imagery and Daydreaming Methods in Psychotherapy and Behavior Modification.* New York: Academic Press.

Singer, J.L. (1977). Imagination and Make-Believe Play in Early Childhood: Some Educational Implications. *Journal of Mental Imagery*, 1, 127–144.

Singer, J.L., & Pope, K.S. (Eds.) (1978). *The Power of Human Imagination: New Methods in Psychotherapy.* New York & London: Plenum.

Siroka, R.W., & Schloss, G.A. (1968). The Death Scene in Psychodrama. *Psychotherapy: Theory, Research & Practice*, 5, 355–361.

Siroka, R.W., Siroka, E., & Schloss, G. (Eds.) (1971). *Sensitivity Training and Group Encounter.* New York, Grossett & Dunlap.

Slavson, S.R. (1951). Catharsis in Group Psychotherapy. *Psychoanalytic Review*, 38, 39–52.

Sloane, R.B., Staples, F.R., Cristol, A.H. Yorkston, N.J., & Whipple, K. (1975). *Psychotherapy Versus Behavior Therapy.* Cambridge: Harvard University Press.

Stanislavski, C. (1936). *An Actor Prepares.* New York: Theatre Art Books.

Starr, A. (1977). *Psychodrama: Rehearsal for Living.* Chicago: Nelson Hall.

Stern, W. (1938). *General Psychology.* New York: Macmillan.

Stone, L. (1981). Notes on the Noninterpretive Elements in the Psychoanalytic Situation and Process. *Journal of the American Psychoanalytic Association*, 29, 89–118.

Strachey, J. (1934). The Nature of the Therapeutic Action of Psycho-Analysis. *International Journal of Psycho-Analysis*, 15, 127–159.

Strupp, H.H. (1972). On the Technology of Psychotherapy. *Archives of General Psychiatry*, 26, 270–278.

Strupp, H.H. (1973). On the Basic Ingredient of Psychotherapy. *Journal of Consulting and Clinicial Psychology*, 41, 1–8.

Strupp, H.H., & Hadley, S.W. (1979). Specific Versus Nonspecific Factors in Psychotherapy: A Controlled Study of Outcome. *Archives of General Psychiatry*, 36, 1125–1136.

Sturm, I.E. (1965). The Behavioristic Aspects of Psychodrama. *Group Psychotherapy and Psychodrama*, 18, 50–64.

Sullivan, H.S. (1953). *The Interpersonal Theory of Psychiatry.* New York: Norton.

Sundberg, N.D. & Tyler, L.E. (1962). *Clinical Psychology.* New York: Appleton-Century-Crofts.

Tavris, C. (1982). Anger Defused. *Psychology Today*, 16, November, 25–35.

Tellegen, A., & Atkinson, G. (1974). Openness to absorbing and self-altering experiences ('absorbtion'), a trait related to hypnotic susceptibility. *Journal of Abnormal Psychology*, 83, 268–277.

Temerlin, M.K., & Temerlin, J.W. (1982). Psychotherapy Cults: An Iatrogenic Perversion. *Psychotherapy: Theory, Research & Practice*, 19, 131–141.

Thorne, F.C. (1973). Conclusion. In. Jurjevich, R.M. (Ed.) *Direct Psychotherapy: American Originals.* Florida: University of Miami Press, (pp.847–884).

Treadwell, T.W., Stein, S., & Kumar, V.K. (1990). A Survey of Psychodramatic Action and Closure Techniques. *Group Psychotherapy, Psychodrama & Sociometry*, 42, 102–115.

Vaihinger, H. (1911). *Philosophie des Als Ob.* Berlin: Reutner & Reinhard. (English translation: The Philosophy of As-If).

Versluis, A. (1986). *The Philosophy of Magic.* London: Arkana.

Viderman, M. (1991). The Real Person of the Analyst and his Role in the Process of Psychoanalytic Cure. *Journal of the American Psychoanalytic Association*, 39, 451–489.

Volkan, V.D. (1980). Narcissistic Personality Organization and "Reparative" Leadership. *International Journal of Group Psychotherapy*, 30, 131–152.

Wachtel, P.L. (Ed.)(1982). *Resistance: Psychodynamic and Behavioral Approaches.* New York: Plenum.

Wallas, G. (1926). *The Art of Thought.* New York: Harcort & Brace.

Warner, G.D. (1975). *Psychodrama Training Tips.* Hagerstown, Md.: Maryland Psychodrama Institute.

Warren, R., & Kurlychek, R.T. (1981). Treatment of Maladaptive Anger. *Journal of Behavior Technology, Methods & Therapy*, 27, 135–139.

Watzlawick, P., Weakland, J. & Fish, R. (1974). *Change—Principles of Problem Formation and Problem Resolution.* New York: Norton.

Weber, M. (1953). *The Sociology of Religion.* Boston: Beacon Press.

Weiner, H.B. (1959). *Psychodrama and the Chronic Alcoholic with a Discussion of the Magic Shop Technique*. Michigan Institute of Group Psychotherapy and Psychodrama. [monograph]

Weiner, H.B. (1967). The Identity of the Psychodramatist. *Group Psychotherapy*, 20, 114–117.

Weiner, H.(1974). Toward a Body Therapy. *Psychoanalytic Review*, 61, 45–52.

Weiner, H.B., & Sacks, J.M. (1969). Warm up and Sum up. *Group Psychotherapy*, 22, 85–102.

Weiner, M.F. (1977). Catharsis: A Review. *Group Process*, 7, 173– 184.

Wheelis, A. (1950). The Place of Action in Personality Change. *Psychiatry*, 13, 135–148.

Whitaker, D.S. & Lieberman, M.A. (1964). *Psychotherapy Through the Group Process*. New York: Atherton Press.

Winnicott, D.W. (1965). *The Maturational Processes and the Facilitating Environment*. London: Hogarth Press.

Winnicott, D.W. (1971). *Playing and Reality*. London: Tavistock Publications.

Williams, A. (1989). *The Passionate Technique: Strategic Psychodrama with Individuals, Families and Groups*. New York: Routledge, Chapman & Hall.

Willis, S.T. (1991). Who goes there?: Group-analytic Drama for Disturbed Adolescents. In P. Holmes & M. Karp (Eds.), *Psychodrama: Inspiration and Technique*. London: Routledge.

Witenberg, E.G. (Ed.)(1973). *Interpersonal Explorations in Psychoanalysis*. New York: Basic Books.

Wittgenstein, L. (1922). *Tractus Logicus-Philosophicus*. London: Routledge and Kegan. (p. 1889).

Witztum, E., van der Hart, O., & Friedman, B. (1988). The Use of Metaphors in Psychotherapy. *Journal of Contemporary Psychotherapy*, 18, 270–290.

Wogan, M., & Norcross, J.C. (1983). Dimensions of Psychotherapists' Activity. *Psychotherapy: Theory, Research & Practice*, 20, 67–74.

Wolberg, L.R. (1977). *The Technique of Psychotherapy*. New York: Grune & Stratton. (3rd edition).

Wolson, P. (1974). Loss of Impulse Control in Psychodrama on Inpatient Services. In I.A. Greenberg (Ed.), *Psychodrama: Theory and Therapy*. New York: Behavioral Publications.

Yablonsky, L. (1976). *Psychodrama: Resolving Emotional Problems Through Role Playing*. New York: Basic Books.

Yablonsky, L., & Enneis, J.M. (1956). Psychodrama Theory and Practice. In F. Fromm-Reichmann and J.L. Moreno (Eds.), *Progress in Psychotherapy, Vol 1*. New York: Grune & Stratton.

Yalom, I.D. (1975). *The Theory and Practice of Group Psychotherapy (2nd rev. ed)*. New York: Basic Books.

Yardley, K.M. (1982). On Enagaging Actors in As-If Experiments. *Journal for the Theory of Social Behavior*, 12, 291–304.

Zaleznik, A. (1974). Charismatic and Consensus Leaders: A Psychological Comparison. *Bulletin of the Menninger Clinic*, 38, 222–238.

Zeligs, M. (1957). Acting In. *Journal of the American Psychoanalytic Association*, 5, 685–706.

Zumkley, H. (1978). *Aggression und Katharsis*. Saarbrucken, Gottingen: Hogrefe.

Subject Index

Name Index

Gender and Romance

in Chaucer's

Canterbury Tales